English-Malay dictionary

Chong Sin **Song**

Alpha Editions

This edition published in 2019

ISBN : 9789353892210

Design and Setting By
Alpha Editions
email - alphaedis@gmail.com

English-Malay Dictionary

BY

SONG CHONG SIN.

SECOND EDITION.

KITAB-LOGAT DARI BAHASA INGGRIS DAN MELAJOE.

oleh

SONG CHONG SIN.

Tjitakan ka tiga kali.

Printed and published by KHO TJENG BIE & Co.

Ditjitak dan dikloearken oleh:
KHO TJENG BIE & Co.,
BATAVIA.
1921.

Preface to the first Edition.

I have seen that it is difficult to obtain an English and Malay dictionary suitable for our beginners in this colony, and so determined to undertake the translation of this book which has not been completed in the proper scheme though, I hope it will be a boon to them.

SONG CHONG SIN.

Batavia, 25th June 1914.

Pendahoeloean bagi tjitakan jang pertama.

Saja soeda menjaksiken bahoea di ini Insulinde ada soesa sekali didapet satoe kitab-logat (woordenboek) dari bahasa Inggris dan Melajoe jang satoedjoe bagi orang-orang jaŋg baroe moelai jakinken bahasa Inggris, ini sebab, saja lantes ambil poetoȩsan boeat salin ini boekoe, jang maski belon sampoerna ȩetoel, tapi saja harep nanti bisa djoega djadi penoeloeng bagi marika itoe.

SONG CHONG SIN.

Batavia, 25 Juni 1914.

A Dictionary of the English and Malay languages.

---—■—---

Kitab-Logat dari bahasa Inggris dan Melajoe.

---—■—---

A.

A	Satoe
Aback	Ka blakang; dengen kaget.
Abandon	Boeang; loepoetken.
Abandoned	Jang soeda diboeang; amat berbahaja.
Abandonment	Pemboeangan.
Abase	Merenda; membikin renda.
Abasement	Merendaän; pembikinan renda.
Abash	Bikin maloe; bikin kaloet.
Abasing	Amat merenda.
Abatable	Jang boleh dikoerangin.
Abate	Koerangin; membikin koerang.
Abatement	Koerangan; pembikinan koerang.
Abba	Ajah; papa.
Abbacy	Kamerdikaännja satoe kepala padri.
Abbe	Gelaran jang tiada mempoenjai pekerdjaän atawa hak; kepala padri.
Abbess	Kepala padri prempoean.
Abbey	Tempat tinggalnja padri lelaki atawa padri
Abbot	Kepala padri lelaki.
Abbreviate	Bikin pendek; ringkesin.
Abbreviation	Pendeknja; ringkesnja.
Abbreviator	Toekang bikin ringkes; orang jang bikin ringkes.
Abdicate	Seraken kekwasaän.
Abdication	Persrahan kekwasaän.
Abdomen	Peroet bagian sebla bawa.
Abdominal	Berhoeboeng dengen peroet.
Abduce	Moendoerken diri.
Abduction	Peroendoeran diri.

Abed	Dalem · pembaringan; atas tempat-tidoer.
Aberrance,	
Aberrancy	Kesalaän; Kakliroean.
Aberrant	Berlaloe dari kabeneran; djadi kliroe.
Aberration	Perboeatan berlaloe dari kabeneran; kekaloetan pikiran.
Abet	Membikin besar hati; bantoein.
Abetter, Abettor	Orangjang membikin besar hati; pembantoe.
Abeyance	Keadaän tiada mempoenjai kepala atawa pemimpin.
Abhor	Tiada soeka atawa bentji dengen sanget.
Abhorrence,	
Abhorrancy	Tabiat jang sanget membentji.
Abhorrent	Membikin orang bentji.
Abhorrently	Dengen sanget membikin orang bentji.
Abide	Tinggal boeat sementara waktoe; menahan.
Abiding	Tempat menahan; menahanan.
Ability	Kapandean.
Abject	Boesoek; tida ada harganja.
Abjection	Kaboesoekan; kedjahatan.
Abjectness,	
Abjectedness	Keadaän dalem baboesoekan atawa kedjahatan.
Abjuration	Soempaän.
Abjure	Soempaken.
Ablative	Menjataken terpisa satoe sama laen.
Ablaze	Menjala.
Able	Bisa; pande.
Able-bodied	Mempoenjai kebisaän atawa kapandean.
Ablution	Tjoetjian; mandian.
Ably	Dengen mempoenjai kapandean atawa kebisaän.
Abnegate	Tiada akoe; tiada trima.
Abnegation	Tabiat tiada soeka akoe atawa trima.
Abnormal	Melanggar atoeran; bertentangan dengen atoeran.

Aboard	Dalem atawa ka dalem kapal.
Abode	Tempat-tinggal.
Abolish	Boeang; laloeken.
Abolishable	Boleh diboeang atawa dilaloeken.
Abolition	Pemboeangan; penghapoesan.
Abolitionist	Orang jang berichtiar boeat memboeang atawa laloeken.
Abominable.	Boleh dibentji; membentji-in.
Abominably	Dalem keadaän jang sanget boleh dibentji.
Abominate	Bentji dengen sanget.
Aboriginal	Pertama; permoela.
Aborigines	Pendoedoek pertama dari sasoeatoe negri.
Abortion	Kelahiran karoeron.
Abortive	Belon sampe waktoenja; karoeron; tiada berhasil.
Abortively	Dalem keadaän jang belon sampe waktoenja; dengen tiada berhasil.
Abound	Banjak.
About	Koeliling; kira-kira; fatsal.
Above	Atas; meliwatin.
Abrade	Gosok bikin ilang.
Abrasion	Gosokan bikin ilang.
Abreast	Berbaris; sebla-menjebla.
Abridge	Bikin ringkes: bikin kisoet.
Abridgement	Pembikinan ringkes; tjerita-ringkes.
Abroad	Di loear roema atawa negri.
Abragate	Laloeken; boeang; pantang atawa tjega.
Abrogation	Perboeatan aken melaloeken.
Abrupt	Petja; terkoenjoeng-koenjoeng.
Abruption	Petjaän dari anggota badan.
Abruptness	Keadaän jang petja; gerakan jang terkoenjoeng-koenjoeng.
Abscess	Bisoel jang menggengem nana.
Abscind	Potong.
Abscond	Semoeniken diri.
Absconder	Orang jang semoeniken diri.

Absence	Keadaän tiada dateng; keadaän tiada hadlir,
Abcent	Tiada dateng; tiada hadlir.
Absentee	Orang jang tiada dateng atawa hadlir.
Absenteeism	Adat-kebiasaän dari orang jang soeka tiada dateng.
Absolute	Tiada berwates.
Absolutely	Dengen tiada berwates.
Absoluteness	Tjoekoep; kekwasaän jang tiada berwates.
Absolution	Pembrian ampoen.
Absolutism	Pengaroe dari kekwasaän jang tiada berwates.
Absolve	Ampoenin; maäfken.
Absorb	Isep.
Absorbable	Boleh di-isep.
Absorbent	Barang jang mengisep: isepan.
Absorptive	Mempoenjai kebiasaän boeat mengisep.
Abstain	Berlaloe; djaoeken.
Abstention	Perboeatan aken laloeken atawa djaoeken.
Abstract	Pisain; tarik; pindaken.
Abstraction	Pisaän; loepa ingetan.
Abstractly	Dengen sendirian.
Abstruse	Soesa diartiken.
Abstrusely	Dengen soesa diartiken.
Absurd	Djaoe dari kabeneran; tiada boleh djadi.
Absurdity	Keadaän jang djaoe dari kabeneran; keadaän jang tiada boleh djadi.
Abundance	Keadaän jang banjak sekali.
Abundant	Banjak sekali.
Abuse	Maki.
Abuse	Behaja.
Abyss	Kadaleman jang tiada bisa didjadjakin.
Academician	Anggota dari satoe sekola tinggi.
Academic,	
Academical	Berhoeboeng dengen sekola tinggi.
Academy	Sekola tinggi.
Accede	Moefakat; kaboelken.

Accent	Tanda boeat dibatja dengen soeara keras.
Accentual	Berhoeboeng dengen tanda boeat dibatja. keras.
Accentuate	Taro tanda boeat dibatja dengen keras.
Accept	Trima.
Acceptable	Boleh ditrima.
Acceptability	Alesan jang boleh ditrima.
Acceptance	Pertrimaän dengen senang hati; kwitantie.
Acceptation	Pertrimaän; maksoed jang oemoem dari satoe perkataän.
Accepter.	
Acceptor	Orang jang menerima.
Access	Tambahan; djalanan masoek.
Accessary	Jang berikoet; orang jang toeroet tjampoer tangan dalem kadosahan.
Accessible	Jang boleh dideketin.
Accession	Tambahan.
Accessorial	Berhoeboeng dengen orang jang toeroet tjampoer tangan dalem kadosahan.
Accidence	Boekoe boeat permoelaän beladjar atoeran soerat.
Accident	Kedjadian; ketjilakaän jang tiada terdoega.
Accdental	Terdjadi dengen tiada terdoega.
Accidentally	Dengen tiada terdoega.
Acclaim	Bersoerak.
Acclamation	Soerakan
Acclimate,	
Acclimatize	Tjotjok dengen hawa tempat.
Acclimation,	
Acclimatation,	
Acclimatization	Keadaän jang tjotjoh dengen hawa tempat.
Acclivity	Tempat djoerang.
Acclivous	Djoerang.
Accommodate	Moeatin; satoedjoe.
Accommodating	Berhati moelia.
Accommodation	Kasatoedjoean; pindjeman oewang.

Accommodations	Kasatoedjoean; logement (tempat menginep)..
Accompaniment	Barang jang diberikoetin atawa ditambain.
Accompanist	Toekang maen muziek jang pegang rol aken mengikoet lagoe
Accompany	Ikoet; pergi bersama-sama.
Accomplice	Orang jang berikoet dosa.
Accomplish	Bikin; kerdjaken.
Accomplished	Soeda bikin atawa soeda kerdjaken sampe abis (klaar).
Accomplishment	Pembikinan sampe abis; penambahan bagi kabagoesan.
Accord	Akoer; perdjandjian.
Accordance	Pengakoeran; karoekoenan: moefakatan.
Accordant	Ingin boeat akoer atawa meloeloesken.
Accordingly	Dengen hati jang ingin akoer atawa meloeloesken; dengen menoeroet..
Accordion	Harmonika (permaenan muziek)..
Accost	Omong bermoela.
Accostable	Soeka bergaoelan; soeka mentjari sobat.
Account	Peritoengan; lantaran; kabaean.
Account	Itoeng atawa memoetoesin; mendjawab.
Accountability	Kapertjajaän boeat kasi peritoengan.
Accountable	Berhoeboeng dengen peritoengan; boleh dipertjaja.
Accountableness	Perhoeboengan atawa kapertjajaän boeat mendjawab; kewadjiban.
Accountant	Orang jang pande atawa dipake boeat simpen peritoengan.
Accoutre	Sertain; lengkepin dengen sendjata.
Accoutrements	Lengkepan dari sendjata.
Accredit	Kasi kapertjajaän atawa kahormatan.
Accrescent	Menamba; menoemboe.
Accretion	Penambahan; pertoemboean.
Accretive	Menamba; menoemboe.
Accrue	Bangoen; ditambaken.

Accumbency	Keadaän lagi reba atawa tidoer.
Accumbent	Bereba atawa bertidoer.
Accumulate	Bertoemploek; bersoesoen; bertamba.
Accumulation	Toemploekan; soesoenan; tambahan.
Accumulative	Jang menoemploek, bersoesoen, atawa menamba.
Accumulator	Orang jang toemploekin, soesoen atawa tamba.
Accuracy	Tjotjoknja; betoelnja.
Accurate	Tjotjok; betoel.
Accurately	Dengen tjotjok; dengen betoel.
Accurse	Soempaken; koetoeken.
Accursed,	
Accurst	Jang disoempaken atawa dikoetoeken.
Accusant	Orang jang berklak atawa mendakwa.
Accusation	Perboeatan berklak atawa mendakwa.
Accusative	Berhoeboeng dengen kelakan atawa dakwaän.
Accuse	Berklak atawa mendakwa.
Accuser	Orang jang mendakwa.
Accustom	Biasa; keseringan; toeman.
Ace	As dari kartoe Olanda (kartoe dji-it).
Aceldama	Lapangan dara.
Acephalous	Tiada berkepala.
Acerbity	Pait dari rasa atawa dari alcohol.
Acescent	Bisa djadi asem.
Acetify	Djadi asem; djadi tjoeka.
Acetous	Mempoenjai rasa sebagi tjoeka.
Ache	Sakit.
Achievable	Jang boleh dibikin atawa dikerdjaken.
Achieve	Bikin; kerdjaken; dapet.
Achievement	Pembikinan; perboeatan.
Aching	Sakit; merasa-sakit.
Achromatic	Polos; tiada bewarna.
Acicular	Beroman dan tadjem sebagi djaroem.
Acid	Barang jang asem, asem sebagi tjoeka.

Acdify	Bikin atawa djadiken tjoeka.
Acidity	Kaäseman ; ketadjeman.
Acidulate	Taroin barang asem.
Acidulous	Rada-rada asem.
Acknowledge	Mengakoe ; akoe.
Acknowledge-ment.	Pengakoean ; pengrasaän trima kasi.
Acme	Poentjak dari soeatoe barang; bagian jang paling tinggi dari soeatoe barang.
Acorn	Boea dari poehoen *oak* (sebagi disini poenja poehoen djati).
Acoustic	Berhoeboeng dengen pendengeran koeping.
Acoustics	Peladjaran ilmoe soeara.
Acquaint	Bersobat ; kasi taoe.
Acquaintanee	Sobat ; persobatan.
Acquanted	Dikasi taoe ; kenal ; bersobat.
Acquiesce	Merasa poeas atawa moefakat.
Acpuiescence	Moefakatan.
Acquiescent	Soeka mengala.
Acquirable	Boleh didapetin.
Acquire	Dapet.
Acquirement	Pendapetan.
Acquisition	Perboeatan aken mendapet; barang jang ditjari.
Acquisitiveness	Kainginan boeat mempoenjai atawa dapet.
Acquit	Membebas ; bikin teges.
Acquitment	Perboeatan boeat membebasken; pembikinan teges.
Acquittal	Pembebasan dari toedoehan.
Acquittance	Penerimaän penoe dari peroetangan.
Acre	Satoe petak tana besarnja 160 rod pesegi ; bouw.
Acreage	Sakoempoelan petak-petak tana dalem peroesahan.
Acred	Mempoenjai petak-petak tana.
Acrid	Getir ; pait.

Acridity	Rasa getir atawa pait.
Acrimonious	Pait.
Acrimony	Kapitan.
Acritude	Rasa pait.
Acrobat	Toekang dansoe atawa soenglap.
Across	Melintang; menjebrang.
Acrostic	Sairan jang apabila diambil kepala barisannja bisa djadi satoe nama.
Act	Berboeat; bikin perboeatan; rol komedi.
Action	Perboeatan; praprangan; prilakoe.
Actionable	Boleh didakwa.
Active	Sebat; radjin.
Actively	Dengen sebat atawa radjin.
Activity	Kasebatan atawa keradjinan.
Actor	Orang jang bermaen komedi; anak-komedi.
Actress	Orang prempoean jang bermaen komedi; anak-komedi prempoean.
Actual	Betoel; tentoe.
Actuary	Krani; djoeroetoelis.
Actuate	Dikerdjaken; dibangoenken.
Acuity	Tadjemnja; oedjoengnja.
Aculeate	Tadjem; beroedjoeng berdoeri.
Acumen	Katadjeman otak.
Acuminate	Tadjem bikin tadjem.
Acumination	Oedjoeng jang tadjem.
Acute	Tadjem.
Acuteness	Katadjeman otak; kasebatan.
Adage	Pribahasa; mistal.
Adamant	Batoe keras; inten.
Adamantine	Keras sebagi batoe.
Adapt	Goenaken; disatoedjoein.
Adaptibility	Keadaän jang boleh digoenaken atawa disatoedjoein.
Adaptable	Boleh digoenaken atawa disatoedjoein.
Adaptation	Perboeatan menggoenaken.
Adapted	Soeda digoenaken atawa disatoedjoein.

Add	Tamba; bikin djadi besar.
Addendum	Barang tambahan.
Addenda	Barang-barang tambahan.
Adder	Oeler santja jang besar.
Addict	Soeka dari kebiasaän; toeman.
Addictedness	Kasoekahan dari kebiasaän; adat jang soeda djadi toeman.
Addiction	Kasoekahan hati.
Addition	Tambahan; itoengan tamba.
Additional	Penambahan.
Additive	Jang boleh ditamba.
Addle	Bikin roesak; bikin tiada bisa branak.
Addled	Roesak; tiada bisa melahirken anak.
Address	Adresin; berbahasain; bikin pertjintahan.
Address	Adres; alamat soerat.
Addressee	Orang jang diadresin atawa dialamatken; orang pada siapa satoe soerat ingin disampeken.
Adduce	Bawa ka depan; boedjoek.
Adducible	Boleh dibawa ka depan; boleh diboedjoek.
Adduction	Pembawahan ka depan.
Adept	Pande; orang pande.
Adeqnate	Satoedjoe.
Adhere	Berlengket.
Adherence	Adat berlengket.
Adherent	Berlengket; berhoeboeng; orang jang ada mempoenjai perhoeboengan; perseroan.
Adherer	Orang jang berlengket dengen pemimpinnja atawa kaoem.
Adhesion	Perboeatan atawa keadaän jang berlengket.
Adhesive	Berlengket.
Adhesively	Dengen mempoenjai adat berlengket.
Adhesiveness	Adat berlengket.
Adieu	Slamat tinggal.
Adjective	Perkataän jang menoendjoekin matjem atawa romannja barang.

Adjoin	Samboeng; ambil bagian.
Adjoining	Tersamboeng; deket; berdamping.
Adjourn	Moendoerken sampe di laen waktoe.
Adjournment	Pemoendoeran di laen waktoe.
Adjudge	Poetoesin perkara; bri hoekoeman,
Adjudgement	Poetoesan perkara; pembrian hoekoeman.
Adjudicate	Poetoesin; bersidang sebagi hakim.
Adjudication	Pamereksaän perkara atawa pembrian. hoekoeman.
Adjunct	Penamba; tamba.
Adjunction	Penambahan.
Adjunctive	Jang menamba.
Adjuration	Soempahan.
Adjure	Angkat soempa.
Adjust	Bikin tjotjok: pasang.
Adjustment	Pembikinan tjotjok; peratoeran.
Adjutancy	Pangkat adjudant.
Adjutant	Adjudant.
Adjutor	Pembantoe.
Administer	Oeroes sebagi administrateur.
Administerial	Berhoeboeng dengen oeroesan administratie
Administration	Oeroesan administratie.
Administrative	Jang mengoeroes.
Administrator	Administrateur; orang jang mengoeroes; pengoeroes.
Administrator-ship	Pangkat atawa pakerdjaännja satoe administrateur.
Administratrix	Pengoeroes prempoean.
Admirable	Bagoes; menjoekain hati; membikin kagoem.
Admirably	Dengen heran; dengen membikin kagoem.
Admiral	Laksamana; kepala prang laoet.
Admiralship	Pangkat atawa pakerdjaännja satoe laksamana.
Admirally	Kantoor boeat oeroes oeroesan angkatan prang laoet.

Admiration	Kaheranan; kakagoeman.
Admire	Kagoem; merasa heran.
Admirer	Orang jang merasa kagoem atawa heran; katjintahan.
Admissibility	Hak atawa keadaän jang boleh dikasi masoek.
Admissible	Boleh dikasi atawa dipermisiïn masoek.
Admission	Permisian masoek.
Admit	Permisiïn; kasi masoek; anggep bener.
Admittance	Hak boleh dikasi masoek.
Admix	Tjampoer.
Admixtion	Tjampoeran.
Admixture	Pertjampoeran; barang jang soeda ditjampoer.
Admonish	Kasi inget kasi advies atawa nasehat.
Admonisher	Orang jang kasi nasehat.
Admonition	Nasehat: omongan baek.
Admonitive	Bergengem nasehat.
Admonitor	Toekang membri nasehat.
Admonitary	Jang bri nasehat.
Ado	Riboet; kasoesahan.
Adolescence, Adolescency	Tempo moeda; tempo masi boleh besar.
Adopt	Poengoet atawa akoe boeat anak; pili.
Adoption	Pengakoean anak; pilihan.
Adoptive	Jang memoengoet anak atawa anak jang dipoengoet.
Adorability	Keadaän jang boleh dipoedja atawa disoedjoet.
Adorable	Boleh dipoedja atawa disoedjoet: soetji.
Adoration	Poedjahan atawa kasoedjoetan hati.
Adore	Poedja atawa bersoedjoet; tjinta dengen sagenep hati.
Adorer	Orang jang memoedja atawa bersoedjoet; orang jang menjinta atawa ditjinta dengen sagenep hati.

Adorn	Riasin; bikin bagoes.
Adornment	Periasan.
Adrift	Anjoet sasoekanja.
Adroit	Pinter; pande.
Adroitly	Dengen pinter; dengen pande.
Adroitness	Kapinteran; kapandean.
Adry	Aoes; maoe minoem.
Adscititious	Tambahan; lampiran.
Adulation	Tabiat bermoeka-moeka.
Adulatory	Jang bertabiat bermoeka-moeka.
Adult	Orang besar; orang jang soeda sampe oemoer.
Adulterate	Bergaoelan dengen orang djahat.
Adulterated	Djahat; berderadjat renda.
Adulteration.	Kalakoean djahat, oepama maen prempoean.
Adulterer	Orang jang soeka maen prempoean.
Adulteress	Orang prempoean jang berdjalan tiada baek
Adulterous	Mempoenjai kelakoean tiada baek.
Adultery	Perboeatan tiada baek antara orang lelaki dan orang prempoean.
Adultness	Keadaän soeda sampe oemoer.
Aduncous	Bengkok sebagi pantjing.
Adust	Panas sebagi terbakar.
Advance	Madjoe; angkat; naekin; bajar lebi doeloe (kasi voorschot).
Advancement	Kemadjoean; Keangkatan ka tingkat jang lebi tinggi.
Advantage	Faedahnja; kagoenaännja.
Advantageous.	Berfaedah; bergoena.
Advent	Kadatengannja; waktoe 4 minggoe sablonnja hari Natal.
Adventitious	Tambahan.
Adventual	Berhoeboeng dengen kadatengannja atawa tempo 4 minggoe sablonnja hari Natal.
Adventure	Perboeatan jang gaga brani.

Adventurous	Gaga brani.
Adverb	Perkataän jang menoendjoekin begimana satoe perboeatan ada dilaloeken.
Adverbial	Berhoeboeng dengen atawa sebagi satoe perkataän jang menoendjoekin begimana satoe perboeatan ada dilakoeken.
Adverbially	Dengen mempoenjai keadaän sebagi satoe perkataän jang menoedjoekin begimana satoe perboeatan ada dilakoeken.
Adversary	Moesoe.
Adverse	Bertentangan ; melawan.
Adversely	Dengen bertentangan; atawa melawan.
Adversity	Nasib djelek.
Advert	Roba haloean; mendoesin; perdoeliken.
Advertence	Perdoelian ; perhatian.
Advertent	Perdoeli; teliti.
Advertise, Advertize	Masoekin dalem halaman advertentie; kasi orang banjak taoe.
Advertisement	Advertentie ; pembrihan taoe pada orang banjak.
Advertiser	Orang jang masoekin advertentie.
Advertising	Bri atawa ada mempoenjai advertentie.
Advice	Advies; nasehat; kabar.
Advice-boat	Praoe pranti membawa kabaran.
Advisable	Boleh dikerdjaken.
Advisableness	Katjoekoepan; kasatoedjoean.
Advisably	Dengen bergengem nasehat; dengen pinter
Advise	Bri nasehat; bri kabar.
Advisedly	Dengen dibri nasehat dengen disengadja.
Adviser	Orang jang membri nasehat; adviseur.
Advisery	Mempoenjai hak aken bri nasehat; kasi nasehat.
Advocacy	Permoehoenan; dakwaän; perlindoengan.
Advocate	Orang jang bikin permoehoenan, dakwaän atawa perlindoengan.

Adynamic	Lema; tiada koeat; kenji.
Adynamy	Kalemahan: kakenjian.
Adytum	Gredja poenja bagian dalem.
Adz, Adze	Linggis kampak.
Aerate	Bikin berhawa sebagi aer Olanda.
Aerated Waters	Minoeman jang berisi hawa gas sebagi aer Olanda, limonade d. l. l.
Aerial	Berhoeboeng dengen hawa oedara; tinggi.
Aerie	Sarang boeroeng groeda atawa arend.
Aeriform	Mempoenjai hawa gas.
Aerify	Bikin berhawa.
Aerolite	Namanja saroepa batoe.
Aerometry	Ilmoe peladjaran hawa gas.
Aeronaut	Orang jang pande dalem ilmoe terbang.
Aeronautic	Berhoeboeng dengen peladjaran ilmoe ter- bang.
Aeronautics	Ilmoe boeat terbang di oedara.
Aerostatics	Ilmoe boeat perhatiken hawa oedara jang diam.
Aerostation	Peladjaran boeat terbang di oedara.
Asthetic	Liat *Esthetic*.
Afar	Djaoe.
Affability	Prikasopanan.
Affable	Sopan.
Affably	Dengen sopan; satjara sopan.
Affair	Pakerdjahan; oeroesan.
Affect	Berlakoe; menggeraken; mengenain; per- toendjoeken.
Affectation	Pertoendjoekan palsoe; pri-lakoe jang di- boeat-boeat.
Affected	Tergerak hati.
Affectedly	Dengen tergerak hati.
Affecting	Bergeraken hati orang.
Affectingly	Dengen maksoed boeat bergeraken hati orang.
Affection	Kasoekahan hati; katjintahan.
Affectionate	Jang tertjinta.

Affiance	Soerat kawin; melamar; toendangken.
Affianced	Soeda ditoendangin.
Affiche	Soerat pembrihan taoe jang ditempel di tembok.
Affiliate	Poengoet boeat anak; bersariket.
Affiliation	Poengoetan boeat anak; persariketan.
Affinity	Perhoeboengan dari kawin.
Affirm	Bilang dengen teroes trang; pastiken; tentoeken.
Affirmable	Boleh dipastiken atawa ditentoeken.
Affirmant	Orang jang mempastiken atawa menentoeken.
Affirmantion	Pembitjarahan jang teroes-terang; kapastian
Affirmative	Jang dirasa boleh dipastiken.
Affirmer	Orang jang mempastiken atawa bitjara teroes-terang.
Affix	Berlengketin; berikoetin.
Affix	Soerat atawa omongan jang ditambaken di boentoet laen perkataän.
Afflict	Kasi sakit; persakiti; menjoesaken.
Affliction	Kesoesahan; kesakitan.
Affluent	Soengei atawa kali ketjil; hartawan atawa kaja.
Afford	Sanggoep pikoel atawa kasi kaloear ongkos.
Affray	Pertengkaran jang heibat
Affright	Ketakoetan; bikin takoet.
Affront	Kesalaän dengon perkataän atawa perboeatan; kasi sala.
Afloat	Mengambang di moeka aer.
Aflore	Lebi doeloe dari; lebi lekas atawa siang
Afraid	Takoet.
Afresh	Baroe-baroe; belon lama.
Aft	Blakang atawa mengadepin ka blakang kapal.
After	Sasoedanja; di blakang.

Afternoon	Lohor; Liwat djam 12 tengahari.
Afterwards	Kamoedian; di laen waktoe.
Again	Lagi sakali; lagi.
Against	Pada; melawan pada.
Agape	Dalem kaheranan.
Agate	Samatjem · batoe permata jang sebagi batoe *quartz*.
Age	Oemoer; toeroenan.
Aged	Beroemoer; toewa.
Agency	Pakerdjahan dari satoe agent.
Agent	Agent; orang jang mengoeroes pakerdjahan boeat laen orang; alesan atawa pengaroe jang koewat.
Agglomerate	Berkoempoel atawa toemboe daiem goemploekan.
Agglutinate	Bikin berlengket.
Aggrandize	Bikin besar; besarken.
Aggravate	Bikin djadi lebi roesak atawa djelek.
Aggregate	Koempoelan atawa djoemblaän; koempoelin atawa djoemblain.
Aggression	Kembang berklai.
Aggressor	Orang jang moelai berklai.
Aghast	Kaget; heran.
Agile	Tjepet; gesit.
Agitate	Ganggoe; bikin bergerek atawa mara·
Ago	Doeloe; jang soeda liwat.
Agog	Soeda naek moerka dan bersedia; dalem pengrasaän kapingin atawa ingin taoe.
Agonize	Merasa sakit.
Agony	Sakit jang heibat.
Agrarian	Termasoek dalem bilangan sawa atawa tana.
Agree	Akoer; moefakat.
Agreeable	Sedap; satoedjoe.
Agreement	Moefakatan; perdjandjian.
Agriculture	Ilmoe menani.

Agriculturist	Orang tani.
Aground	Kandas.
Ague	Meriang dingin.
Ah !	Oetjapan dari kaget.
Ahead	Madjoe.
Aid	Pertoeloengan; toeloeng.
Ail	Sakit.
Ailment	Penjakit.
Aim	Haloean ; toedjoehan ; djoedjoe; berichtiar.
Air	Hawa oedara; laga atama prilakoe; kering·
Airing	Menoenggang atawa djalan dalem hawa oedara.
Airpump	Pompa angin.
Aisle	Samping gredja.
Ajar	Terboeka sedikit.
Akimbo	Bengkok; legat-legot.
Akin	Sama; berhoeboeng-familie.
Alack !	Ai !
Alacritry	Persediaän jang girang.
Alarm	Ketakoetan; bikin takoet; kasi tanda.
Alarm-clock.	Wekker: lotjeng ketjil jang disertain bel.
Alarum	Pekakas dalem lotjeng boeat bangoenin orang.
Alas !	Ai !; seboelan dari tanda soesa hati.
Alb	Rompi dari linnen poeti.
Albatross	Boeroeng laoet jang besar.
Albeit	Maski begitoe; kendati begitoe.
Albino	Orang bangsa Negro jang poeti; orang atawa binatang jang mempoenjai ramboet poeti dan mata mera.
Albion	Nama laen boeat negri Inggris.
Album	Album; boekoe pranti taro potret atawa kartoe-post.
Albumen	Poeti telor.
Alcohol	Alcohol; arak api; spiritus.

Alderman	Pembesar kota.
Ale	Bier; minoeman jang terbikin dari tape.
Alert	Mendjaga; pasang mata-mata.
Algebra	Ilmoe itoeng dalem mana ada digoenaken hoeroef.
Alias	Alias; atawa; sebaliknja.
Alibi	Dimana mana.
Alien	Orang asing; asing.
Alienate	Bawa ka laen keadaän; bikin asing.
Alight	Mentjlok; laloe.
Alike	Saroepa; samatjem.
Aliment	Makanan; pikoeat badan.
Alive	Hidoep; berdjiwa.
All	Semoea; antero.
Allay	Bikin toeroen; bikin dingin.
Allege	Moefakat; minta maäf.
Allegiance	Kewadjiban; kesetiaän.
Allegory	Omongan jang dipetain; sindiran.
Alleviate	Bikin senang; bikin koerang.
Alley	Djalanan jang sempit; gang.
Alliance	Persariketan; kontract.
Alliteration	Perkata-perkataän jang moelai dengen letter jang sama.
Allot	Kasi; briken; bagi.
Allotment	Pembrian; bagian dari tana.
Allow	Bri idjin; akoe.
Allowance	Idjin; korting atawa potongan procent.
Alloy	Logam tjampoeran.
Allude	Maksoedi dengen menjimpang; sindirin.
Allure	Boedjoekan; pikatan.
Allusion	Maksoed jang menjimpang; sindiran.
Alluvial	Beraeran.
Ally	Bersobat; bersariket.
Almanac	Almanak; kalender; tarich.
Almighty	Toehan-Allah; semoea koewat.
Almond	Samatjem kenari.

Almoner	Orang jang soeka berboeat amal.
Almost	Ampir; deket.
Alms	Amal; sedeka.
Aloe,	Tetaneman jang pait.
Aloft	Tinggi; di atas.
Alone	Sendiri; sendirian.
Along	Sapandjang; bersama-sama.
Aloof	Djaoeken.
Aloud	Soeara keras; njaring.
Alphabet	Soerat atawa letter menoeroet djalannja a b c.
Already	Soeda; dalem tempo jang soeda liwat.
Also	Djoega; begitoepoen.
Altar	Medja sembajang.
Alter	Tockar; berlaenan.
Alteration	Penoekaran.
Alternate	Dengen giliran.
Altenative	Pilihan antara doea; kasi pilihan.
Although	Maskipoen; kendatinja.
Altitude	Tingginja; bangoennja dari moeka tana.
Altogether	Sama sekali; anteronja.
Alum	Tawas.
Aluminium	Aluminium; logam jang paling enteng.
Always	Selaloe; senantiasa.
Am	Ada; mendjadi.
Amain	Dengen sakoewat-koewatnja.
Amalgam	Aer perak tertjampoer dengen laen logam.
Amalgamate	Tjampoer; djadiken satoe.
Amanuensis	Secretaris; djoeroe soerat.
Amass	Koempoelin; djadiken satoe.
Amateur	Orang jang soeka dengen berbagi-bagi ilmoe aloes; mendateng; boekan pakerdjahannja jang sedjati.
Amaze	Kaget; terkedjoet.
Amazon	Prempoean gaga perkasa; nama dari satoe soengei besar di Amerika Selatan.

Ambassador	Kong-soe; peganti atawa wakil radja atawa keizer begitoepoen President dari satoe negri.
Ambiguous	Sangsi; tjoeriga.
Ambition	Kagiatan; kagoembirahan.
Ambulance	Hospitaal atawa roema sakit di lapangan peprangan.
Ambush	Semoeni; baijhok.
Amen!	Demikianlah! Amin!
Amend	Bikin lebi baek; memperbaiki; djadi lebi baek.
Amends	Pembalesan.
Amenity	Kealoesan dari omongan atawa adat.
Amerce	Hoekoem denda
Amethyst	Batoe permata jang mempoenjai warna biroe toea.
Amiable	Boleh diboeat kagoem; boleh ditjintai.
Amicable	Satjara sobat; satjara dami.
Amid	Antara.
Amiss	Sala; kliroe.
Amity	Persobatan; perdamian.
Ammonia	Ammonia; aer asem jang mempoenjai baoe pesing.
Ammunition	Obat pasang; barang jang perloe dipake oleh balatentara.
Amnesty	Pembrian ampoen jang loear biasa.
Among	Antara.
Amorous	Soeka; tjinta.
Amorphous	Tiada beroman.
Amount	Djoembla; totaal; sampeken.
Amphibious	Bisa hidoep dalem aer dan di hawa oedara.
Amphitheatre	Gedong atawa pekarangan jang beroman boender atawa londjong pranti komedi maen.
Ample	Banjak; rojaal.
Amplify	Bikin banjak; bikin rojaal.

Amputate	Potong kaki.
Amuiet	Djimat; goena-goena.
Amuse	Bikin senang; hiboerin.
An	Satoe, dipake di hadepan perkataän jang moelai dengen a, e, i, o, u.
Anaesthetic	Obat tidoer.
Analogy	Roman jang mirip atawa bersamaän.
Analysis	Petjahan dari bebrapa bagian.
Analyze, Analyse.	Petja djadi bebrapa bagian; balik ka pikiran jang pertama.
Anarchy	Hoeroe-hara; gerakan anak-rahajat jang melawan pada pamerenta.
Anatomy	Ilmoe potong toeboe menoesia; tengkorak menoesia.
Ancestor	Leloehoer; kake-mojang.
Anchor	Djangkar; brenti atawa singga.
Anchorite	Saorang pertapaän; orang jang djaoeken diri dari orang banjak.
Ancient	Toea; dari djeman dahoeloe kala.
And	Dan; perkataän dipake boeat samboeng omong.
Anecdote	Tjerita pendek.
Aneroid	Oekoeran hawa-oedara.
Anew	Baroe; lagi sekali.
Angel	Bidadari; perikajangan.
Angelic	Termasoek dalem bilangan bidadari atawa peri-kajangan.
Anger	Rasa amarah; goesar hati; bikin mara atawa goesar.
Angle	Oedjoeng dari doea garisan.
Angler	Toekang pantjing ikan dengen satoe djoran
Angry	Mara; goesar.
Anguish	Sakit heibat dari pikiran atawa toeboe.
Angular	Mempoenjai poloksok atawa pepodjok.
Animal	Machloek; binatang; termasoek dalem bilangan machloek atawa binatang.

Animalcule	Machlock atawa binatang jang paling aloes.
Animate	Bikin berdjiwa; bikin hidoep.
Animosity	Kebentjian jang sanget.
Ankle	Mata kaki.
Anklet	Periasan boeat mata kaki.
Annals	Hikajat; tjerita dari dahoeloe kala.
Annex	Samboeng; hoeboengken.
Annextion	Samboengan; hoeboengan.
Annihilate	Binasaken; bikin abis.
Anniversary	Hari saban taon.
Annotate	Bikin tjatetan.
Announce	Kata; wartaken.
Annoy	Ganggoe; bikin mara.
Annual	Tetaneman jang toemboe dan mati dalem satoe taon; saban taon.
Annuity	Djoembla oewang jang dibajar saban taon.
Annul	Bikin abis; singkirken.
Annular	Boender sebagi tjintjin.
Annunciate	Kata; wartaken.
Anoint	Gosok dengen gemoek atawa minjak.
Anomaly	Soeatoe keadaän jang tiada ketetepan.
Anon	Lekas; dengen tjepat.
Anonymous	Anoniem; tiada disertain nama.
Another	Laen; tiada sama.
Answer	Djawab; djawaban.
Answerable	Boleh didjawab; boleh diitoeng.
Ant	Semoet.
Antagonist	Moesoe.
Antarctic	Di sebrang djoeroesan Oetara.
Antecedent	Barang atawa perkataän jang djalan lebi doeloe atawa di hadepan; berdjalan lebi doeloe atawa di hadepan.
Antedate	Sablonnja tanggal jang ditentoeken.
Antelope	Binatang samatjem domba dan mendjangan.

Antemeridian	Sablonnja poekoel 12 tengahari.
Anteroom	Kamar jang menoentoen ka laen kamar.
Anthem	Lagoe soetji; njanjian keradjaän.
Anthology	Koempoelan dari sairan jang terpili; omongan pri-hal kembang atawa boenga.
Antic	Heran; loear biasa.
Antichrist	Orang jang bertentangan pada Nabi Jesus Kristus.
Anticipate	Berboeat lebi doeloe.
Antidote	Obat boeat poenaken ratjoen atawa kedjahatan.
Antiquary	Orang jang pande dengen hikajat dahoeloe kala.
Antiquated	Beroman koeno; djadi koeno.
Antique	Sisa peninggalan dari djeman koeno,
Antiqiuty	Djeman koeno; hikajat dari djeman koenoe atawa dahoeloe kala.
Antiseptic	Bisa bri rawatan baek.
Antithesis	Bertentangan dalem perkataän atawa pikiran.
Antitype	Barang atawa toelisan jang lebi doeloe dihoendjoek dengen tjitakan.
Antler	Tjabang tandoek.
Anus	Lobang pantat.
Anvil	Talenan besi pranti ketok besi panas.
Anxiety	Kekwatiran; kedoekaän.
Anxious	Kwatir; doeka.
Any	Sasoeatoe; sembarang.
Anywhere	Dimana-mana; di sasoeatoe atawa sembarang tempat.
Apace	Dengen tjepet; lekas.
Apart	Terpisa.
Apartment	Kamar; pangkeng.
Apathy	Tiada lengkep pengrasaän; botjeng; tiada inget orang poenja boedi.
Ape	Monjet; tiroe atawa adjokin.

Aperient	Obat bikin boewang aer; bikin djadi boewang aer.
Aperture	Lobang; gowa.
Apex	Oedjoeng; poentjak.
Apiece	Satoe potong; satoe bidji.
Apologize	Minta maäf; moehoen ampoen.
Apologue	Tjerita dongeng; tjerita sindiran
Apology	Permintaan maäf; permoehoenan ampoen pembelaän diri.
Apoplexy	Lingloeng pikiran.
Apostle	Mantri atawa orang soeroehan.
Apostolic	Termasoek dalem bilangan mantri atawa orang soeroehan.
Apostrophe	Tanda (') menjataken ada soerat jang ditinggalken atawa *poenja* dalem bahasa Inggris.
Apothecary	Toekang djoeal obat; orang jang djaga roema obat.
Appal	Ilang pengharepan; terkedjoet.
Apparatus	Pekakas atawa perabot.
Apparel	Pakean.
Apparent.	Djarang; bening.
Apparition	Setan; iblis.
Appeal	Appel; teeken appel.
Appear	Beroepa; keliatan.
Appearance	Roepa; roman.
Appease	Diam; dami.
Appellant	Orang jang teeken appel.
Appelation	Nama.
Append	Gantoeng atawa tambaken pada.
Appendix	Penambahan.
Appertain	Terbilangan; terpoenja.
Appetite	Napsoe makan.
Applaud	Bersoerak.
Applause	Soeara soerakan.
Apple	Boea appel; anak-anakan mata.

Appliance	Barang atawa oeroesan jang diminta dengen soerat.
Application	Permintaän dengen soerat.
Apply	Minta dengen soerat.
Appoint	Angkat; benoemd.
Appointment	Keangkatan.
Apportion	Bagi: pisa.
Apposite	Satoedjoe; sedeng.
Appraise	Taro harga.
Appreciate	Hargain; kagoemin.
Apprehend	Mengarti.
Apprehension	Maksoed; pengrasaän takoet; tangkepan.
Apprentice	Orang jang magang atawa bekerdja zonder gadji; magang atawa bekerdja zonder gadji.
Approach	Dateng deket; deketin atawa hampirin; begrooting; tambahan.
Approbation	Perkenanan.
Appropriate	Satoedjoe: dipisaken.
Approval	Perkenanan.
Approve	Soeka: perkenanken.
Approximate	Kira-kira: didoega paling deket.
April	Boelan ka ampat dari satoe taon: Yanglek Si-gwee.
Apron	Oto: toetoepan dada: tatakan pakean.
Apt	Tersangkoet: tiada loepoet: sedeng atawa satoedjoe.
Aptitude	Kasatoedjoean: kainginan.
Aptly	Dengen betoel: sasoenggoenja.
Aquarium	Glas pranti piara ikan atawa tetaneman.
Aquatic	Tinggal atawa hidoep dalem aer.
Aqeduct	Djalanan pranti angkoet aer: solokan atawa got.
Aqueous	Beraer: seperti aer,

Aquiline	Bengkok sebagi patok boeroeng.
Arable	Satoedjoe aken diloekoe.
Arbiter	Hakim; orang jang bri poetoesan dalem satoe perkara.
Arbitrary	Despotiek; tjoan-tji; berkwasa sendiri.
Arbitration	Pendengeran atawa pengakoean di hadepan satoe hakim; poetoesan dari satoe hakim.
Arbitrator	Orang jang dipili aken memoetoesken pertengkaran.
Arbour	Tempat tedoe; peseban di kebon atawa taman.
Arc	Bagian dari satoe boenderan.
Arcade	Djalanan jang atasnja tertoetoep.
Arch	Pembikinan sebagi roema pana atawa boelan sebla; jang oetama; bisa bermoeka-moeka.
Archaeology	Ilmoe peladjaran tentang djeman koeno atawa dahoeloe kala.
Archbishop	Padri kepala.
Archer	Toekang pana jang pande,
Architect	Ingineur; toekang bikin peta roema.
Architecture	Peta atawa model dari pembikinannja satoe roema, gedong dan sebaginja.
Archives	Harta peninggalan dari djeman koeno atawa gedong dalem mana barang itoe ada disimpen.
Arctic	Di djoeroesan Oetara; termasoek dalem djoeroesan Oetara.
Ardent	Ingin dengen sanget; goembira.
Ardour	Kainginan dengen sanget; kagoembirahan
Arduous	Biasa bekerdja berat; soesa dipandjet.
Area	Moeka berisinja.
Arena	Tempat terboeka bagi segala orang aken bertanding.
Argeu	Meroendingin.

Argument	Peroendingan; kalimat peroendingan.
Arid	Kering; glintingan.
Aright	Betoel; sampoerna.
Arise	Bangoen; naek.
Aristocracy	Pamerentahan jang dioeroes oleh pembesar negri; keangkeran.
Aristocrat	Orang jang menoendjang haloean pemerentahan jang dioeroes oleh pembesar negri.
Arithmetic	Ilmoe itoeng.
Ark	Peti kajoe.
Arm	Lengen; tjabang poehoen; moeara ketjil; lengkepin dengen alat-sendjata.
Armada	Pasoekan kapal prang.
Armament	Balatentara disediaken aken berprang; angkatan prang.
Armistice	Toendahan prang boeat samentara waktoe
Armlet	Gelang tangan.
Armour	Pakean prang terbikin dari besi.
Armourer	Pembikin alat sendjata.
Armoury	Goedang atawa tempat dimana alat-sendjata disimpen.
Arms	Alat-sendjata; alat paprangan.
Army	Balatentara; angkatan prang darat.
Aroma	Baoe jang enak.
Aromatic	Berbaoe enak; wangi.
Around	Koeliling; sakiternja.
Arouse	Bangoen; berkiser.
Arraign	Panggil mengadep di hadepan pengadilan.
Arrange	Atoer; bikin rapi.
Array	Barisan prang; pakean; atoer.
Arrears	Oetang jang belon terbajar loenas.
Arrest	Tangkep; tahan dalem pendjara.
Arrive	Sampe dari perdjalanan.
Arrow	Anak pana; boengsoer pana.

Arrowroot	Arrowroot; samatjem obi jang bisa mengaloearken sagoe jang baek didahar oleh orang sakit.
Arsenal	Fabriek sendjata; goedang alat-sendjata
Arsenic	Ratjoen jang sringkali terdapet di dalem parit dan bisa binasaken djiwa menoesia.
Arson	Pembakaran roema jang dilaloeken dengen sengadja.
Art	Kapandean; pengatahoean.
Artery	Oerat mera jang angkoet dara bersi.
Artesian	Soemoer bor.
Artful	Berakal; berdaja.
Article	Artikel; keadaän; barang.
Artificial	Terbikin dengen kapandean menoesia.
Artillery	Barisan meriam.
Artisan	Orang jang pande bekerdja; achli pakerdjahan.
Artist	Toekang teeken gambar atawa laen-laen ilmoe aloes.
Artiess	Zonder pake akal; gampang.
As	Seperti; samantara.
Ascend	Naek; bangoen.
Ascension	Naeknja; bangoennja.
Ascent	Naek; djoerangnja boekit.
Ascertain	Menentoeken; memboektiken.
Ash	Namanja saroepa poehoen jang termashoer di Europa.
Ashamed	Maloe.
Ashes	Aboe; sisa peninggalan dari barang jang dibakar.
Ashore	Di darat; di atas darat.
Aside	Di satoe sebla; terpisa.
Asinine	Bodo sebagi kerbo.
Ask	Minta; tanja; oendang.
Asleep	Poeles.

Asp	Samatjem oeler jang berbisa atawa bera-tjoen.
Aspect	Roepa; roman.
Asperity	Kekasaran.
Aspirate	Omong dengen bernapsoe.
Aspiration	Napsoe.
Aspire	Napsoein; djoedjoein.
Assail	Labrak; poekoel.
Assailant	Orang jang melabrak; orang jang me-moekoel.
Assassin	Pemboenoe.
Assult	Labrakan; poekoelan; labrak; poekoel.
Assay	Pertjobaän; oedjan; tjoba; oedji.
Assemble	Berkoempoel; berhimpoen.
Assembly	Vergadering; koempoelan; perhimpoe-nan.
Assent	Moefakat; kaboelken; trima baek.
Assert	Tanggoeng; menjataken betoel.
Assess	Taksiran atas padjek; taksir padjek.
Assets	Harta peninggalan jang moesti digoena-ken boeat bikin bersi oetang.
Assiduous	Radjin.
Assign	Bikin over; bikin baroe lagi; overdrag.
Assignation	Keangkatan.
Assignment	Pindahan pangkat atawa tempat.
Assist	Bantoe; toeloeng.
Assistant	Pembantoe; penoeloeng.
Assize	Pengadilan.
Associate	Temen bergaoelan; persero; tjampoer gaoel.
Assort	Atoer menoeroet matjemnja; pili.
Assortment	Pilihan.
Assume	Ambil; tanggoeng.
Assurance	Assurance; kapertjajaän; tanggoengan, prilakoe koerang sopan.
Assure	Tentoeken; akoe sah.

Aster	Tetaneman jang mempoenjai kembang sebagi binatang.
Asterisk	Tanda (*) dalem pertjitakan.
Asthma	Sakit sengal-sengal.
Astonish	Kaget; terkedjoet; heran.
Astound	Kaget; terkedjoet.
Astray	Kasasar.
Astride	Melintang; menjebrang.
Astringent	Obat mengoewatin badan; jang bikin kisoet atawa menarik.
Astrology	Ilmoe petang-petang dengen meliat bintang di langit.
Astronomy	Ilmoe peladjaran dari benda-benda jang ada di langit; thian-boen.
Asunder	Terpisa; djaoe.
Asylum	Roema sakit; roema gila.
At	di: pada.
Atheist	Orang jang tiada pertjaia Toehan Allah.
Athletic	Koewat; perma=nan sport.
Atlas	Boekoe peta boemi.
Atmosphere	Hawa oedara jang mengoeroengin boemi.
Atom	Sakeping ketjil dari barang.
Atone	Bikin commentaar; kasi sedikit pikiran.
Atrocity	Kedjahatan atawa kedosahan jang besar
Attach	Hoeboengken; menangken; tangkep.
Attachment	Ketjintahan jang kentel; penangkepan.
Attack	Poekoel; labrak.
Attain	Sampeken; hampirken.
Attempt	Pertjobaän; tjoba.
Attend	Hadlir rawatin balik pikiran.
Attendant	Pengikoet; djoeroe-rawat; boedjang.
Attention	Perhatian; pemandangan.
Attentive	Soeka perhatiken; teliti.
Attire	Pakean; berpake.
Attorney	Agent; advocaat; procureur.
Attract	Tarik; pikat.

Attractive	Bisa menarik hati; bisa mempikat.
Attribute	Qualiteit; matjem.
Attribute	Terbilang; didjadiken.
Auction	Lelang; pendjoewalan di hadepan orang banjak.
Audaclous	Gaga brani.
Audacity	Kegagahan; kebranihan.
Audible	Boleh didenger.
Audience	Pendengeran; perhimpoenan; audentie.
Audit	Pemereksaän atas peritoengan; preksa peritoengan.
Auger	Bor; kotrek.
Aught	Soeatoe barang; segala barang.
Augment	Tambahken; bikin lebi besar.
Augment	Tambahan.
August	Boelan ka delapan; Yanglek-Pe-gwee.
Aunt	Entjim, Koh, atawa Ie; tante.
Aurora	Terang tana.
Auspicious	Baek; terang.
Authentic	Toelen; betoel.
Author	Pengarang tjerita.
Authority	Kekwasaän; pengaroe.
Authorize	Bikin mempoenjai kekwasaän; akoe sah.
Autobiography	Riwajat dari satoe orang jang ditoelis oleh ianja sendiri.
Autocrat	Radja atawa pamerenta jang berkwasa besar atawa tjoan-tji.
Automobile	Automobiel; kreta motor.
Auxiliary	Pembantoe; bantoe.
Avail	Kagoenaän; kafaedahan; bergoena; berfaeda.
Avalanche	Goemploekan saldjoe jang djato di selat goenoeng.
Avast	Diam; tahan.
Avenge	Bales sakit hati.
Avenue	Djalanan di bawa-bawa poehoen.

Aver	Kata teroes trang.
Average	Poekoel rata; itoengan poekoel rata.
Averse	Tiada soedi; tiada ingin.
Aversion	Hati jang tiada soedi atawa tiada ingin.
Avert	Toekar; roba.
Aviation	Penerbangan; ilmoe tebang.
Aviator	Toekang terbang; orang jang toenggang kapal terbang.
Avoid	Singkirken; djaoeken.
Avow	Bitjara teroes trang.
Avowal	Pembitjaraän atawa pengakoean jang teroes trang.
Await	Toenggoe; menoenggoe,
Awake	Mendoesin; bangoen.
Award	Hoekoem; poetoesin; bales; koerniaken.
Aware	Taoe; mengatahoei.
Away	Pergi; djaoe.
Awe	Takoet; pengrasaän takoet.
Awful	Boleh ditakoet; ngeri.
Awfully	Dengen ngeri.
Awhile	Samentara waktoe; sabentaran.
Awkward	Djelek.
Awl	Poesoet; bor.
Awn	Koemis djagoeng atawa roempoet.
Awning	Tenda; toetoepan.
Awry	Tiada rata; gendjal-gendjoel.
Axe, Ax	Kampak.
Axiom	Mitsal; kabeneran jang tiada bisa dibantah.
Axis	Besi atawa kajoe poeteran; as roda.
Axle	As roda.
Ay	Ya; baek.
Aye	Selaloe; senantiasa.
Azure	Langit biroe; biroe.

B.

Babble	Mengatjo.
Babe	Anak ketjil; anak orok.
Babel	Kalang-kaboetan; kekaloetan.
Baboon	Saroepa monjet jang paling besar.
Baby	Anak ketjil; anak orok.
Bachelor	Orang lelaki jang belon kawin atawa menika; djedjaka.
Back	Blakang; di blakang; balik toendjang.
Backbone	Toelang blakang.
Background	Tana atawa pekarangan jang pernanja di blakang; halangan.
Backsheesh	Persenan oewang.
Backward	Ka blakang; moendoer.
Bacon	Daging babi jang diasinin atawa diasep; ham.
Bad	Djahat; djelek.
Badge	Tanda.
Baffle	Kalaken; menangin.
Bag	Kantong; kantongin.
Baggage	Perabot dari balatentara; barang bekelan.
Bail	Tanggoengan; kasi tanggoengan.
Bairn	Nama Scotch boeat anak ketjil.
Bait	Oempan; taroken oempan.
Bake	Bakar; panggang.
Baker	Toekang roti.
Balance	Timbangan; timbang.
Balcony	Djoebin di hadepan djendela lankan.
Bald	Botak.
Bale	Baal; boengkoesan besár; tiada tertjampoer aer.
Baleful	Menjilakain; berbahaja.
Balk	Penglari roema; halangin.
Ball	Bola; pesta dansa.

Ballad	Lagoe jang gampang dan disoekai oleh orang banjak.
Ballast	Barang berat boeat imbangin kapal.
Balloon	Balon.
Ballot	Keangkatan dengen resia; angkat dengen resia.
Balm	Obat gosok.
Balmy	Bisa menjemboeken; enak.
Balsam	Zalf; kojo.
Baluster	Lankan; pilar ketjil.
Balustrade	Derekan lankan.
Bamboo	Bamboe.
Ban	Soempaken; koetoekin; soempahan; koe-toekan.
Band	Bán; angkin iketan pinggang; koempoe-lan; berkoempoel.
Bandage	Iketan; verband.
Bandy	Bengkok; toekar.
Bane	Asal-oesoelnja ketjilakaän; keroesakan.
Baneful	Menjilakain; berbahaja.
Bangle	Periasan boeat kaki atawa tangan.
Banish	Singkirken; laloeken.
Bank	Toemploekan; pinggir kali; bank pranti simpen oewang koempoelin; berniaga dengen bank.
Banker	Bankier; pengoeroes bank.
Bankrupt	Bankroet; tiada bisa bajar oetang; failliet.
Banner	Bendera.
Banquet	Pesta atawa perdjamoean besar.
Bantam	Ajam kate.
Baptism	Mandihan dengen aer soetji.
Baptist	Orang jang mandiken laen orang dengen aer soetji; orang jang dimandiken de-ngen aer soetji pada waktoe soeda beroemoer dewasa.
Baptize	Dimandiken dengen aer soetji; dinasaraniken.

Bar	Palangan; bagian dalem permaenan mu-siek; halangan; palangin.
Barbarian	Orang biadab; asing; koerang adjar; tiada sopan.
Barbarous	Kasar; tiada sopan; biadab.
Barber	Toekang goenting ramboet; toekang tjoe-koer; coiffeur.
Bard	Toekang muziek; pengarang sair.
Bare	Telandjang; tiada berpakean; telandjan-ngin.
Bargain	Tawaran; pembikinan kontract tawar.
Barge	Kapal besar.
Bark	Koelit kajoe; kapal tiga tiang; gonggo-ngan andjing; menggonggong sebagi andjing; keset koelit poehoen.
Barley	Saroepa gandoem; trigoe.
Barm	Dek; ragi; tape.
Barn	Loemboeng; goeboek.
Barnacle	Sipoet ketjil; kiong ketjil.
Barometer	Oekoeran hawa oedara.
Baron	Pangkat di bawa burggraaf; gelaran dari satoe hakim.
Baronet	Gelaran di bawa baron.
Barrack	Tangsi; benteng.
Barrel	Tong atawa tahang; taro dalem tong atawa tahang.
Barren	Tiada gemoek; tiada bisa mengaloearken boea; tiada bisa melahirken anak.
Barricade	Pakerdjahan boeat mendjaga moesoe.
Barrier	Wates negri; halangan.
Barrister	Advocaat.
Barrow	Kreta atawa grobak jang disoeroeng de-ngen tangan.
Barter	Toekaran; toekar-menoekar.
Base	Fondament; tatakan; renda; hina; ber-diriken.

Baseless	Tiada mempoenjai fondement; tiada kedjakdjak.
Baseness	Kedjahatan; kehinaän.
Beshful	Taoe adat; pemaloean.
Basilisk	Tjetjek kiber.
Basin	Bin-poen; bintang; ember.
Basis	Fondament; tatakan, toendjangan.
Basket	Bakoel; tetampa.
Baas	Soeara jang paling renda dalem permaenan muziek; renda; dalem.
Bastard	Anak tjampoeran; anak gladak.
Baste	Taroin gemoek atawa minjak; djait pelahan-pelahan.
Bat	Poekoelan bola; kampret atawa kalong.
Batch	Koempoelan barang jang sama roepanja.
Bath	Tempat mandi; mandian.
Bathe	Mandi.
Baton	Roejoeng.
Battalion	Bataljon divisie balatentara.
Batten	Papan jang tiada lebar; kentjengin.
Batter	Tjampoeran; adoeken atawa adonan; tepoeng pisang goreng; kopiok.
Battery	Pemoekoelan; batterij; koempoelan atawa barisan meriam.
Battle	Paprangan.
Bawl	Bertriak; berseroe.
Bay	Moeara; kwala; warna kenari; menggonggong sebagi andjing.
Bayonet	Bajonet; pedang di oedjoeng senapan; toesoek.
Bazaar	Pasar; tempat pendjoealan.
Be	Mendjadi; biar.
Beach	Pinggir laoet; kandasan.
Beacon	Penerangan boeat kasi tanda kesoesaän; roema api.
Bead	Moetee; merdjan.

Beak	Patok.
Beam	Kajoe; penglari; tjahia matari.
Bean	Katjang boentjis.
Bear	Biroewang; melahirken; mengaloearken; tahan; bawa.
Beard	Tjambang; djenggot.
Bearer	Pembawa soerat; soeroehan.
Bearing	Pri-lakoe.
Bearish	Kasar; koerang adjar.
Beast	Binatang boewas.
Beastly	Sebagi binatang; liar.
Beat	Poekoel; poekoelan.
Beatitude	Bagoes; tjantik.
Beautiful	Berkah.
Beauty	Kabagoesan; katjantikan.
Because	Sebab; oleh kerna.
Beck	Tanda jang dibikin dengen kepala atawa tangan.
Beckon	Kasi tanda dengen kepala atawa tangan.
Become	Mendjadi.
Becoming	Boleh djadi; bagoes.
Bed	Tempat tidoer; randjang; dasarnja kali atawa soengei; taro dalem tempat tidoer.
Bedding	Perabot boeat tempat tidoer.
Bedlam	Roema-gila.
Bedridden	Selaloe berbaring dalem tempat tidoer; tiada bisa bangoen dari tempat tidoer.
Bedroom	Kamar tidoer; pankeng.
Bedstead	Besi randjang.
Bee	Tawon.
Beech	Poehoen kenari.
Beef	Daging sampi.
Beer	Bier.
Beet	Samatjem obi jang boleh diboeat bikin goela; obi biet.
Beetle	Koembang; saroepa tawon; gantoeng.

Befall	Terdjadi.
Befit	Sedengin.
Before	Sablonnja; lebi doeloe.
Beforehand	Waktoe; sablonnja; lebi doeloe.
Beg	Minta dengen sanget.
Beget	Lahirken; mendjelemaken.
Beginning	Permoelaän.
Begone	Soeda liwat.
Beguile	Tipoe; hiboerin hati.
Behalf	Kabaean; kaoentoengan; kagoenaän; bagian.
Behave	Berlakoe.
Behaviour	Tingka-lakoe; pri-lakoe.
Behead	Potong kepala.
Behest	Prenta; titaken.
Behind	Di blakang.
Behold	Liat.
Beholden	Mengoetang; teroetang.
Beholder	Pengliat; orang jang meliat.
Behoof	Kabaean; kaoentoengan; kagoenaän.
Behove	Djadi bergoena; djadi kaoentoengan.
Being	Mendjadi; machloek.
Belfry	Tempat klenengan.
Belief	Kapertjaiaän.
Believe	Pertjaia.
Bell	Klenengan; lotjeng.
Belle	Prempoean bagoes.
Bellicose	Sebagi orang paprangan.
Belligerent	Koempoelan orang jang mengadep di medan prang.
Bellow	Bertriakan jang seroe; mengeroeng.
Bellows	Perkakas pranti tioep api; hong-kwie.
Belly	Peroet.
Belong	Terpoenja; djadi miliknja.
Below	Di bawa.
Belt	Band; tali iketan pinggang; angkin.

Bench	Bangkoe; kadoedoekannja hakim; koempoelan hakim.
Bend	Bengkokin; eloek.
Beneath	Di bawa.
Benedictine	Baek-boedi; berhati baek.
Benediction	Berkah kaslamatan.
Benefactor	Orang jang berboeat kabaean pada laen orang; toean-penoeloeng; in-djin.
Beneficial	Aken goenanja; kaoentoengannja.
Benefit	Kagoenaän; kaoentoengan.
Benevolence	Boedi-kabaean.
Benign	Baek; berhati lembek.
Bent	Kainginan; bengkok.
Benzine	Benzine; minjak gasoline.
Bequeath	Lepas atas kamaoehan sendiri.
Bequest	Kalepasan atas maoe sendiri.
Bereave	Loepoetken; bebasken.
Berry	Bidji; roekem.
Berth	Tempat tidoer di atas kapal; station kapal.
Beryl	Batoe permata idjo.
Beseech	Minta dengen sanget.
Beset	Koeroeng; kiterin.
Besetting	Kebiasaän.
Beside	Di sebla; di samping.
Besides	Salaennja; katjoewali.
Besiege	Koeroeng; kepoeng; kepoengan.
Bespeak	Tanja lebi doeloe; bitjara lebi siang.
Best	Paling baek; No. 1.
Bestial	Kotor; mesoem; djorok.
Bestow	Kasi; seraken.
Bet	Tarohan; bertaro.
Betide	Terdjadi.
Betimes	Dalem tempo jang baek.
Betray	Tipoe; tjilakain: djoewal.
Betroth	Bertoendangan.
Better	Lebi baek; bikin lebi baek.

Betters	Orang jang mempoenjai penghidoepan lebi bagoes.
Between	Antara; terapit.
Beverage	Minoeman dari segala matjem.
Bewail	Doekaken; sediïn.
Beware	Ati-ati.
Bewilder	Bingoeng.
Bewitch ·	Dimasoeken setan atawa iblis; angker.
Bey	Pembesar bangsa Toerki.
Beyond	Di sebrang.
Bias	Kabengkokan; keserongan hati.
Bib	Tatakan iler.
Bible	Kitab soetji; boekoe sembajang.
Biblical	Berhoeboeng dengen kitab soetji.
Bibulous	Seperti spons; bisa melar.
Bicker	Katain; omelin; maki.
Bicycle	Sepeda; roda angin,
Bid	Tawaran di lelang; soeda soeroe: tawarin harga.
Bidding	Oendangan.
Bide	Tinggal; berdiam.
Bier	Kreta mati.
Bifurcate	Bergarpoe; bertjagak.
Big	Besar; hamil.
Bigamy	Kadosahan lantaran mempoenjai doea istri atawa soeami.
Bight	Moeara jang tjetek; goeloengan tambang
Bigot	Kaoem jang bandel; kaoem koeno atawa koekoet.
Bigotry	Kakoenoan; kakoekoetan.
Bile	Njali.
Bilious	Berhoeboeng dengen njali.
Bill	Patok boeroeng; peritoengan rekening.
Billet	Tjatetan; potongan kajoe; soldadoe pendjaga boeat sementara waktoe.
Billiards	Permaenan bola di atas medja; billiard,

Billion	Million-million; joeta-joeta.
Billow	Ombak besar.
Bin	Peti atawa kas pranti simpen beras atawa djagoeng.
Bind	Iket; rentjengin; djait.
Binding	Iketan; boengkoesan; djaitan; koelit boekoe.
Biography	Riwajat orang termashoer.
Bioscope	Bioscoop; gambar idoep.
Biped	Binatang kaki doea; berkaki doea.
Birch	Samatjem poehoen.
Bird	Boeroeng.
Birth	Kelahiran.
Birthday	Hari kelahiran; hari she djit.
Biscuit	Biscuit; roti kering.
Bisect	Potong doea.
Bishop	Bisschop; kepala padri.
Bishopric	Pakerdjahan dari satoe bisschop.
Bison	Banteng oetan.
Bit	Besi moeloel koeda; keping; pekakas ngebor.
Bitch	Andjing prempoean.
Bite	Gigitan; keping; gigit.
Bitter	Pait; getir.
Bitterness	Kapaitan; kagetiran.
Bivouac	Tangsi; tenda balatentara.
Bizarre	Heran loear biasa.
Blab	Mendongeng; membilang atawa kasi tjerita.
Black	Orang bangsa Niger; warna jang paling gelap; item; gelap; bikin item atawa gelap.
Blackguard	Bangsat; orang djahat; djahanam; badjingan.
Blackleg	Penipoe; bangsat.
Blackmail	Oewang atawa barang tjoerian,

Blacksmith	Toekang besi.
Bladder	Karet jang bisa melar; karet dalem bola-kaki; beledoengan; belendoeng.
Blade	Salembar roempoet; tadjemnja piso; sampingnja pengajoe atawa pedang.
Blain	Beroentoesan.
Blame	Kasi sala; toedoe.
Blanch	Bikin poeti.
Bland	Baek; lema-lemboet.
Blank	Kertas kosong; kosong; zonder toelisan.
Blanket	Selimoet.
Blarney	Oempakan.
Blaspheme	Tjela Toehan-Allah.
Blast	Tioepan angin; meledakan; lajoe; petjaken karang dengen kakoewatannja obat pasang.
Blaze	Menjela; tersiar di koeliling doenia.
Bleach	Bikin poeti; tjelep.
Bleak	Dingin; soenji.
Blear	Rasa sakit; sakit mata.
Bleat	Boenjinja kambing; berboenji sebagi kambing.
Bleed	Berdara; kaloear dara.
Blemish	Loeka; loekain.
Blend	Tjampoer sama-sama; djadiken satoe.
Bless	Berkahin; mintain keslamatan.
Blessing	Berkah kaslamatan.
Blight	Lajoe.
Blind	Kere; boeta; bikin gelap.
Blindness	Kaboetaän; kailangan pengliatan.
Bliss	Berkah kaslamatan.
Blissful	Mendapet berkah; kliwat senang.
Blister	Belendoengan jang tipis; belendoeng.
Blithe	Bagoes; bergirang.
Bloat	Bengkak.
Block	Kerekan; belokan; halangan; kajoe; belok; halangin.

Blockade	Kepoengan jang rapet; toetoep.
Blockhead	Orang bodo atawa geblèk.
Blood	Dara.
Bloodshed	Pemboenoehan.
Bloody	Soeka memboenoe; kedjem.
Bloodvessel	Oerat jang mengangkoet dara.
Bloom	Kembang; berkembang.
Blossom	Kembang; berkembang.
Blot	Titik; noda; maloe bikin noda; bikin maloe.
Blotch	Melintang; titik; toetoel.
Blow	Poekoelan; kasialan; telor laler; tioep; bertelor sebagi laler.
Blubber	Gemoek atawa minjak ikan paoes.
Bludgeori	Roejoeng besar.
Blue	Biroe; bikin biroe.
Bluestocking	Prempoean jang soeka tjari peladjaran; prempoean jang mempoenjai peladjaran tinggi.
Bluff	Karang jang tergantoeng; melendoeng.
Blunder	Kasalaän; bikin sala.
Blunderbuss	Senapan pendek.
Blunt	Poentoel; bikin poentoel.
Blur	Titik; noda
Blush	Moeka mera lantaran maloe; bikin mara.
Bluster	Soeara mengaoeng; bikin riboet.
Boa	Oeler besar; boeloe toetoepan leher.
Boar	Babi oetan lelaki.
Board	Papan; medja; makanan; perhimpoenan; toetoep dengen papan; naekin kapal; bri makanan dan tempat menginep.
Boarder	Anak sekola menginep.
Boast	Menjombongin; kasombongan.
Boat	Praoe; kapal.
Bob	Gandoelan; gentak.
Bobbin	Djaroem boeat goeloeng benang.

Bodkin	Djaroem poentoel.
Body	Badan atawa toeboe; pongkot; koempoelan.
Bog	Tempat loempoer.
Boil	Bisoel; masak; sedoe; mendidiïn.
Boiler	Kettel.
Boisterous	Soeka bikin riboet.
Bold	Brani.
Boldness	Kabranihan.
Bolster	Bantal peloek; toendjang.
Bolt	Palangan pintoe; tapelan pintoe; palang; tapel.
Bomb	Bomb; barang letoesan.
Bombard	Tembak; petjaken.
Bombardier	Orang atawa soldadoe jang menembak.
Bombardment	Tembakan; pembikinan petja.
Bond	Persariketan; tali iketan; toetoep atawa boei; iket; djadiken boedak.
Bondage	Pakerdjahan boedak.
Bondsman	Tanggoengan; borgtoch.
Bone	Toelang.
Bonfire	Api jang dipasang boeat menjataken kegirangan.
Bonnet	Topi prempoean.
Bonny	Tjakep; senang.
Book	Boekoe; masoeken dalem boekoe.
Bookkeeping	Boekhouding; ilmoe pegang boekoe.
Boom	Kajoe pentangan lajar; kajoe jang dilintangin di kali atawa soengei; mengaoeng.
Booming	Soeara mengaoeng atawa menggereng; toebroekan jang heibat.
Boon	Kabaean; barang pengasian; penoeloeng; girang.
Boor	Orang bodo dan kasar.
Boot	Sepatoe bootin.

Booth	Pondok; roema atep.
Bootless	Tida membawa kaoentoengan.
Booty	Barang rampasan.
Borax	Tjampoeran jang terbikin dari ilmoe pisa.
Border	Wates; watesin.
Bore	Bor; lobang; ganggoean; bangoennja aer pasang; bikin berlobang; toesoek; gangoe.
Born	Diberanakin; terlahir.
Borne	Soeda angkat atawa bawa.
Borough	Kota jang bersarikat; kong-sie.
Borrow	Oetan; pindjem.
Bosom	Dada; tete; bertemen.
Boss	Kantjing knob; chef atawa thauw-kee.
Botany	Ilmoe peladjaran tetaneman.
Botch	Pekerdjahan jang dilakoeken dengen dje-lek; betoelken dengen djelek.
Both	Doewa-doewa; djoega.
Bother	Ganggoe; oesil.
Bottle	Botol; masoeken dalem botol.
Bottom	Bawanja; dasarnja: fondament.
Bourgeois	Rahajat klas tenga.
Bough	Tjabang poehoen.
Boulder	Batoe jang besar dan boender.
Bounce	Lompat atawa lontjat; menjombongin; lompatan; kasombongan.
Bound	Lompat atawa lontjat; wates; pergi; watesin; lompat atawa lontjat.
Boundary	Wates negri.
Bountiful	Rojaal; kaborosan.
Bounty	Karojaalan; kaborosan.
Bourn	Wates.
Bout	Poeteran; karangan.
Bow	Manggoetan kepala; moekanja kapal; manggoet; menjera; atawa menggala.
Bow	Roema pana atawa gandewa; bengko-kan; boentelan pita.

Bowels	Peroet: oesoes.
Bower	Tempat tedoe.
Bowl	Mangkok.
Box	Samatjem poehoen kajoe; peti; loge; tempat - doedoek koesir; poekoelan; koen-tauw; poekoel.
Boy	Anak lelaki; boedjang.
Brace	Bartel; pasangan; iket atawa gesperin; bikin koewat.
Bracelet	Gelang tangan.
Bracksih	Asin.
Brag	Omong besar; sombong.
Braggart	Orang jang soeka omong besar; orang jang sombong,
Braid	Pembikinan betoel; kepang atawa lipet.
Brain	Otak; pengartian.
Brake	Tana jang penoe aer; kreta boeat adjar koeda; rem.
Branch	Tjabang.
Brand	Kajoe jang soeda dibakar; tanda; merk; pengrasaän maloe; bakar sama besi panas; kasi merk.
Brandish	Gojang; poeter.
Brandy	Brandy; cognac; twa-hwee.
Brasier, brazier	Toekang tembaga; kwali besi pranti taro areng.
Brass	Tembaga mera.
Brat	Anak ketjil.
Brave	Brani.
Bravery	Kebranihan.
Brawl	Riboet moeloet; perbantahan; berbantah.
Brawn	Daging babi oetan; oerat.
Brawny	Beroerat; koewat.
Bray	Soeara boenjinja kalde; berboenji sebagi kalde.
Braze	Kerdja dengen tembaga.

Brazen	Terbikin dari tembaga.
Breach	Keriboetan moeloet; lobang; bikin lobang di tembok.
Bread	Roti; makanan.
Breadth	Lebarnja.
Break	Petjahan; lobang; pauze; bikin petja atawa petjaken; bikin djinek; terang tana.
Breakfast	Makan pagi.
Breast	Dada; bertemoe moeka.
Breath	Napas; djiwa.
Breathe	Bernapas.
Breathless	Tiada bernapas; tiada berdjiwa atawa tiada bernjawa.
Breech	Bagian blakang dari senapan.
Breeches	Tjelana jang sesak.
Breed	Bangsa; peranakan; lahirken; netesin.
Breeding	• Rawatan; pembrian peladjaran; opvoeding; pri-lakoe; adat.
Breeze	Angin aloes.
Brevity	Ringkesnja.
Brew	Bikin bier atawa laen-laen minoeman.
Brewery	Tempat pranti bikin bier atawa laen-laen minoeman.
Bribe	Sogokan; smeer; sogok; kasi smeer.
Brick	Batoe bata; terbikin dari batoe bata.
Bridal	Nikahan atawa kawinan; berhoeboeng dengen kemanten.
Bride	Penganten prempoean.
Bridegroom	Kemanten lelaki.
Bridge	Djembatan.
Bridle	Besi moeloet koeda berikoet les; tahan les.
Brief	Pendek; ringkes.
Brigade	Divisie atawa bagian dari balatentara
Bright	Terang; pinter.

Brilliant	Brilliant; terang; mengkilap.
Brim	Pinggir.
Brine	Aer garem.
Bring	Bawa.
Brink	Pinggirnja.
Brisk	Mengkilap; gesit.
Bristle	Boeloe babi; berdiri.
Britain	Negri Inggris.
Briton	Orang Inggris; pendoedoek dari tana Britain.
Brittle	Amo; gampang petja.
Broach	Boeka.
Broad	Lebar.
Broil	Keriboetan moeloet; panggang.
Broker	Commissie agent; makelaar.
Brokerage	Commissie.
Bronchitis	Gondok.
Bronze	Brons; tjampoeran dari tembaga dan tima.
Brooch	Peneti.
Brood	Toeroenan; netesin; pikir.
Brook	Kali; djalanan aer; tahan.
Broth	Boeboer; koewa.
Broom	Sesapoe.
Brow	Djidat; alis; pinggiran.
Brown	Koening toea; mera sawo.
Browse	Makan sajoer-sajoeran; tjiah-tjay.
Bruise	Loeka; bikin loeka.
Bruit	Kabar angin; rapport.
Brunette	Prempoean jang koelitnja gelap.
Brunt	Gojangan; langgaran.
Brush	Sikatan; sikat.
Brusque	Koerang-adjar; kasar.
Brutal	Biadab; tida sopan; kedjem.
Brute	Binatang boewas; kasar; kedjem.
Bubble	Boesa aer; berboesa.
Buccaneer	Badjak laoet.

Buck	Mandjangan lelaki.
Bucket	Ember; tahang kaleng.
Buckle	Gesper.
Buckler	Tameng.
Bud	Moentjoek; bermoentjoek.
Budge	Bergojang; bergerak.
Budget	Kantong; Staat oewang.
Buff	Koelit lemes; warna koening toea.
Buffalo	Kerbo.
Buffet	Poekoelan sama kepelan; poekoel sama kepelan.
Buffoon	Banjolan; badoet.
Bug	Koetoe; bangsat.
Bugle	Trompet.
Build	Bikin; berdiriken.
Building	Pembikinan roema; gedong.
Bulb	Obi; akar jang boelet.
Bulge	Bengkak di tenga-tenganja.
Bulk	Besarnja; toemploekannja.
Bulky	Besar.
Bull	Banteng; mahloemat atawa firman dari pope (paus) atawa radja agama.
Bullet	Pelor atawa peloeroe.
Bullion	Plongkotan dari emas atawa perak.
Bulloch	Anak banteng; banteng jang masi moeda.
Bully	Penipoe; bangsat; bikin takoet; antjem.
Bulwark	Benteng; tembak kota.
Bump	Bantrokan; bantrokin.
Bumper	Saglas penoe; saglas moendjoeng.
Bun	Koewe ketjil.
Bunch	Tangke; rentjeng.
Bundle	Boengkoesan; pakkan: boengkoes; pak.
Bung	Perof; soempel; soempel sama perof.
Bungalow	Roema jang tiada mempoenjai loteng.
Bungle	Barang jang dikerdjaken koerang baek, kerdjaken dengen djelek.

Bunk	Tempat tidoer di atas kapal.
Bunker	Peti pranti taro areng.
Bunting	Tjay-ki; kaen-kaenan.
Buoy	Pelampoeng; ngambang.
Buoyant	Mengambang; enteng.
Burden	Moewatan; pikoelan; refrein atawa koor dari satoe njanjian; moewatin; tindi.
Burdensome	Soesa dibawa; terlaloe berat.
Bureau	Rak latji; kantoor.
Burglar	Perampok; penjamoen.
Burial	Berhoeboeng dengen koeboeran mait orang.
Burly	Besar.
Burn	Melepoe; kali ketjil; bakar
Burnish	Warna jang mengkilap; polis.
Burrow	Lobang binatang di dalem tana; gali lobang.
Bury	Tanem; koeboer.
Bush	Oetan ketjil; gompiokan poehoen-poehoen.
Bushel	Oekoeran dari 8 gallon.
Bushy	Bergompiok.
Business	Pakerdjahan; keadaän jang tida sempet.
Bust	Gambar atawa anak-anakan dari kepala sainggan poendak.
Bustle	Kariboetan; bo-eng atawa tiada sempet.
Busy	Bo-eng atawa tiada sempet; ripoe; rame.
But	Tetapi.
Butcher	Toekang potong binatang; toekang djagal.
Butler	Boedjang atawa djongos jang oeroesin minoeman; kepala; boedjang.
Butt	Oedjoeng; kepala; tanda; satahang dari 126 gallons.
Butter	Mentega.
Butterfly	Koepoe-koepoe.
Buttock	Pantat.
Button	Kantjing.
Buttress	Toendjangan boeat tembok.
Buxom	Hidoep; gesit.

Buy	Beli.
Buzz	Soeara mengaoeng dari tawon.
By	Di sebla; di samping; oleh.
By-and-by	Sabentar lagi.
Bye	Tempat tinggal; slamat tinggal.
Bygone	Jang soeda liwat.
Bypath	Djalanan samping; djalanan ketjil.
Byroad	Djalanan semoeni; tempat jang soenji.
Byroom	Kamar samping; kamar prive.
Bystander	Pengliat; orang jang meliat.
By-way	Djalanan samping; sekalian; berbareng.
By-word	Mitsal pepata; isi moeloet.

C.

Cab	Kahar.
Cabal	Tipoe-daja; pakoempoelan resia; berdaja.
Cabbage	Kool atawa kole.
Cabin	Kamar di kapal; berdiam di kamar kapal.
Cabinet	Rak latji-latji; Kabinet atawa ministers jang mengoeroes pamerentahan negri.
Cabinet-photo-graph	Potret Kabinet.
Cable	Kawat atawa tambang jang koewat; kawat dalem laoet.
Cacao	Poehoen cacao.
Cackle	Soeara riboet dari ajem bersoeara riboet sebagi ajam.
Cad	Orang bangsa renda; kreta; pengawal pintoe.
Caddy	Peti pranti taro thee.
Cadence	Djatonja soeara.
Cadet	Moerid dari sekola militair atawa marine.

Cafe	Waroeng-koffie; restauràtie.
Cage	Koeroengan; koeroeng.
Cairn	Toemploekan batoe jang beroman boen- der atawà londjong.
Cajole	Tipoe dengen djalan mengocmpak.
Cake	Koewe; bergoempel.
Calamity	Ketjilakaän; bahaja.
Calcine	Toemboek; antjoerken.
Calculate	Reken; itoeng.
Calculation	Rekenan; itoengan.
Caldron	Toko besar.
Calendar	Almanak; takwim.
Calender	Tindi dengen besi panas; bikin litjin; besi tindian jang panas.
Calf	Anak sampi; peroet kaki; saroepa koelit.
Caliber, Calibre	Moeloet senapan jang dalemnja terlitit; kaliber; kapandean.
Calico	Kaen dari kapas.
Caligraphy	Toelisan-tangan.
Calisthenics	Gerak-gerakan badan.
Call	Panggilan; koendjoengan; panggil; di namaken; bertreak; koendjoengin ata- wa mampir.
Calling	Pakerdjahan.
Callous	Keras; tiada terasa.
Calm	Diamnja; kesoenjian; diam; soenji.
Calumniate	Toedoe boeta toeli.
Calumny	Toedoehan boeta-toeli.
Calve	Malahirken anak sampi.
Calves	Anak-anak sampi (lebi dari satoe).
Cambric	Saroepa kaen linen jang aloes.
Camel	Oenta.
Camp	Pasanggrahan; tenda soldadoe.
Campaign	Temponja balatentara ada berdiam di lapangan peprangan.
Camphor	Kamfer; kapoer-baroes.

Can	Kaleng'; bisa.
Canal	Djalanan aer; kanaal.
Canary	Samatjem anggoer; sabangsa boeroeng menjanji.
Cancel	Oeroengken; bikin abis.
Cancer	Bisoel ketjil.
Candid	Berhati toeloes; teroes-trang.
Candidate	Candidaat; orang jang mentjari paker-djahan atawa djabatan.
Candle	Lilin.
Candour	Hati jang toeloes; hati jang teroes-trang.
Cane	Rotan; rotanin.
Canine	Sebagi andjing; bangsa andjing.
Canister	Peti ketjil boeat taro daon thee.
Canker	Penjakit dalem binatang dan tetaneman; bikin abis.
Cannibal	Orang makan orang; orang biadab.
Cannon	Mariam.
Cannonade	Labrak dengen meriam.
Canoe	Praoe kolek.
Canon	Wet dalem oedjar-oedjar agama.
Canopy	Pajoeng; klamboe.
Cant	Djatoan; lemparan atawa gentakan ba-hasa renda; djato; lempar atawa gentak; omong dengen bahasa tangsi.
Canteen	Ember boeat minoeman; kantine atawa waroeng minoeman dalem tangsi sol-dadoe.
Canticle	Njanjian; lagoe
Canto	Bagian dari sairan.
Canvas	Kaen lajar.
Cap	Kopia; topi pet.
Capability	Kepandean kebisahan.
Capable	Pande; bisa.
Capakious	Lebar mempoenjai; banjak tempat.
Capacity	Moewatnja.

Cape	Tandjoeng; mantel orang prempoean.
Caper	Lompatan; lompat.
Capillary	Oerat dara jang sebagi ramboet.
Capital	Kapitaal atawa modal dagangan; letter besar; iboe-kota; atasnja kolom; oetama.
Capitulate	Menjera atas perdjandjian.
Capon	Ajam kebiri.
Capsize	Terbalik; karem.
Capstan	Pekakas pranti angkat barang berat.
Capsule	Koelit bidji; tapoek.
Captain	Kaptein; pangkat lebi atas dari luitenant.
Captious	Braligasan; bo-sioh,
Captive	Orang tahanan.
Captivity	Tahanan; tangkepan.
Capture	Tangkepan; tangkep.
Car	Kahar.
Caravan	Kawanan orang pelantjongan; kreta besar.
Carbine	Senapan pendek.
Carbon	Areng jang toelen.
Carcass	Mait; bangke.
Card	Kartoe; kaartjis-nama; sisir benang wool; sisirin benang wool.
Cardinal	Pangkat padri dalem gredja Roomsch Katholiek; oetama; kepala.
Care	Djagaän; djaga; perdoeli.
Careen	Miringin; dojongin.
Career	Haloean; djalanan; bergerak dengen tjepet.
Careful	Ati-ati; mempoenjai kekwatiran.
Careless	Teledor; koerang perhatian.
Caress	Pelokan; pelok.
Cargo	Moewatan kapal.
Caricature	Gambar sindiran.
Carmine	Mera bagoes.
Carnage	Pemboenoehan,

Carnal	Berisi; mempoenjai napsoe tiada baek.
Carnation	Warna daging; boenga atawa kembang.
Carnivorous	Berdahar daging machloek atawa binatang.
Carol	Njanjian kagirangan.
Carp	Ikan kakap; tjari kesalaän.
Carpenter	Toekang kajoe.
Carpet	Goedri.
Carping	Pentjarian sala.
Carriage	Kreta; moewatan.
Carrion	Daging jang tiada baek didahar.
Carry	Angkat; bawa.
Cart	Grobak; angkoet.
Cart-de-visite	Portret visite.
Cartilage	Toelang moeda.
Cartridge	Patroon senapan.
Carve	Oekir; potong.
Carver	Toekang oekir.
Cascade	Djatoan aer
Case	Peti; perkara; keadaän.
Casement	Djendela jang pake engsel,
Cash	Oewang kontant; toekar dengen oewang.
Cashier	Kassier; omslag.
Cask	Tahang; tong.
Casket	Trommel mas-inten.
Casque	Topi prang.'
Cassock	Pakean padri.
Cassowary	Boeroeng Kasuarie.
Cast	Barang boewangan; sisa restant; boewang; djadiken; kalaken.
Castaway	Orang jang diboewang atawa disiasiaken
Casting	Barang boewangan; barang jang terbikin dengen tjitakan.
Castle	Benteng; gedong; kasteel.
Casual	Sringkali; tempo-tempo.
Casualty	Ketjilakaän jang terdjadi tiada dengen sengadja.

Cat	Koetjing.
Catecomb	Tempat mengoeboer mati.
Catalogue	Catalogus; prijscourant; lijst.
Cataract	Toempahan aer; penjakit dalem mata.
Catarrh	Rasa dingin dalem kepala.
Catastrophe	Ketjilakaän; bahaja.
Catch	Tangkepan; njanjian; tangkep.
Catechise	Adjar dengen pake pertanjaän.
Catechism	Boekoe pertanjaän dan djawaban.
Cater	Lengkepin dengen barang makanan.
Caterpillar	Koetoe jang beroman seperti tjatjing; oeler boeloe.
Cathedral	Gredja dari Bisschop atawa kepala padri.
Catholic	Sama rata; agama atawa orang jang memoedja agama Roomsch Katholiek.
Cattle	Heiwan, seperti sampi, kerbo, kambing; dan sebaginja.
Caul	Topi prempoean; oesoes besar.
Cauldron	Teko besar.
Cauliflower	Kool atawa kole jang moeda.
Cause	Sebabnja; lantarannja; perkara; bikin; terdjadi.
Causeway	Djalanan jang boleh diangkat.
Caustic	Barang jang bisa menjala; menjala.
Cauterise	Panggang.
Caution	Perhatian; kasi inget.
Cautious	Berati-ati; teliti.
Cavalier	Orang jang menoenggang koeda; sombong.
Cavalry	Soldadoe koeda.
Cave	Lobang gowa.
Cavern	Gowa besar.
Cavil	Tjari kesalaän; toedoe.
Cavity	Tempat jang berlobang.
Cease	Brenti; mandek.
Cede	Seraken; menjera.

Ceiling	Langit-langit roema.
Celandine	Saroepa tetaneman.
Celebrate	Rajaken.
Celebration	Kerajahan.
Celebrity	Nama jang termashoer.
Celerity	Kakentjengan.
Celestial	Berhoeboeng dengen langit atawa sorga.
Cell	Kamar ketjil; lobang ketjil.
Cellar	Kamar di bawa roema.
Cellular	Berisi lobang-lobang ketjil.
Cement	Cement; kapoer; lengketin.
Cemetery	Tandjoeng orang mati; tempat orang di-koeboer.
Censor	Mantri jang diwadjibken boeat bikin cri-tiek atawa perdendingan atas oeroesan negri; gie-soe; kritiek atawa peroen-dingan.
Censorious	Ingin boeat tjari kesalaännja orang.
Censure	Kasalaän; toedoehan.
Census	Tjatja djiwa.
Cent	Oewang cent; saperatoes.
Centenarian	Orang jang beroemoer 100 taon toea.
Centurion	Officier jang berkwasa di atas 100 orang.
Central	Di tenga-tenga; deket tenga-tenga.
Centre, center	Tenga-tenga; berdiam.
Century	Saratoes taon; satoe abad.
Ceremonious	Dengen oepa tjara; dengen satjara ofii-cieel atawa sah.
Ceremony	Oepa-tjara; adat-istiadat; atoeran.
Certain	Tentoe; pasti.
Certainty	Katentoean; kepastian.
Certificate	Certificaat; soerat ketrangan.
Certify	Bri ketrangan.
Cessation	Pembrentian; pauze.
Cession	Penjerahan; pengalaän,
Chafe	Gosokan; gosok,

Chaff	Koelit; gaba; barang jang tiada di pake.
Caffer	Tawar-menawar.
Chagrin	Keadaän koesoet pikiran; oering-oeringan.
Chain	Rante; rantein; iket dengen rante.
Chair	Korsi.
Chairman	Voorzitter; president.
Chaise	Kreta jang bisa ladjoe tjepet.
Chaldron	Takeran dari 30 bushels.
Chalk	Kapoer.
Challenge	Pertandingan; bertanding.
Chamber	Kamar.
Chamberlain	Penggawe pengadilan.
Champ	Gigitan; koenjaän.
Champagne	Champagne; minoeman jang paling aloes.
Champion	Kampioen; orang jang petjoendangin orang laen.
Chance	Tempo jang baek; kedjadian; ketjilakaän; terdjadi.
Chancel	Bagian sebla Timoer dari gredja.
Chanceller	Hakim pertama; professor jang paling tinggi dalem midrasa atawa sekola besar.
Chandelier	Besi gas.
Chandler	Toekang klontong.
Chandlery	Barang tjampoer-tjampoer; barang klontong.
Change	Penoekaran; perobahan; toekar; roba.
Changeable	Boleh ditoekar-toekar atawa diroba-roba.
Channel	Djalanan aer; kanaal.
Chant	Njanjian; njanji.
Chaos	Kekaloetan; kalang-kaboetan; bintjana.
Chap	Meleka di koelit; orang atawa anak lelaki.
Chapel	Gredja ketjil.
Chaplain	Padri; goeroe dalem sekola militair atawa marine.
Chaplet	Krans atawa boeket kembang.

Chapter	Bagian dari satoe boekoe; hoofdstuk.
Char	Bekerdja dengen itoeng hari; bakar dengen pisa-pisa.
Character	Tingka-lakoe atawa pri-lakoe.
Charcoal	Areng kajoe.
Charge	Djagaän; pembajaran; toedoehan; toebroekan; kenain pembajaran; toedoe; toebroek.
Charger	Basi atawa piring jang besar; koedapeprangan.
Chariot	Kreta jang enteng, ladjoenja.
Charitable	Dermawan; mempoenjai hati baek.
Charity	Kadermawaän; hati jang baek.
Charlatan	Pendjoesta; toekang poera-poera.
Charm	Kasoekahan; goena-goena atawa djimat; kaset horlogie; bikin girang; kalaken.
Charming	Menggirangin; bagoes.
Chart	Peta negri.
Charter	Kaboelan; kamerdikaän; sewa kapal.
Chase	Pemboeroean; pengoedekan; boeroe; oedek.
Chaste	Tiada bernoda; poeti-bersi.
Chasten	Bikin betoel; roba.
Chastise	Hoekoem.
Chastity	Keadaän poeti-bersi.
Chat	Omongan antara temen.
Chattels	Barang-barang.
Chatter	Omong iseng-iseng; kata.
Chauffeur	Chauffeur; djoeroe-moedi dari kreta motor atawa automobile.
Cheap	Moera; biasa.
Cheat	Tipoean; tipoe.
Check	Tahanan; tahan.
Cheek	Pipi; prilakoe jang koerang-adjar.
Cheer	Soeara soerakan; bikin girang.
Cheerful	Penoe kagirangan; gesit.

Cheese	Kedjoe.
Cheetah	Matjan toetoel jang terdapet di Hindia Inggris.
Chemist	Orang jang pande dalem ilmoe pisa; toekang djoeal obat.
Cheque	Bon; kiriman oewang.
Cherish	Rawat dengen baek.
Cherub	Bidadari.
Chest	Peti besar; dada.
Chew	Koenja; mama; papak.
Chick	Anak ajam.
Chicory	Saroepa poehoen koffie.
Chide	Tjomelin.
Chief	Pemimpin; kepala; oetama; teroetama.
Chiefly	Teroetama; kebanjakan; sebagian besar.
Chilblain	Meleka lantaran hawa dingin.
Child	Anak lelaki atawa prampoean.
Childbed	Pakerdjahan; kelahirannja anak.
Childhood	Keadaän masi ketjil.
Childish	Seperti anak-anak; tiada beharga.
Chill	Rasa dingin; bikin dingin; dingin.
Chime	Klenengan atawa soeara klenengan; ber- soeara dengen stem atawa akoer.
Chimney	Semprong.
China	Perabot percelein jang aloes; Tiongkok.
Chink	Tempat petja; menganga.
Chintz	Kaen tjita.
Chip	Tatal; potong tipis-tipis.
Chiropodist	Doktor padi.
Chirp	Soeara tjetjrowetan boeroeng; bertjetjro- wet.
Chisel	Pahat; pahatin.
Chivalrous	Gaga brani.
Chivalry	Perboeatan gaga-brani.
Chloroform	Aer keras.
Chocolate	Chocolade atawa tjoklat.

Choice	Pilihan; pili.
Choir	Koempoelan orang njanji sama-sama.
Choke	Tjekek.
Choler	Rasa amarah; goesar hati.
Cholera	Penjakit cholera atawa boewang-boewang. aer.
Choleric	Gampang dibikin mara; brangasan.
Choose	Pili.
Chop	Potongan daging; pipi; potong.
Chops	Lak lakan moeloet; sampingnja moeloet; djalanan aer atawa kanaal.
Chop-sticks	Soempit.
Chord	Benang; tali.
Chorus	Koempoelan orang njanji sama-sama; koor.
Chough	Sabangsa gaok atawa gowak.
Christ	Nabi Jeusus Kristoes; Nabi Mesehi.
Christen	Kaoem jang memoedja agama Kristen.
Christianity	Agama Kristen.
Christmas	Kertsmis; hari natal, djato pada December 25.
Chronic, Chronical	Jang soeda berdiri lama; jang soeda djadi koeno.
Chronicle	Hikajat.
Chronology	Ilmoe mengitoeng tanggal.
Cronometer	Oekoeran tempo jang dipake di laoet.
Chrysalis	Anak blatoeng soetra.
Chrysanthemum	Kembang seroni: kiok-hwa.
Chubby	Bermoeka boender.
Chuckle	Tertawaän jang ditahan; tertawa dengen ditahan.
Chum	Temen; pengikoet.
Church	Gredja.
Churchwarden	Pendjaga gredja.
Churchyard	Pekarangan gredja pranti koeboer orang.

Churl	Orang doesoen; badoet.
Churlish	Bermoeka asem; koerang adjar.
Churn	Tempat bikin mentega; bikin mentega.
Cider	Pati boeat appel.
Cigar	Lisong atawa seroetoe.
Cincture	Band; gesper.
Cinder	Areng jang baroe terbakar saparo.
Cinematograph	Gambar idoep; bioscoop.
Cipher	Nummer atawa nomor; soerat potong-letter; itoeng pake nummer.
Circle	Boenderan; barang jang boender.
Circuit	District.
Circuitous	Pergi mengider.
Circular	Circulaire atawa soerat ideran; boender.
Circulate	Terpoeter.
Circumference	Watesnja boenderan; djaoenja koeliling satoe boenderan.
Circumflex	Tanda soeara (ô).
Circumnavigate	Belajar mengiderin.
Circumscribe	Koeroeng; kiderin.
Circumspect	Ati-ati; teliti.
Circumstance	Keadaän hal; kedjadian.
Circumstantial	Terdjadi dengen boekan sengadja; terdjadi di loear doegahan.
Circumvent	Tipoe.
Circus	Komedi koeda.
Cistern	Pantjoran; bak aer.
Citadel	Benteng soldadoe.
Citation	Soerat panggilan; rentjana.
Cite	Panggil mengadep; rentjenaken.
Citizen	Pendoedoek negri.
City	Kota besar.
Civic	Berhoeboeng dengen kota besar.
Civil	Berhoeboeng dengen negri; civiel; taoe adat; sopan.
Civilian	Orang vrijman atawa preman.

Civility	Kasopanan.
Civilization	Kasopanan; pendidikan jang baek; beschaving.
Civilize	Bikin djadi sopan.
Claim	Permintaän; minta.
Claimant	Orang jang minta atawa menagi.
Clamber	Mandjet meliwatin tempat ngandangain.
Clammy	Lengket.
Clamour	Soeara riboet; bikin riboet.
Clamp	Pakoe koeda; pakoe besi.
Clan	Kaoem.
Clang	Soeara njaring.
Clank	Soeara krentjengan; berkrentjengan.
Clap	Tepokan tangan; tepok tangan.
Clarify	Bikin terang.
Clarion	Samatjem trompet.
Clash	Bentoeran dengen mengaloearken soeara; * bentoer dengen mengaloearken soeara; gangoe.
Clashing	Berlawanan; bertentangan.
Clasp	Sangketan; peloekan; peloek; pegang dengen kentjeng.
Class	Klass; prangkatan.
Classify	Atoer djadi bebrapa koempoelan.
Clatter	Soeara krentjengan jang tjepet.
Clause	Bagian dari satoe omongan.
Clavicle	Toelang leher.
Claw	Koekoe machloek.
Clay	Tana lempoeng.
Clean	Bersi; bikin bersi; sama-sekali.
Cleanliness	Kabersihan.
Cleanse	Bikin bersi.
Clear	Terang; bening; tiada bersala; saderhana; laloeken; bikin sebagi kaoentoengan.
Clearance	Pembikinan bersi; pembikinan abis.

Cleave	Tjengkerem; pegang dengen kéras.
Cleaver	Golok toekang djagal.
Cleft	Lobang; melekaän.
Clematis	Saroepa tetaneman jang bisa merajap.
Clemency	Kalema-lemboetan; kabaean.
Clement	Lema-lemboet; baek.
Clergy	Pembesar dari gredja.
Clerical	Berhoeboeng dengen pembesar gredja atawa krani.
Clerk	Krani; djoeroe-toelis; tjaij-hoe.
Clever	Pinter.
Clew	Bola berisi benang; toentoenan.
Client	Orang jang memake advocaat
Cliff	Karang jang djoerang.
Climate	Hawa.
Climax	Naekan ka tingkatan jang lebi tinggi.
Climb	Mandjet.
Clime	Hawa; tempat.
Cling	Melengket.
Clinical, Clinic	Berhoeboeng dengen tempat-tidoer.
Clink	Bikin bersoeara ketjil.
Clinker	Batoe-bata jang djadi angoes; raroentoekan logam.
Clip	Potong pendek-pendek.
Clipper	Kapal jang tjepet ladjoenja.
Clique	Partij; kaoem.
Cloak	Mantel orang prampoean; semoeniken.
Clock	Lotjeng.
Clod	Goempelan tana.
Clog	Bakkiak; tjegahan; tjega.
Cloister	Roema tinggalnja padri lelaki atawa prempoean.
Close	Lapangan ketjil; tertoetoep; pelit terdjaga.
Close	Toetoepnja; tamatnja; toetoep; tamatin.
Closet	Kamar ketjil.

Cloth	Kaen.
Clothe	Berpakean; pake.
Cothes	Pakean.
Cloud	Awan.
Clout	Tambelan; tambel.
Clown	Badoet.
Club	Roejoeng; pakoempoelan.
Clue	Haloean; pimpinan.
Clump	Gompiokan poehoen.
Clumsy	Djelek.
Cluster	Tangke; bertangke.
Clutch	Tjengkerem.
Coach	Kreta.
Coachman	Koesir.
Coal	Areng batoe.
Coalition	Djadian satoe; hoeboengan.
Coarse	Kasar.
Coast	Pinggir laoet.
Coat	Badjoe.
Coating	Toetoepan; koelit.
Coax	Boedjoek; pikat.
Cobble	Betoelin dengen satjara kasar.
Cobbler	Toekang betoelin sepatoe.
Cobweb	Sarang lawa-lawa atawa kawa-kawa.
Cock	Ajam djago; moeloet senapan; djaroem timbangan; bikin berdiri.
Cockney	Nama sindiran boeat pendoedoek kota London.
Cockade	Boentelan atas topi.
Cockpit	Tempat adoe ajam djago; kamar di bawa dek kapal.
Cocoa	Chocalade atawa tjoklat.
Cocoon	Telor blatoeng soetra.
Cod	Sabangsa ikan.
Coddle	Bikin lembek.
Code	Code atawa atoer-atoeran jang terkoempoel dan teratoer.

Coerce	Paksa; tjega.
Coercion	Tjegahan; paksaän.
Coffee	Koffie atawa kopi.
Coffin	Peti mait.
Cog	Gigi roda.
Cogent	Berpengaroe; penting.
Coffer	Kofter; peti; peti oewang.
Cogitate	Pikir lagi.
Cognate	Mempoenjai hoeboengan.
Cognizant	Taoe; mengatahoei.
Cohabit	Hidoep satjara soeami-istri.
Coheir	Samboeng toeroenan.
Cohere	Melengket.
Coherent	Jang melengket.
Coign	Peloksok atawa pepodjok.
Coil	Goeloengan tambang atawa oeler; goeloeng.
Coin	Oewang; doewit
Coincide	Beroekoen; djadi satoe.
Coke	Areng jang baroe terbakar saparo.
Cold	Kadinginan; pilek; dingin; tawar.
Colic	Penjakit dalem peroet.
Collapse	Terbaliknja; terbalik; keleboe; karem.
Collar	Krah atawa niah leher; tangkep.
Colleague	Collega atawa temen satoe pakerdjahan; persero.
Collect	Koempoelin.
Collect	Sembajang jang dilakoeken sabentaran.
Collection	Koempoelan.
Collector	Collecteur atawa toekang mengoempoelin.
College	Sekola tenga.
Collide	Kabentoer; beradoe.
Collier	Toekang gali areng batoe; kapal jang moewat areng batoe.
Colliery	Parit areng batoe.
Collision	Bentoeran; beradoean.

Collusion	Pesarikatan resia boeat melakoeken perboeatan chianat.
Colon	Tanda (:).
Colonel	Kolonel atawa officier kepala dari satoe regiment soldadoe.
Colonial	Termasoek dalem bilangan djadjahan.
Colonize	Doedoekin tana djadjahan.
Colony	Tana djadjahan; koempoelan orang jang djadi pendoedoeknja tana djadjahan.
Colour, Color	Warna; bewarna.
Colt	Anak koeda lelaki.
Colter	Besi di hadepan pekakas loekoe.
Column	Kolom atawa bagian lembaran; pillar. atawa tiang.
Comb	Sisir; djengger ajam djago; sarang tawon; sisirin.
Combat	Perklaihan; berklai.
Combine	Samboeng; hoeboengin.
Combustible	Barang jang gampang menjala; gampang menjala.
Combustion	Penjalaän.
Come	Dateng; sampe.
Comedy	Komedi atama opera bangsawan.
Comely	Bagoes; molek.
Comet	Bintang sesapoe.
Comfort	Hiboeran; kasenangan; hiboerin; senangin.
Comfortable	Enak; senang.
Comforter	Penghiboer; meleikat jang soetji.
Comic	Loetjoe; berbadoet.
Coming	Datengnja; tempo jang bakalan dateng.
Comma	Tanda (,).
Command	Tita; prentahan; titaken bri prenta.
Commander	Commandeur atawa kepala dari satoe barisan.
Commanding	Mempoenjai pengaroe atawa kekwasaän.
Commandment	Oedjar-oedjar agama; tita.

Commemorate	Rajaken; bikin rame.
Commemoration	Kerajahan; pembikinan rame.
Commence	Moelai.
Commencement	Permoelaän.
Commend	Poedji; pertjaiaken.
Comment	Commentaar atawa noot ketrangan; taro noot ketrangan.
Commerce	Perniagaän; dagangan; berniaga; berdagang.
Commercial	Berhoeboeng dengen perniagaän atawa dagangan.
Commination	Antjeman dengen hoekoeman.
Commission	Commissie; kapertjaiaän atawa tanggoengan; potongan procent; kasi kekwasaän
Commissioner	Commissionair atawa orang jang dibri kekwasaän boeat berlakoe.
Commit	Bikin; masoeken dalem pendjara
Committee	ᴉ Comite atawa koempoelan orang jang bekerdja.
Commodious	Satoedjoe.
Commodity	Barang-barang perniagaän.
Common	Tana terboeka; orang banjak; biasa.
Commoner	Orang particulier atawa orang biasa.
Commonly	Biasanja; loemrahnja.
Commons	Orang biasa tweede kamer dalem sidang pamerentahan.
Commonweal	Kabaean orang banjak.
Commonwealth	Negri jang merdika; republiek.
Commotion	Ganggoean.
Commune	Bitjara; mempoenjai hoeboengan.
Communicate	Bagi kabar; wartaken; toelis soerat.
Communication	Kabaran; soerat; hoeboengan.
Community	Koempoelan orang dengen hak sama rata.
Commute	Toekar.
Compact	Tebel; bergoempel.
Compact	Persariketan; persakoetoean.

Companion	Temen di djalan.
Company	Koempoelan; persero; maatschappij.
Comparative	Terbanding.
Compare	Bandingken.
Compartment	Disivie atawa bagian.
Compass	Wates; derekan; padoman.
Compasses	Djangka atawa pekakas boeat teeken. boenderan; koeroeng; berdaja.
Compassion	Pengrasaän kesian.
Compatible	Satoedjoe; sedeng.
Compel	Paksa; perkosa.
Compendious	Jang dibikin pendek: jang dibikin ringkes.
Compensate	Bikin pembalesan.
Compensation	Pembalesan.
Compete	Bersaing; bertanding.
Competence	Katjoekoepan; kasampoernäan.
Competent	Tjoekoep; sampoerna.
Competition	Persaingan; pertandingan.
Competitor	Saingan; orang jang bertanding.
Compile	Bikin boekoe.
Complacent	Menggirangin.
Complain	Mengroetoe; menggrendeng; mengadoe.
Complainant	Orang jang menggroetoe atawa mengadoe.
Complaint	Menggroetoean; menggrendengan; pengadoean.
Complaisant	Taoe adat; berprilakoe baek.
Complement •	Nummer jang berdjoembla penoe.
Complete	Sampoerna; lengkep; bikin sampoerna lengkepin.
Completion	Kasampoernaän; kalengkepan.
Complex	Teradoek; mempoenjai banjak bagian.
Complexion	Paras moeka.
Compliant	Gampang menjara atawa mengala.
Complicate	Bikin teradoekan.
Complication	Keadaän jang teradoekan.

Compliment	Poedjihan; .pembrian slamat; bri slamat.
Compliments	Oetjapan pri-kasopanan.
Comply	Kaboelken; loeloesken.
Campose	Karang tjerita.
Camposed	Diam.
Camposition	Karangan.
Compositor	Letterzetter.
Compost	Boemboe bikin gemoek tana jang ter-tjampoer.
Composure	Kadiamannja.
Compound	Tjampoeran; tjampoer.
Comprehend	Mengarti.
Comprehension	Pengarti.
Compress	Tindi sama-sama.
Comprise	Berisi.
Compromise	Perdjadjian dengen concessie atawa pe-ngalaän; bikin slese dengen perdjan-djian jang baek.
Compulsion	Paksahan.
Compunction	Seselan.
Computation	Peritoengan.
Compute	Itoeng; reken.
Comrade	Temen; sobat.
Concave	Tjeglok.
Conceal	Semoeni.
Concealment	Semoenian.
Concede	Kaboelken; bri-idjin.
Conceit	Kaägoengan diri sendiri; ·pikiran jang samar-samar.
Conceited	Mangagoengin diri sendiri; sombong atawa tokkong.
Conceive	Doega doega; pikir.
Conception	Doega-doegahan; pikiran.
Concern	Pakerdjahan; oeroesan; kekwatiran; ber-hoeboeng.
Concerning	Berhoeboeng pada.

Concert	Persariketan; permaenan muziek.
Concert	Berdaja sama-sama.
Concession	Concessie atawa pengalaän.
Conciliate	Menangken; pertjoendangin.
Concise	Pendek; ringkes.
Conciave	Pembitjaraän resia.
Conclude	Abisin; berpikir tetep.
Conclusion	Abisnja; pikiran jang soedah tetep.
Concoct	Pertjenaken atawa antjoerken; berdaja.
Concord	Persariketan.
Concordant	Bersariket.
Concourse	Perhimpoenan; koempoelan.
Concubine	Nona piarahan; dji-ngeh.
Concur	Moefakat hoeboengken.
Concussion	Bergojangan sama-sama; toebroekan satoe sama laen.
Condemn	Toedoe sala; bri hoekoeman.
Condemnation	Hoekoeman.
Condense	Djadi kentel.
Condensed	Kentel.
Condescend	Merenda; mengala.
Condescension	Prilakoe jang rendah; penggalaän.
Condign	Haroesnja.
Condition	Keadaän; perdjandjian.
Condole	Menoeroet doeka tjita atawa soesa hati.
Condolement	Toeroetan doeka tjita atawa soesa hati.
Condone	Maäfin; ampoenken.
Conduce	Mengiring; mengadepin.
Conduct	Tingka-lakoe atawa prilakoe.
Conduct	Toentoen; pimpin.
Conductor	Conducteur atawa Pengoeroes kreta api atawa tram; pemimpin; barang jang bisa menoeroenin hawa panas.
Conduit	Pipa-aer.
Cone	Roman sebagi koekoesan.
Confectioner	Toekang koewe; toekang bikin manis-manisan.

Confederate	Bersariket dalem satoe peroesahan.
Confederation	Persariketan dalem satoe peroesahan.
Confer	Kasi; loeloesken; bitjara pada.
Conference	Conferentie atawa pembitjaraän besar.
Confess	Mengakoe.
Confession	Pengakoean.
Confide	Pertjaja sampe abis.
Confidence	Kapertjaiaän besar.
Configuration	Roman di loear.
Confine	Watesin; toetoep.
Confinement	Toetoepan.
Confirm	Pastiken; tentoeken.
Confiscate	Rampas milik.
Conflagration	Api njalaän jang besar.
Conflict	Perklaihan; pertandingan.
Conflict	Perklai; bertanding.
Confluence	Anjoetan sama-sama.
Conform	Kaboelken bikin sabanding.
Confound	Soesa hati binggoeng.
Confront	Hadepken.
Confuse	Bikin kaloet.
Confusion	Kekaloetan.
Confute	Trangken ada bersala.
Congeal	Djadi keras; bikin tebel.
Congenial	Akoer; mempoenjai haloean sama.
Conger	Mowa laoet.
Congestion	Toemploekan; bergoempelnja dara.
Congratulate	Bri slamat.
Congratulation	Pembrian slamat.
Congregate	Ketemoe sama-sama.
Congregation	Pertemoean sama-sama; koempoelan.
Congress	Persidangan; sidang pamerentahan dari Amerika Sariket.
Congruous	Satoedjoe; sedeng.
Conjecture	Badean; bade.
Conjoin	Hoeboengken; djadiken satoe.

Conjugal	Berhoeboeng dengen nikahan atawa per-kawinan.
Conjugate	Koempoelan djadi satoe; toekar keadaän-nja *verb*.
Conjugation	Koempoelan djadi satoe; penoekaran ke-adaännja *verb*.
Conjunction	Samboengan; perkataän menjamboeng.
Conjuncture	Tempo jang penting.
Conjure	Badein; maen ilmoe hikmat atawa soenglap
Conjurer	Toekang soenglap.
Connect	Hoeboengin; samboeng.
Connection	Hoeboengan; samboengan.
Connive	Kedipin mata.
Conubial	Berhoeboeng dengen oeroesan kawin.
Conquer	Kalaken; petjoendangin.
Conqueror	Orang jang dapet kemenangan.
Conquest	Kamenangan.
Consanguinity	Kaoem koelawarga atawa familie; tong-pauw.
Conscience	Pikiran; kabisahan aken membedaken barang jang baek dari jang djahat.
Conscious	Taoe; mengatahoei.
Consecrate	Bikin alim.
Consecutive	Meroentoen; menoeroet tingkatan.
Consent	Moefakatan; moefakat; kaboelken.
Consequence	Kedjadian; boeanja; achirnja.
Consequential	Jang berhoeboeng; berkepala besar.
Conserve	Manisan.
Conserve	Bikin manisan.
Consider	Pikir; timbang.
Considerable	Perloe; penting.
Consideration	Pikiran atawa timbangan jang mateng.
Considering	Berhoeboeng; tentang hal.
Consign	Kirim.
Consist	Berisi; terbikin dari.
Consistence	Moefakatan; kategoehan badan,

Consistent	Termoefakat; tegoe.
Consolation	Hiboeran; kasenangan.
Console	Hiboerin; bri kasenangan.
Consols	Oewang ganti keroegian; oetangnja ke-radjaän Inggris.
Consonant	Letter jang diboenjiken dengen *vowel*.
Consort	Soeami atawa istri.
Consort	Bergaoelan; bertemenan.
Compicuous	Terang; teges; njata.
Conspiracy	Persariketan doerhaka.
Conspirator	Orang jang ingin berboeat doerhaka.
Conspire	Ingin berboeat doerhaka.
Constable	Schout.
Constant	Tetep; tiada beroba.
Constellation	Koempoelan binatang-binatang.
Constenation	Ketakoetan besar.
Constituency	Koempoelan orang jang bikin pemilihan.
Constitute	Angkat; benoemd.
Constitution	Keadaän badan atawa pikiran; constitutie atawa wet pamerentahan negri.
Constrain	Paksa; perkosa.
Contraint	Paksahan; perkosahan.
Constrict	Tarik sama-sama; iket.
Construct	Bikin; berdiriken.
Construction	Pembikinan; pendirian.
Construe	Kasi mengarti.
Consul	Consul atawa wakil keradjaän di negri asing.
Consult	Berdami; bermoefakatan.
Consultation	Perdamian.
Consume	Goenaken; abisin; makan.
Consummate	Soeda abis; soeda lengkep; bikin abis; bikin lengkep.
Consumption	Sakit paroe; tering.
Contact	Perhoeboengan; djadian satoe.

Contain	Berisi.
Contemn	Tiada liat mata; bentji.
Contemplate	Pikir; timbang; oekoer.
Contemporary	Orang pantaran oemoer; orang jang hidoep di djeman bersamaän.
Contempt	Kabentjian; pemandangan renda pada laen orang.
Contemptible	Renda; hina.
Contend	Bertanding; begoelet.
Content	Rasa poewas hati; berpoewas hati; bikin poewas hati.
Contention	Pertandingan; pergoeletan.
Contentment	Rasa poewas hati.
Contents	Berisinja.
Contest	Pertandingan; pertengkaran.
Contest	Bertanding; bertengkar.
Context	Omongan jang ada di sebla atas atawa bawa.
Continence, Continency	Pendjagaän diri sendiri.
Continent	Binoewa.
Contingent	Waktoe jang kabetoelan atawa jang tiada didoega lebi doeloe; kabetoelan tiada didoega lebi doeloe.
Continuation	Berikoetnja; teroesannja.
Continue	Berikoetin; teroesin.
Contour	Roman di loear.
Contraband	Gelap; terpantang.
Contract	Kontract atawa perdjandjian.
Contracted	Kisoet; sempit; temaha.
Contraction	Kisoetannja; djadi pendeknja.
Contradict	Bantah; moengkir.
Contrariwise	Sabaliknja.
Contrary	Sebaliknja; bertentangan; melawan.
Contrast	Bertentangannja; bantahannja.
Contrast	Bandingken.

Contravene	Bantah; halangin.
Contribute	Kasi masoek oewang; mempoenjai andeel atawa bagian.
Contribution	Contributie atawa oewang jang dikasi masoek.
Contrite	Sanget menjesel.
Contrition	Seselan jang sanget.
Contrivance	Daja; peta pikiran.
Contrive	Berdaja; tjari akal.
Control	Prentahan; djagaän; prenta; djaga.
Controversy	Perselisihan; pertengkaran.
Contumacious	Bandel; bengal.
Contumacy	Kabandelan; kabengalan.
Contumely	Hinaän; oesikan.
Contuse	Antjoerken; loekain.
Contusion	Loeka; bagian jang antjoer.
Conundrum	Badean; tebakan.
Convalescence	Semboehan dari penjakit.
Convene	Berkoempoel; berhimpoen.
Convenience	Kasatoedjoean; kalengkepan.
Convenient	Satoedjoe; lengkep.
Convent	Tempat tinggalnja padri prempoean.
Conventicle	Tempat berkoempoel; roema perhimpoenan.
Convention	Perhimpoenan dari wakil-wakil keradjaän; moefakatan.
Conventional, Conventionary	Brasa; menoeroet perdjandjian.
Converge	Berkoempoel di tenga.
Conversant	Mateng; paham.
Conversation	Omongan.
Converse	Omong; bertentangan atawa berlawanan.
Converse	Omong; bitjara.
Conversely	Dalem atoeran jang bertentangan atawa berlawanan.
Conversion	Toekarnja keadaän.

Convert	Toekang toekar pikiran atawa haloean.
Convert	Toekar dari satoe keadaän ka dalem jang laen.
Convex	Noendjoel kaloear; boender moekanja.
Convey	Angkat; angkoet.
Conveyance	Kreta; angkatan; angkoetan.
Convict	Persakitan; orang jang berdosa.
Conviction	Pendapetan sala; pikiran jang tegoe.
Convince	Boedjoek; tetepken dengen ketrangan.
Convivial	Bersobat baek; soeka bergaoelan dengen orang; soeka koendjoengin pesta orang.
Convoke	Panggil mengadep.
Convoy	Barisan pendjaga.
Convulse	Sala-lakoe kisoet.
Convulsion	Sala lakoe jang koenjoeng-koenjoeng; keriboetan jang boekan biasa-biasanja.
Cony	Sabangsa klintji.
Cook	Koki atawa toekang masak; masak.
Cookery	Ilmoe masak-masakan; koki-bitja.
Cool	Adem; memegang deradjat; bikin adem.
Coop	Koeroengan ajam; koeroeng.
Cooper	Toekang tahang.
Cooperate	Bersariket; bersatoe hati.
Cooperation	Bersariketan; pakerdjahan jang dilakoeken dengen satoe hati; karoekoenan.
Coot	Saroepa ajam rawa.
Cope	Badjoe padri; bersaingan.
Coping	Boetjaknja tembok.
Copious	Banjak.
Copper	Tembaga; kettel besar.
Copse	Oetan lebet.
Copula	Samboengan; hoeboengan.
Copy	Copij atawa tjonto; tiroean; menjonto; tiroe.
Coquet	Tjari katjintahan dengen kebagoesan diri.
Coquette	Prempoean jang tjari katjintahan dengen kabagoesan; prempoean berhati palsoe.

Cord	Tali; iket.
Cordage	Tambang kapal.
Cordial	Obat mengoewatken badan; baek hati.
Corduroy	Kaeii kapas jang tebel.
Cordwainer	Toekang sepatoe.
Core	Hati; bagian sebla dalem.
Cork	Perop; soempelan; soempel dengen prop.
Corn	Djagoeng; gandoem.
Corned	Diasinin, sebagi daging.
Corner	Pepodjok atawa peloksok.
Cornet	Samatjem trompet muziek.
Coronation	Penerimaän makota keradjaän.
Coroner	Pembesar jang diwadjibken boeat tjari taoe tentang meninggalnja orang jang koenjoeng-koenjoeng.
Coronet	Makota jang dipake oleh pembesar.
Corporal	Korporaal atawa pembesar ketjil dalem barisan; berhoeboeng dengen koempoelan dagang.
Corporation	Pakoempoelan dagang; gemeenteraad.
Corps	Balatentara; barisan soldadoe.
Corpse	Mait; bangke.
Corpulence	Kagemoekan jang terlaloe.
Correct	Bikin betoel; memperbaiki; betoel tjotjok.
Correction	Pembikinan betoel.
Correctness	Kabetoelannja; katjotjokannja.
Correspond	Moefakat; rasa satoedjoe; berhoeboeng dengen soerat.
Correspondence	Moefakatan; perhoeboengan dengen soerat.
Corridor	Djalanan jang pandjang.
Corrode	Makan abis; bikin roesak.
Corrosion	Pemakanan, abis; pembikinan roesak.
Corrupt	Sogokan; nodahan; bernoda; makan sogokan.
Corruption	Kenodahan; kaboesoekan.

Corsair	Badjak laoet.
Corse	Mait; bangke.
Corselet	Tembaga toetoepan dada jang enteng.
Corset	Korset atawa pakean dada bagi orang prempoean.
Cosmopolitan	Pendoedoek doenia.
Cost	Harga pembikinannja; modal atawa poentjinja; beharga.
Costive	Tiada bisa boewang aer; mempoenjai djelek pentjernaän makan.
Costly	Beharga; mahal.
Costume	Pakean; model pakean.
Cosy	Anget; enak.
Cot	Pondok ajoenan.
Coterie	Partij atawa kaoem jang terpili.
Cottage	Roema pondok; roema kampoengan.
Cotton	Kapas; lawe; terbikin dari kapas atawa lawe.
Couch	Tempat-doedoek; randjang; reba tengkoeroep; seboet; laloeken kelilipan dalem mata.
Coulter	Besi di hadepan loekoean.
Council	Koempoelan orang jang membikin timbangan tentang oeroesan negri.
Counsel	Nasehat; advocaat; kasi nasehat.
Count	Peritoengan; perkenahan pembajaran; nama gelaran jang bermaksoed graaf; itoeng; hargaken.
Countenance	Paras moeka; toendjangan; toendjang.
Counter	Medja toko; bertentangan atawa berlawanan.
Counteract	Tjega; halangin.
Counterfeit	Tiroean; tiroe; tertiroe.
Countermand	Atoeran jang bertentangan atawa berlawanan.
Counterpane	Toetoepan tempat tidoer.

Countersign — Tanda resia.

Countersign — Taro tanda resia.

Countess — Gravin atawa istrinja graaf.

Countless — Tiada bisa teritoeng.

Country — Oedik; negri.

Countryman — Orang oedik.

County — Afdeeling.

Couple — Sapasang; doea; samboeng.

Couplet — Doea sairan; sapasang.

Coupon — Coupon atawa kaartjis.

Courage — Kebranihan.

Courageous — Brani; gaga.

Courier — Soeroehan jang diprenta dengen terboe-roe-boeroe.

Course — Djalanan; lapangan adoe-koeda; boeroe.

Courser — Koeda jang bisa lari kentjeng; koeda-adoean.

Coursing — Pemboeroean klintji dengen memake andjing.

Court — Paleis atawa kraton radja; pengikoet ra-dja; pengadilan; pekarangan; meminang atawa melamar.

Courteous — Taoe adat; berprilakoe hormat.

Courtesy — Prilakoe jang taoe adat atawa hormat.

Courtier — Penoenggoe di kraton radja atawa di pengadilan; orang jang bisa mengoem-pak atawa bermoeka-moeka.

Courtmartial — Pengadilan militair atawa marine.

Courtship — Minangan atawa lamaran.

Cousin — Soedara misan; soedara tjintong atawa piauw.

Cove — Moeara ketjil.

Covenant — Moefakatan; kontract; membikin moefa-katan atawa kontract.

Cover — Toetoepan; lindoengan; maäfan; toetoepin pakein; lindoengin; semoeniken.

Covert	Oetan lebet; tempat semoeni; tersemoeni.
Covet	Serakain.
Covetousness	Kaserakaän atawa kasekakeran.
Cow	Sampi; bikin takoet.
Coward	Penakoet atawa pengetjoet.
Cowardice	Hati jang penakoet.
Cower	Mengkeroet atawa kisoet lantaran keta-koetan.
Cowl	Topi padri; toetoepan semprong.
Cowslip	Samatjem kembang *primrose,*
Coxcomb	Djengger ajam djago; kembang djengger ajam; orang jang perlente; kongtjoe. idoeng poeti.
Coxswain	Pembesar ketjil jang berkwasa atas ma-troos-matroos kapal.
Coy	Taoe adat; pemaloean.
Coyness	Adat jang pemaloean; pendjaga.
Cozon	Tipoe.
Cozy	Anget; enak.
Crab	Kepiting; asem; kasar.
Crabbed	Gampang mara; bo-sioh.
Crack	Soeara barang meleka; meleka; petja.
Crakle	Bikin soeara kerekekan.
Cradle	Ajoenan.
Craft	Kepandean; tipoe-daja; praoe ketjil.
Crag	Karang-djoerang.
Cram	Isi sampe loeber.
Cramp	Kasemoetan; toetoep.
Crane	Boeroeng bango; pekakas pranti angkat. barang berat.
Crank, Crankle	Bengkokan roda; gampang terbalik.
Cranny	Lobang meleka.
Crape	Kaen tioe atawa djiauw-see.
Crash	Soeara barang djato atawa petja.
Crate	Naja atawa bakoel jang terboeka.
Crater	Moeloet dari goenoeng api.

Crave	Minta dengen sanget.
Craving	Kainginan jang sanget; mengileran.
Craw	Glondongan boeroeng.
Crawl	Merajap; merangkang.
Crayon	Potlood dari-kapoer.
Craze	Kagendengan; kageloan.
Cracy	Gendeng atawa gelo.
Creak	Bikin soeara bekrikik.
Cream	Kepala soesoe.
Crease	Lipet atawa lepit; tanda lipetan atawa lepitan.
Create	Bikin; djadiken.
Creator	Jang membikin atawa djadiken; Toehan Jang Berkwasa,
Creature	Machloek; barang pembikinannja Allah.
Credence	Kapertjaiaän.
Credible	Boleh dipertjaia.
Credit	Kapertjaiaän; pertjaia.
Creditor	Pioetang; orang jang kasi oetang.
Credulity	Kagampangan aken pertjaia.
Creed	Kapertjaiaän; artikel dari kapertjaiaän.
Creek	Moeara laoet.
Creep	Merajap; merangkang.
Cremation	Pembakaran.
Crest	Djengger boeroeng; poentjak goenoeng atawa boekit.
Crevass, Crevasse	Lobang meleka jang dalem.
Crevice	Melekahan.
Crew	Matroos kapal.
Crib	Krib atawa brand card; gotongan orang; toetoep koeroeng.
Gricket	Djangkrik; permaenan bola dengen tamparan.
Crier	Pembesar kota jang membri wartaän dari pamerenta pada pendoedoek negri.

Crime	Dosa.
Criminal.	Orang jang berdosa; djahat.
Criminate	Toedoe.
Crimp	Amo; gampang petja; kakedoetan.
Crimson	Mera toea.
Cringe	Merendaän diri; manggoetan kepala; rendain diri; manggoetin kepala.
Cripple	Orang pintjang; pintjang.
Crisis	Tempo jang sanget penting.
Crisp	Amo atawa renja: bikin mengkeroet; bikin kriting.
Critic	Timbang toekang timbang.
Critical	Penting; pengabisan.
Criticism	Critiek atawa pertimbangan pikiran.
Croak	Soeara kodok; bersoeara; dengen serak; soeda larang.
Crochet	Pakerdjahan dari benang; pinggiran jang tersoelam.
Crock	Pot; teko.
Crockery	Perabot jang terbikin dari tana.
Croft	Lapangan ketjil jang berdamping dengen roema.
Crone	Prempoean toea.
Crook	Bengkokan; toengket toekang angon; bengkokin.
Crooked	Bengkok; berhati serong.
Crop	Hasil dari peroesahan; potongan padi; glondongan boeroeng; petik; potong.
Croquet	Permaenan croquet jang dimaenken di atas roempoet.
Crossier	Toengket dari bisschop atawa kepala padri.
Crossness	Adat jang gampang mara; oering-oeringan.
Crotchet	Noot dalem muziek.
Crouch	Djongkok; berboeat dengen hina.
Croup	Penjakit pipa napas; bebokong koeda.
Croupier	Pembantoe atas medja perdjoedian.

Crow	Gaok atawa gowak; berkroejoek menjombongin,
Crowd	Koempoelan orang; berdesek.
Grown	Makota radja; oewang Inggris dari 5 *shillings;* kamenangan; pake makota; abisin.
Crucify	Dipakoein di atas pergantoengan.
Crude	Menta; kasar.
Cruel	Bengis; kedjem.
Cruelty	Kabengisan; kakedjeman.
Cruise	Perlajaran; belajar.
Crumb	Antjoeran roti.
Crumble	Antjoer; djadi reroentoekan.
Crumple	Mengkeroet; letjek.
Crupper	Koelit dibawa boentoet koeda boeat menahan blakang sela.
Crusade	Prang agama; expeditie.
Cruse	Botol ketjil.
Crush	Remoekan; bikin remoek; kalaken.
Crust	Koelit keras; batok; toetoep denden batok.
Crusty	Keras di loearnja; bertabiat djelek.
Crutch	Toengket boeat orang pintjang.
Cry	Tangisan; soeara treakan; menangis; bertreak.
Crypt	Tempat di bawa gredja.
Crystal	Kristal atawa tjoei-keng.
Cub	Anaknja binatang dari bangsa andjing.
Cube	Roman jang mempoenjai anam pesegi; kekoewatan ka tiga.
Cubit	Oekoeran dari sikoet sampe di oedjoeng djeridji.
Cucumber	Ketimoen.
Cud	Makanan jang dimama kedoea kali.
Cuddle	Reba deket-deket.
Cuddy	Kamar di kapal jang ketjil.
Cudgel	Toengket jang berat.

Cue	Mengsolnja perkataän; nummer gelap; boentoet.
Cuff	Oedjoeng tangan badjoe; poekoel.
Cuirass	Tembaga djagaän dada.
Cull	Pili; koempoelin.
Cullender	Saringan.
Culm	Batang padi; areng jang potongannja ketjil.
Culminate	Sampeken poentjaknja.
Culpable	Haroes dikasi sala.
Culprit	Bangsat; orang jang tertoedoe sala.
Cultivate	Sediaken tana; loekoe; memperbaiki.
Cultivation	Persediaän tana; loekoehan; tana; oeroesan memperbaiki priboedi kesoetjian.
Culture	Haloean aken memperbaiki; perloekoean tana.
Cumber	Tjega; tahan; moewatin.
Cumulate	Soesoen; toemploekin.
Cunning	Akal; berakal.
Cup	Mangkok; tjangkir atawa thee-auw.
Cupboard	Lemari makanan.
Cur	Andjing jang galak: orang jang berparas asem.
Curb	Les koeda; pamerentahan; pinggiran soemoer atawa djalanan jang diplester; tahan.
Curd	Soesoe jang dibikin kentel; tauw-hoe.
Curdle	Djadi kentel
Cure	Obat; obatain; semboeken.
Curiositiy	Kaheranan; rasa penasaran.
Curious	Heran; penasaran.
Curl	Meringkoekan; kritingan; meringkoek; kriting.
Currency	Oewang jang dipake.
Current	Djalanan aer; anjoet; berdjalan.
Currier	Toekang tjelep koelit.
Curry	Sajoer kari; gosok dan bersiken.

Curse	Soempahan; koetoekan; bersoempa; koetoekin.
Curt	Pendek; ringkes.
Curtail	Bikin pendek; potong.
Curtain	Klamboe; bangta.
Curtsey	Berloetoetan; berkoeian; berloetoet; berkoei.
Curvature	Meringkoekan; bengkokan.
Curve	Meringkoekan; bengkokan; meringkoek; bengkok.
Cushion	Bantal.
Custard	Soesoe dan telor dimasak.
Custard-apple	Siri kaja; boea nona.
Custody	Pendjagaän; toetoepan.
Custom	Adat-kebiasaän; pemblian barang.
Customs	Bea atas barang.
Customer	Langganan.
Cut	Potongan; potong.
Cute	Tadjem; pinter.
Cutlass	Pedang jang lebar.
Cutler	Toekang bikin pekakas tadjem, oepama piso, goenting dan sebaginja.
Cutlet	Potongan ketjil dari daging.
Cutter	Praoe belajar jang ketjil.
Cutting	Galian; keping jang terpotong; bengis.
Cutwater	Kepala kapal jang memotong ombak.
Cycle	Terpoeternja tempo; sepeda.
Cyclone	Angin besar di negri-negri panas.
Cyclopedia	Boekoe ilmoe peladjaran.
Cygnet	Anak gangsa.
Cylinder	Cylinder atawa pipa jang pandjang.
Cymbal	Tjetjer.
Cynic	Orang jang bertabiat binatang.
Cynosure	Bintang oedjoeng-langit.
Cypher	Liat. *Cipher.*
Cypress	Samatjem poehoen pipee.
Cyprus	Kaen pangsi jang tipis dan djarang; na= manja satoe poelo di Laoetan tenga.

Cyriologic	Berhoeboeng dengen letter besar.
Cyst, Cystis	Klemboengan; bisoel.
Cystitis	Penjakit klemboengan atawa bengkaknja kemaloean.
Czar	Keizer dari Rusland.
Czarevna	Istri dari poetra makota Rusland.
Czarine	Permisoeri dari keizer Rusland.
Czarowits	Gelaran dari poetra makota di Rusland.

D.

Dab	Poekoelan jang enteng; ikan sebela; poekoel dengen enteng.
Dabble	Tjelep di dalem aer; ganggoe.
Dado	Bagian sebla bawa dari tembok.
Daffodil	Saroepa kembang; boenga soei-sian.
Dagger	Pedang pendek.
Dailay	Sahari-hari; saban hari.
Dainty	Kabagoesan; kelema-lemboetan; bagoes; lema-lemboet.
Dairy	Kamar pranti simpen soesoe dan mentega.
Dairyman	Toekang peres soesoe sampi.
Daisy	Kembang daisy; kembang; mata-hari.
Dale	Lemba; selat-goenoeng.
Dam	Iboe atawa biang binataug; dam atawa gili-gili boeat tahan madjoenja aer; tahan madjoenja aer.
Damage	Keroesakan; bikin roesak.
Dame	Njonja; orang prampoean.
Damp	Hawa jang semek atawa demek; semek atawa demek; bikin semek atawa demek.
Damsel	Gadis; anak prawan.
Dance	Dansa; mengigel atawa tandak.

Dandelion	Saroepa tetaneman jang mengaloearken kembang koening; poehoen pouw-kong-eng.
Dandle	Bergerak di atas loetoet.
Dandy	Anak moeda jang perlente; kong-tjoe. idoeng poeti.
Danger	Ketjilakaän; bahaja.
Dank	Semek; basa.
Dapper	Gesit; netjis.
Dapple	Bertoetoel sebagi koeda.
Dare	Brani.
Daring	Kabranihan; brani.
Dark	Gelap goelita; kabodohan; gelap; bodo.
Darkness	Kaglapan.
Darling	Katjintahan; orang jang sanget ditjinta; jang ditjinta.
Darn	Tambel lobang.
Dart	Djemparing; lempar; toebroek.
Dash	Toebroekan; tanda (-); toebroek.
Dastard	Penakoet; pengetjoet.
Date	Tanggal; korma; tetepin tanggalnja.
Daugther	Anak prempoean; gadis; poetri.
Daunt	Tjega; bikin ketjil hati.
Dauntless	Tida penakoet; brani.
Dauphin	Gelaran jang doeloe dari poetra kasatoe dari radja prasman.
Dawn	Terang-tana.
Day	Hari; 24 djam; siang.
Dazzle	Bikin silo; bikin goerem.
Dead	Kasoenjian; mati.
Deaden	Bikin mati.
Deadly	Bakal mati. membikin kematian.
Deaf	Toeli.
Deal	Bagian; toemploekan; papan; bagi; berniaga; rawatin.
Dealer	Orang jang berniaga; toekang djoeal.
Dear	Tertjinta; mahal.

Death	Kematian.
Deathless	Tiada bisa mati.
Debar	Tjega; singkirken.
Debase	Membikin toeroen; membikin renda.
Debate	Pertengkaran; bertengkar.
Debility	Kalemahan; keamohan.
Debit	Masoekan dalem bagian Dr. dari boekoe peritoengan; masoekan boeboe; kenaken harga.
Debt	Peroetangan.
Debtor	Orang jang mengoetang.
Decade	Djoembla atawa nomor dari sapoeloe.
Decadence	Djadi boesoek.
Decamp	Pinda boeroe-boeroe.
Decant	Toewang bikin kering.
Decanter	Goblet atawa botol pranti taro minoeman.
Decay	Djadi boesoek; kaboesoekan.
Decease	Kematian; mati.
Deceit	Tipoe-daja.
Deceive	Tipoe; akalin.
Deception	Tipoe daja.
Decide	Tetepken pikiran; poetoesken.
Decided	Njata; teges; soeda di poetoesin atawa ditetepin.
Decimal	Kasapoeloe; diitoeng dengen sapoeloe.
Decision	Katetepan hati.
Decisive	Soeda tetep pikiran.
Deck	Deck kapal; riasin.
Declaim	Omong begiat-giatan.
Declaration	Kenjataän pikiran.
Declare	Njataken; bilang.
Decline	Djadi boesoek atawa noewa; moengkir.
Declivity	Dojongan ka bawa.
Decomposition	Djadi boesoek; kanoewahan.
Decorate	Riasin; bikin bagoes.
Decorous	Mendjadi.

Decoy	Oempan; djebakan; oempanin; djebak.
Decrease	Koerangin; bikin koerang; pembikinan koerang.
Decree	Firman soeda djadi tetep; persembahken
Decrepit	Roesak lantaran soeda toea.
Decry	Bertriak; tjela; hinaken.
Dedicate	Dipersembahken; dihatoerken.
Dedication	Persembahan; hatoeran.
Deduce	Tarik; koerangin.
Deduct	Potong.
Deduction	Potongan.
Deed	Perboewatan.
Deem	Pikir; kira.
Deep	Laoetan; dalem; djaoe ke bawa; beril- moe.
Deepen	Bikin dalem.
Deer	Mendjangan.
Deface	Bikin djadi tida kroewan matjem.
Defalcation	Petjahan dari kapertjaiaän.
Defamation	Tjelahan; hinaän.
Defame	Tjela; hinain.
Default	Tida perhatiken; kateledoran.
Defect	Kakoerangan; kesalaän.
Defective	Tida tjoekoep; masi ada jang koerang.
Defence	Pendjagaän; perlindoengan.
Defend	Djaga; lindoengin.
Defer	Lantoetin; lambatin.
Deference	Kahormatan; mengalaän.
Defiance	Pertengkaran; gaga-brani.
Deficient	Kakoerangan; tida tjoekoep.
Defile	Djalanan jang sempit; djalan berbaris; kotor; mesoem.
Defilement	Kakotoran; kamesoeman.
Define	Watesin; kasi ketrangan.
Definite	Pasti; tetep; tentoe.
Definition	Ketrangan; maksoed.

Deform	Bikin tida kroewan matjem.
Deformed	Tida kroewan matjem.
Defraud	Tipoe.
Defray	Bajar sebagi ongkos.
Deft	Netjis; moengil.
Defunct	Mati; meninggal doenia.
Defy	Brani; bertengkar.
Degenerate	Bikin lebi djelek.
Degrade	Toeroenin; bikin renda.
Degree	Deradjat gelaran.
Deign	Merenda; menoendoek.
Deity	Toehan-Jang Maha kwasa.
Deject	Ganggoe pikiran; bikin kesel; mengoewatirken.
Dejection	Kekwatiran hati; ilang niatan.
Delay	Kalambatan; lambatin; tinggalken; toenda.
Delegate	Wakil; oetoesan; dikirim sebagi wakil atawa oetoesan.
Deliberate..	Pelahan; tetep hati; timbang; pikir.
Delicacy	Kalemboetan; kelembekan.
Delicious	Goeri; enak rasanja.
Delight	Kagirangan besar; bergirang.
Delirium	Roesak. pikiran; lingloeng.
Deliver	Lepas; bri kamerdikaän; kasi.
Deliverance	Kalepasan; pembrian kamerdikaän.
Dell	Lemba ketjil.
Deluge	Aer bandjir; bikin bandjier; tenggelemin.
Delusion	Kesalaän; kapertjaiaän jang palsoe.
Demagogue	Pemimpin jang disoekai.
Demand	Minta; madjoeken permintaän.
Demean	Berlakoe; bikin renda.
Demeanour	Pri-lakoe.
Demerit	Kedjahatan; kesalaän.
Demi	Perkataän tambahan jang bermaksoed sa-tenga.
Demise	Kematian; meninggalnja; sewahan; bawa; tinggalken.

Democracy	Pamerentahan jang dioeroes oleh orang banjak.
Demolish	Bikin roesak.
Demon	Iblis jang djahat.
Demonstrate	Kasi ketrangan jang tjoekoep.
Demur	Toendahan; toenda.
Demure	Taoe adat; mempoenjai prilakoe hormat.
Den	Gowa; sarang binatang boewas.
Denominate	Namaken; panggil.
Denominator	Nomor dalem itoengan *fraction*,
Denote	Hoendjoek; bermaksoed.
Denounce	Antjem; toedoe.
Dense	Penoe orang; tebel.
Density	Ketebelan; kerapetan.
Dent	Gigi; lobang.
Dental	Berhoeboeng dengen gigi.
Dentist	Doktor gigi.
Denude	Reba telandjang.
Denunciation	Antjeman; toedoehan.
Deny	Moengkir; bantah.
Depart	Brangkat pergi; tepisa.
Department	Kantoor; tjabang tempat pakerdjahan.
Departure	Brangkat perginja; terpisanja.
Depend	Bergantoeng; mengandelin.
Dependence	Hoeboengan; andelan.
Dependent	Pengrawat tetamoe; mengandel; berlengket.
Deplore	Berdoeka.
Deportment	Adat; tabiat; prilakoe.
Depose	Ditoeroenken dari tachta keradjaän; membri ketrangan dengen soempa.
Deposit	Barang simpenan; tanggoengan; menginep.
Deposition	Keadaän ditoeroenken dari tachta keradjaän; kesaksian dengen soempa.
Depot	Depot; goedang; tempat pendjoewalan,

Deprave	Bikin djelek.
Depravity	Kadjelekan pikiran.
Depress	Toeroenin; boewang.
Depression	Lobang; ilangnja pengharepan atawa niat.
Deprivation	Kakoerangan; karoegian.
Depth	Dalemnja; djakdjakannja.
Deputation	Commissie atawa oetoesan loear biasa.
Depute	Wakilken.
Deputy	Wakil; oetoesan.
Derange	Kalang-kaboet; adoek.
Deranged	Kalang-kaboetan dalem pikiran.
Deride	Tertawaken; lewein.
Derision	Tertawaän; lewean.
Derive	Dapet; dateng dari.
Descend	Toeroen.
Descendant	Toeroenan.
Descent	Toeroennja ka bawa; toeroenan; anak-tjoetjoe.
Describe	Tjeritaken; rentjanaken.
Description	Tjerita; rentjana.
Desert	Kaharoesan; tinggal; memboeron.
Desert	Padang pasir; laoetan pasir; kosong.
Deserter	Soldadoe atawa matros jang boeron.
Deserve	Haroes; katoela.
Design	Peta; tjonto; kasi pikiran; kasi tjonto.
Designate	Hoendjoek atawa toendjoek.
Designing	Berakal.
Desire	Kainginan; ingin; kapingin.
Desirous	Mempoenjai kainginan; mempoenjai hati; kapingin.
Desist	Tahan; brentiken.
Desk	Medja sekola.
Desolate	Tersia-sia; tida enak.
Despair	Kailangan pengharepan; ilang pengharepan.
Despatch	Kiriman; soeroehan; keadaän jang boeroe-boeroe; kirim; abisin.

Desperate	Di loewar harepan; berkoetet-koetetan.
Despise	Liat tida mata; pandang renda.
Despite	Dendeman hati; tida perdoeli.
Despond	Ilang pengharepan.
Despot	Djago; orang jang berkwasa sendiri.
Despotic	Berkwasa sendiri; tjoan-tji.
Dessert	Boea-boeahan; kwee-tji.
Destine	Korbanken; teriket.
Destiny	Nasib; peroentoengan
Destitute	Perloe; kakoerangan.
Destry	Roesaken; boewang.
Destruction	Keroesakan; pemboenoehan.
Destructive	Membawaken keroesakan.
Detach	Pisaken.
Detachment	Kiriman sabagian dari soldadoe.
Detail	Ketrangan sampe aloes.
Detail	Trangken sampe aloes.
Detain	Tahan; Tjega.
Detect	Bikin sampe trang; bikin sampe resianja petja.
Detective	Mata-mata.
Deter	Tahan; tjega.
Determination	Katetepan pikiran.
Determine	Tetepken pikiran; ambil poetoesan.
Dethrone	Toeroenken dari tachta keradjaän.
Detract	Tjela; nistà.
Detriment	Kailangan; keroesakan.
Devastate	Sia-siaken.
Develop	Boeka; pentang.
Deviate	Djalan-djalan; kesasar.
Device	Daja; tanda peringetan.
Devil	Iblis; setan.
Devious	Kesasar.
Devise	Mentjari daja; tinggalken.
Devoid	Kosong; tida ditempatin.
Devote	Goenaken; persembahken; soenggoe-soenggoe hati; sampeken maksoed.

Devotee	Orang jang bersoedjoet.pada maleikat ata-wa agama.
Devotion	Hati jang soedjoet; katjintahan jang loear biasa.
Devour	Makan dengen rakoes.
Devout	Alim.
Dew	Emboen.
Dexterous	Pande; paham.
Diabetes	Sakit kentjing manis.
Diagonal	Dari oedjoeng ketemoe oedjoeng.
Diagram	Tjonto; roman; peta.
Dial	Piring boeat menoedjoeken tempo.
Dialogue	Pembitjaraän antara doea orang.
Diameter	Oekoeran dari pinggir sampe ka tenga.
Diamond	Inten.
Diarrhoea	Sakit mentjret; sakit boewang-boewang aer.
Diary	Boekoe tjatetan.
Dictate	Prentahan; prenta; batjaken perkataän. boeat laen orang toelis.
Dictation	Batjahan perkataän boeat laen orang toelis; beksoe.
Dictator	Radja atawa orang jang pegang pameren-tahan dengen berkwasa besar.
Dictionary	Kitab logat; djie-tian; woerdenboek.
Die	Mati; meninggal doenia; tjitakan atawa stempel; dadoe atawa tjimplong.
Diet	Makanan; perhimpoenan; makan dengen atoeran; kasi makan.
Differ	Berlaenan; berbeda.
Different	Laen; beda.
Difficult	Soesa.
Difficulty	Kesoesaän; halangan.
Diffuse	Siarken; boleh ditiroe atawa ditoeroet.
Diffusion	Tersiarnja.
Dig	Gali.

Digest	Koempoelan wet-wet.
Digest	Antjoerken atawa pentjernaken barang makanan di dalem peroet.
Digit	Djeridji; nomor dari 1 sampe 9.
Dignify	Agoengin; bikin tinggi.
Dignity	Keagoengan; pangkat.
Dike	Solokan; tembok.
Dilapidate	Roesakan; roeboeken.
Dilate	Melarin.
Dilemna	Kabingoengan.
Diligence	Keradjinan.
Diligent	Radjin.
Dilute	Bikin entjer.
Dim	Goerem; gelap.
Dimension	Besarnja, tingginja, dalemnja, dan pandjangnja.
Diminish	Koerangin.
Diminutive	Ketjil.
Dimple	Sidjen.
Din	Soeara keras.
Dine	Dahar; makan; bersantap.
Dinner	Barang makanan; barang santapan.
Dint	Poekoelan; poekoel.
Dip	Tjelepan; tjelep.
Diplomatist	Staatsman atawa diplomaat; orang jang pande dalem oeroesan bergaoel dengen laen negri.
Dire	Penakoet; gelap.
Direct	Teroes; tida menjimpang; atoer; toentoen.
Direction	Djoeroesan; toentoenan; atoeran; penoentoen.
Directly	Dengen sigra; dengen lantes.
Director	Directeur; pengoeroes.
Dirge	Njanjian dari poedjian bagi orang jang soeda meninggal doenia.

Dirt	Kekotoran; nadjis; tana; bikin kotor.
Dirty	Kotor; mesoem; bikin kotor; bikin me-soem.
Disable	Bikin djadi tida bisa.
Disadvantage	Keadaän jang koerang enak; tida ada ke-faedahan.
Disagree	Tida akoer; tida roekoen.
Disagreeable	Tida sedap; tida roekoen.
Disappear	Ilang dari pemandangan.
Disappoint	Bikin sjah hati; bikin mendongkol.
Disapprove	Toedoe; sangka djelek.
Disarm	Rampas sendjata.
Disaster	Ketjilakaän.
Disband	Lepas, seperti balatentara.
Disc	Barang jang boender dan litjin; moeka dari matahari, remboelan dan sebagi-nja.
Discard	Oesir; omslag.
Discern	Liat; tengok.
Discharge	Angkatan moewatan; meletoesan; oesir; angkat moewatan; tembak.
Disciple	Moerid; pengikoet.
Discipline	Pengadjaran; adjar.
Disclaim	Moengkir; tida akoe.
Disclose	Boeka.
Discolour	Toekar warna; nodain.
Discomfit	Kalaken.
Discompose	Bikin djadi kalang-kaboet.
Disconcert	Toenda; oeroengin.
Disconnect	Pisaken.
Disconsolate	Berdoeka; tida mempoenjai hati girang.
Discord	Perselesihan; perbantahan.
Discordant	Tida roekoen.
Discount	Potong pro cent.
Discourage	Bikin ilang pengharepan; bikin hati dja-di ketjil.

Discourse	Pembitjaraän omongan; bitjara; omong.
Discourtesy	Prilakoe jang koerang adjar.
Discover	Dapet taoe; boeka.
Discovery	Pendapetan taoe; ketrangan.
Discreet	Tjerdik.
Discrepancy	Koerangnja karoekoenan.
Discriminate	Liat dan bedaken.
Discursive	Tida tentoe.
Discuss	Meroending; roendingken.
Discussion	Peroendingan.
Disdain	Makian; tjomelan; maki; tjomel.
Disease	Penjakit; bikin sakit.
Desembark	Naek ka darat.
Disengage	Lepas; bri kalongaran.
Disentangle	Bri kalepasan atawa kamerdikaän.
Disfavour	Tida soeka; bentji.
Disfigure	Tida kroewan matjem; tida beroman betoel.
Disgorge	Toempaken; moentaken.
Disgrace	Pengrasaän maloe; bikin maloe.
Disguise	Menjaroe; salin roepa.
Disgust	Pengrasaän bentji; membentji-in.
Dish	Piring; basi.
Dishearten	Bikin hati ketjil.
Dishonest	Tida djoedjoer; berhati serong.
Dishonour	Pengrasaän maloe; atawa djenga; bikin maloe atawa djenga.
Disinfect	Bikin bersi linjapken penjakit.
Disinter	Kaloearken dari koeboeran.
Disjoin	Pisaken.
Disjointed	Tida menjamboeng atawa berhoeboeng.
Dislike	Pengrasaän tida soeka atawa bentji; tida soeka atawa bentji.
Dislocate	Kaloearken dari samboengan; lotjotken.
Dislodge	Oesir.
Disloyal	Tida setia; tida berhati lempeng.

Dismal	Glap; soenji.
Dismantle	Telandjangin.
Dismay	Ketakoetan; bikin takoet dan kalang-kaboet.
Dismember	Potong anggota toeboe.
Dismiss	Oesir.
Dismount	Toeroen dari koeda; pinda.
Disobedience	Tabiat tida denger kata atawa berbakti; poet-hauw.
Disobey	Tida menoeroet; tida denger kata; tida berbakti.
Disorder	Kalang-kaboetan; kekaloetan; bikin kalang kaboet; bikin kaloet.
Disorderly	Dalem keadaän kalang-kaboet atawa kaloet.
Disorganize	Sala atoer.
Disown	Tida akoe; moengkir.
Disparity	Perbedahan.
Dispatch	Kirim; anterken.
Dispel	Pentjarken; bikin terpisa.
Dispensary	Roema-obat.
Dispensation	Kamerdikaän aken perboeat satoe hal jang terlarang; takdir Allah.
Dispense	Kasiken; pantarken.
Disperse	Sebarken; siarken.
Displace	Laloeken dari tempatnja.
Display	Pertoendjoekan; toendjoeken.
Displease	Bikin tida senang hati.
Displeasure	Hati jang koerang senang.
Disport	Permaenan; memaen.
Disposal	Oeroesan; atoeran.
Dispose	Atoer; ingin; djoeal.
Disposition	Perangi; tabiat; kainginan.
Disproof	Kesaksian palsoe.
Disprove	Djadi saksi palsoe.

Dispute	Pertengkaran; peroendingan; sangka; bertengkar.
Disqualify	Bikin tida satoedjoe.
Disquiet.	Keadaän jang tida bisa diam; kekwatiran; tida bisa diam; ganggoe.
Disrespect	Keadaän tida sopan.
Dissatisfaction	Hati jang tida merasa poewas.
Dissatisfy	Tida bisa bikin poewas.
Dissect	Potong atawa belek peroet.
Dissemble	Semoeni; poera-poera atawa belaga; menjaroe atawa salin roepa.
Dissembler	Penghianat; pendjoestà.
Dissension	Pikiran jang koerang tjotjok.
Dissenti	Koerang tjotjok pikiran.
Dissimilar	Tida sama; tida mirip.
Dissipate	Pentjarken; siarken.
Dissipation	Kailangan djiwa; keadaän terlaloe banjak plezir.
Dissociate	Pisaken; djaoeken.
Dissolute	Latjoerken; bikin tjilaka.
Dissolution	Pemisahan; kematian.
Dissolve	Loemerin; pisaken.
Dissyllable	Perkataän dari doea soeara-batjaän.
Distance	Djaoenja; terpisanja; tinggalken di blakang.
Distant	Djaoe; tida bergoembira; pemaloean.
Distaste	Tida soeka; bentji.
Distemper	Penjakit; penjakit andjing.
Distend	Bikin bengkok; melarin.
Distil	Diato dengen berketel; tarik dengen hawa panas; bikin minoeman keras.
Distiller	Toekang bikin minoeman keras.
Distinct	Teges; njata.
Distinction	Perbedahan; kategesan; kenjatahan.
Distinguish	Bikin beda; bikin tegas atawa njata.
Distinguished	Termashoer; ternama tinggi; terkenal.

Distract	Bikin bingoeng.
Distrain	Tangkep oetang.
Distraint	Tangkepan oetang.
Distress	Kesoesaän; kemiskinan; bikin soesa.
Distribute	Bagi; kasiken.
District	District; bagian afdeeling.
Distrust	Katjoerigaän; sangkahan; tjoeriga; sangka
Disturb	Ganggoe; bikin soesa.
Disuse	Kateledoran dalem memake.
Disuse	Berenti memake; tida pake lagi.
Ditch	Solokan; gali solokan.
Ditto	Sebagimana terseboet di atas; sama sebagi di atas.
Ditty	Lagoe; njanjian.
Divan	Pertengahan pranti mengoempoelin tetamoe.
Dive	Seloeloep.
Diverge	Siarken.
Divers	Banjak matjem; tjampoer-tjampoer.
Diverse	Laen matjem; beda.
Diversity	Bikin djadi matjem-matjem.
Diversion	Berlaloen dari djalanan atawa atoeran. jang betoel; permaenan sport.
Diversity	Perbedahan; roepa jang matjem-matjem.
Divert	Berlaloe dari djalanan atawa atoeran jang betoel; senangin diri.
Divest	Telandjangin; tjopotin.
Divide	Bagi nummer.
Dividend	Dividend; nummer jang dibagi; boenga atawa rente atas bagian atawa aandeel.
Divine	Minister dari gredja: soetji; ramalin.
Divinity	Toehan Allah; ilmoe peladjaran tentang barang jang soetji.
Division	Pembagian.
Divisor	Nummer jang membagi.

Divorce	Bertjerehan ; bertjere.
Divulge	Bikin terkenal.
Dizzy	Mabok; poejeng.
Do	Bikin; boewat; apa.
Dicile	Gampang diadjar.
Dock	Dok; tempat betoelin kapal.
Docket	Soerat ketrangan; kaartjis; bri tanda dengen kaartjis.
Doctor	Doktor; thabib.
Doctrinal	Berhoeboeng. dengen oedjar-oedjar agama.
Doctrine	Oedjar-oedjar agama.
Document	Kertas; ketrangan jang tertoelis.
Dodge	Semoeniken; pedengin.
Doe	Mendjangan prempoean.
Doer	Pemboewat; pembikin.
Doff	Toenda.
Dog	Andjing; ikoetin.
Dogged	Bermoeka asem.
Dogma	Haloean; tali kapertjaiaän.
Dogmatical	Pasti; tentoe.
Doily	Serbeta ketjil.
Doings	Perboewatan.
Dole	Bagian; barang bingkisan bagi; persembahken.
Doleful	Kesel; berdoeka.
Doll	Anak-anakan; boneka.
Dollar	Ringgit.
Dolorous	Penoe kadoekahan.
Dolphin	Saroepa binatang samatjem ikan paoes.
Dolt	Orang goblok.
Domain	Djadjahan; peroesahan.
Dome	Woewoengan roema jang beroman sebagi satenga bola.
Domestic	Boedjang piaraän; berhoeboeng dengen roema atawa tempat-tinggal; djinek; tida asing; aseli.

Domicile	Gedong.
Dominant	Jang berkwasa; jang berpengaroe.
Domineer	Mendjagoin atas sekalian orang.
Dominion	Pengaroe besar; tana djadjahan.
Donate	Derma; soembang.
Donation	Dermahan; soembangan; derma; soembang.
Donkey	Kalde.
Donor	Orang jang menderma atawa menjoembang.
Doom	Hoekoeman; koetoekan.
Doomsday	Hari poetoesan; hari kiamatnja doenia.
Door	Pintoe.
Dormant	Tida gesit; bebel.
Dormitary	Kamar tidoer.
Dorsal	Termasoek bilangan blakang.
Dose	Obat jang dimakan sakali; obatin.
Dot	Titik; toetoel.
Dotage	Kalemahan pikiran.
Dote	Tjinta dengen kliroe.
Double	Dubbel; doea kali; lipet-ganda; tipoedaja; mempoenjai tipoe daja; bikin lipet ganda; mengiterin doenia.
Doublet	Pasangan; rompi.
Doubt	Sangkahan; katjoerigaän; sangka; tjoeriga.
Doubtful	Sangsi; penoe sangkahan atawa katjoerigaän.
Doubtless	Tida sangsi; tetep; tida ada sangkahan atawa katjoerigaän apa-apa.
Douche	Ketelan aer.
Dough	Dek pranti bikin koewe atawa roti.
Doughty	Gaga-brani; koewat.
Douse	Terdjoen atawa lompat ka aer.
Dove	Boeroeng dara.
Dowager	Prempoean djanda jang mempoenjai anak soeda menika.

Dowdy	Bodo; goblok.
Dowel	Tjantoem dengen djaroem pentol.
Dower	Pembagian boeat istri.
Down	Boekit jang tida toemboe poehoen; boeloe aloes; di bawa; toeroenin.
Downfall	Binasanja; djatonja.
Downright	Teroes-trang; teges; njata; dengen teroes-trang.
Dowry	Bagian harta boeat saorang prempoean jang menika.
Doxology	Njanjian dari poedji-poedjihan.
Doze	Lajap-lajap; tidoer lajap-lajap.
Dozen	Dozijn; doea-blas.
Drab	Koening toea poetjet.
Draft	Wissel; kiriman oewang; kenaken pembajaran.
Drag	Tarik; seret.
Dragon	Naga; liong.
Dragon-fly	Tjapoeng.
Dragoon	Barisan soldadoe koeda.
Drain	Solokan; djalanan aer; bikin kering; kasi aer berdjalan.
Drake	Bebek lelaki.
Drama	Permaenan komedi.
Draper	Toekang djoeal kaen.
Drapery	Barang kaen-kaen; gantoeng-gantoengan.
Drastic	Bisa tjoetji peroet; keras.
Draught	Tioepan angin atawa hawa oedara; minoeman keras; soeda minoem kering; peta atawa daja; sakoempoelan ikan jang soeda ditangkep; dalemnja kapal jang masoek dalem aer.
Draughtsman	Toekang djoeal wissel.
Draw	Tarik; kenaken pembajaran.
Drawback	Bea jang dikirim; halangan atawa tjegatan.

Drawer	Latji; tokkwi.
Drawing	Gambar teekenan.
Drawl	Omongan dengen pelahan.
Dread	Pengrasaän takoet atawa ngeri; menakoetin; bikin takoet.
Dreadful	Menakoetin.
Dreadnought	Samatjem kapal prang jang paling besar
Dream	Impihan; mengimpi.
Dreary	Glap; soenji.
Dredge	Djala-tirem; kepretin aer.
Dredger	Peti tepoeng; toekang pantjing tirem; kapal keroek.
Dregs	Ampas; dedekan.
Drench	Bikin lepek atawa basa.
Dress	Pakean; berpakean; masak; obatin loeka.
Dresser	Lemari dapoer; orang jang meriasin atawa masak.
Dribble	Djato berketel.
Drift	Haloean, toemploekan; ngambang; anjoet.
Drill	Bor atawa poesoet; bor bikin berlobang; adjar baris.
Drink	Minoeman; minoem.
Drip	Djato berketel.
Drive	Pasiaran atas kandaran; oesir atawa geba.
Drizzle	Oedjan grimis.
Droll	Bikin orang djadi tertawa; loetjoe.
Dromedary	Oenta Arab jang melaenken mempoenjai satoe bongkok.
Drone	Tawon lelaki.
Droop	Bersoesa hati; lajoe.
Drop	Ketelan; giwang; berketel; kasi djato.
Dropsy	Sakit menjenje atawa beraer.
Drought	Moesim kering.
Drove	Kawanan heiwan; soeda oesir atawa geba.
Drown	Tenggelem; kalelep.
Drowsy	Ngantoek; ingin berbaring.

Drub	Poekoel; labrak.
Drubbing	Poekoelan; labrakan.
Drudge	Boedak; berkerdja soesa.
Drug	Boemboe obat-obatan; makan obat; bikin bodo.
Drugget	Saroepa kaen jang kasar.
Druggist	Toekang djoeal obat.
Drum	Drenden atawa tamboer; bagian pendengeran koeping; poekoel.
Drunk	Mabok; soeda minoem.
Drunkard	Pemabokan.
Dry	Kering; djemoer.
Dryness	Keaoesan; moesim kering.
Dual	Satoe sama satoe; terbilangan doea.
Ducal	Berhoeboeng dengen *Duke (hertog)*.
Duchess	Istri dari satoe *duke* atawa *hertog*,
Duchy	Tana jang terprenta oleh satoe *duke* atawa *hertog*.
Duck	Bebek; kaen lajar; seloeloep; djongkok.
Duct	Pipa; semprong; djalanan.
Ductile	Gampang ditarik keloear.
Dudgeon	Kaäseman atawa katjeriwisan adat.
Due	Oetangan; hak; bermilik; sah.
Duel	Pertandingan satoe sama satoe atawa antara doea orang.
Duet	Muziek dalem doea bagian.
Dug	Tete binatang; soeda gali.
Duke	*Hertog;* orang berpangkat jang paling agoeng.
Dulcet	Enak; merdoe.
Dull	Bodo; poentoel; bikin bodo atawa poentoel.
Dulness	Kabodohan; kapoentoelan.
Duly	Dengen satoedjoe; dengen betoel.
Dumb	Bisoe; gagoe.
Dump	Lemparken atawa banting.
Dun	Koening toea; tagi oetang dengen paksa.

8,

Dune	Boekit pasir.
Dunce	Orang jang bladjar dengen lambat atawa pelahan; orang jang geremet; orang bodo.
Dung	Hadjad koeda; kotoran.
Dunghill	Vuilbak; tempat boewang kotoran.
Dungeon	Kamar gelap.
Dupe	Orang jang gampang ditipoe; tipoe.
Duplicate	Duplicaat; salinan jang bersamaän; bikin dubbel atawa lipet ganda.
Duplicity	Tipoe daja.
Durable	Tahan lama; koewat; oelet.
Durance	Tahanan dalem pendjara.
Duration	Waktoe; tempo; masa.
During	Pada waktoe; pada tempo; pada masa.
Dusk	Menggerip; gelap-gelap.
Dust	Aboe atawa deboe.
Dutiful	Berbakti; denger kata.
Duty	Kewadjiban; kabaktian.
Dwarf	Orang kate.
Dwell	Tinggal; berdiam.
Dwelling	Tempat tinggal; tempat berdiam.
Dwindle	Djadi lebi koerang.
Dye	Tjelep warna; warnain,
Dyer	Toekang tjelep,
Dynamite	Dynamiet; letoesan.
Dynasty	Toeroenan radja-radja; keradjaän,
Dysentery	Sakit medjen.
Dyspepsia, Dyspepsy	Sakit soesa boewang aer.
Dyspeptic	Orang jang mempoenjai pentjernaän djelek; orang jang tjia-bee-siauw; jang tiada bisa dipentjernaken atawa diantjoerken didalem peroet.
Dysphagia, Dysphagy	Penjakit tenggorokan jang bikin soesa menelen barang makanan.

Dysphony   Kailangan soeara; kesoesaän aken bitjara.
Dyspnoea   Sakit asthma; sakit napas sengal-sengal.
Dysury   Sakit lobang kentjing tertoetoep; sakit soesa
           kentjing.

E.

Each   Soeatoe; sembarang.
Eager   Kapingin; ingin
Eagle   Boeroeng groeda atawa arend.
Ear   Koeping; tangke.
Earl   Graaf; gelaran di bawa Markies.
Early   Siang-siang; pagi-pagi; siang; pagi;
Earn   Tjari oentoeng; tjari.
Earnest   Pembajaran voorschot dari sabagian oewang;
            jang kapingin; jang ingin.
Eart   Tana; boemi atawa doenia; toetoepin de-
            ngen tana.
Earthen   Terbikin dari tana.
Earthly   Termasoek dalem bilangan boemi atawa
            doenia.
Earthquake Tana gojang; gempa boemi; linoe.
Ease   Kasenangan; kagampangan; bikin senang;
            bikin gampang.
Easel   Kajoe berdirian papan boord atawn gambar.
East   Timoer; wetan; mengadep timoer atawa
            wetan.
Easter   Kerajahan dari bangoennja Nabi Jesus dari
            koeboeran.
Eastern   Di timoer atawa wetan; dari timoer atawa
            wetan.
Easy   Gampang; senang.
Eat   Makan; dahar.
Eatable   Barang jang boleh di makan; boleh di makan.
Eaves   Pinggiran woewoengan roema jang ber-
            gantoeng.

Ebb	Aer soeroet ; soeroet.
Ecclesiastical	Termasoek dalem bilangan greoja.
Echo	Soeara berbalik ; balikin soeara.'
Eclectic	Terpili.
Eclipse	Kapangan ; djadi glap.
Ecliptic	Djalanan remboelan.
Economy	Ilmoe himat ; kahimatan ; rawatan jang baek.
Ecatasy	Kagirangan besar.
Eczema	Broentoesan di atas koelit.
Eddy	Aer terpoeter ; oeseran aer; aer beroeser.
Edentate	Tiada bergigi.
Edge	Pinggiran ; pinggiran jang tadjem ; bikin tadjem ; watesin.
Edging	Watesin ; betoelin.
Edict	Mahloemat ; firman.
Edifice	Gedong ; roema.
Edify	Memperbaeki ; kasi adjaran ;
Edit	Ditjitak boeat orang banjak.
Edition	Tjitakan boeat orang banjak.
Educate	Rawatin ; briken peladjaran ; didik.
Education	Rawatan : peladjaran ; pendidikan.
Eel	Mowa.
Efface	Blontoran.
Effect	Kedjadiannja ; boeanja ; kaloearken kerdjaken.
Effects	Barang-barang.
Effective	Satoedjoe boeat pakerdjahan ; bisa berkerdja.
Effectual	Bisa membawaken hasil atawa boea.
Effeminate	Termasoek dalem fihak prempoean.
Effete	Lela ; tjape.
Efficacy	Kapandean boeat mengaloearken hasil atawa boea.
Efficient	Pande bekerdja.
Effigy	Bajangan ; gambar.

Effluent	Kaloearken ; terbitken.
Effluvium	Baoe jang tiada enak.
Efflux	Anjoet keloear.
Effort	Pertjobaän ; ichtiar.
Effrontery	Adat atawa prilakoe jang koerang adjar.
Egg	Telor.
Eider	Saroepa bebek ; blibis.
Either	Sala satoe ; soeatoe ; dipakenja sama perkataän *or*.
Ejaculation	Bertreakan jang koenjoeng-koenjoeng.
Eject	Kaloear ; ondjolin.
Eke	Bikin pandjang ; selaennja.
Elaborate	Didjadiken dengen soenggoe-soenggoe hati.
Elapse	Liwat ; selang.
Elastic	Bisa melar ; bisa membal.
Elasticity	Adat jang bisa berbalik sebagimana roepanja jang aseli atawa bener.
Elbow	Sikoet.
Elder	Orang jang lebi toea ; lebi toea.
Eldest	Paling toea.
Elect	Pili ; angkat.
Election	Pemilihan ; kaängkatan.
Elector	Orang jang memili atawa mengangkat.
Electric	Electrisch atawa electris ; mempoenjai hawa electris.
Electricity	Electriciteit ; tenaga jang memang djadi sendiri bersamaän dengen kilat.
Electrify	Masoeken hawa electriciteit ; bikin kaget.
Elegance	Kebagoesan ; katjantikan.
Elegant	Bagoes ; tjantik.
Elegy	Sairan jang mennjedi-in.
Element	Dasarnja.
Elephant	Gadja.
Elevate	Angkat ; goembiraken.
Elf	Maleikat ketjil.
Elicit	Madjoe ka hadepan.

Eligible	Setoedjoe ; sedeng.
Eliminate	Tarik koloear.
Ell	Elo ; oekoeran dari 45 duim.
Ellipse	Roman jang londjong sebagi telor.
Elm	Saroepa poehoen di oetan.
Elocution	Atoeran mengomong.
Elope	Lari ; boeron.
Eloquence	Kapandean aken mengomong.
Else	Lagi ; poela ; kaloe tida.
Elsewhere	Dimana-mana poela.
Elucidate	Kasi mengarti ; bikin trang.
Elude	Singkirken ; kalaken.
Emaciate	Djadi koeroes ; ilang daging.
Emanate	Kaloearken ; terbitken.
Emancipate	Lepas ; bri kamerdikaän.
Emancipation	Kalepasan ; pembrian kamerdikaän.
Embalm	Simpen dengen ditaroïn obat.
Embankment	Gili-gili.
Embark	Belajar ; melakoeken pakerdjahan.
Embarrass	Bingoeng.
Embassy	Minister dan pengikoetnja dalem pengadilan bangsa asing ; gezantschap.
Embellish	Riasin.
Embers	Tai atawa sisa peninggalannja api.
Emblem	Tanda.
Embody	Berkoempoel.
Embolden	Bikin djadi brani.
Embrace	Peloek ; peloekan ; trima.
Embrazure	Lobang boeat taro meriam.
Embrocation	Obat gosok.
Embroider	Soelam.
Embroidery	Soelaman.
Embroil	Bikin soesa.
Emerge	Kaloear ; bangoen.
Emergency	Kaperloean jang koenjoeng-koenjoeng atawa tida terdoega.

Emetic	Obat moenta.
Emigrant	Orang jang dateng pinda; pendoedoek.
Emigratie	Pinda dari satoe ka laen negri.
Eminence	Kahormatan; kaägoengan; nama jang termashoer; gelaran.
Eminent	Agoeng; bergelar; termashoer.
Emit	Kirim.
Emollient	Obat jang membikin lemes.
Emolument	Kaoentoengan.
Emotion	Gerakan; kahilapan pikiran.
Emperor	Keizer; hongtee.
Emphatic	Koewat; bertenaga.
Empire	Kekwasaän besar; keradjaän; negri jang terprenta oleh satoe keizer atawa hongtee.
Employ	Pakerdjahan; pake.
Employment	Pakerdjahan; penghidoepan.
Empower	Kasi koeasa besar.
Empress	Permisoeri dari satoe keizer; hong-hoúw.
Empty	Kosong; bikin kosong.
Emulate	Adoe; bersaingan.
Emulation	Saingan.
Emulsion	Santen.
Enable	Bikin djadi bisa; toeloeng
Enact	Berdiriken dengen menoeroet wet.
Enamel	Moeka jang tertjat mengkilap; tjat bikin mengkilap.
Encamp	Berdiriken tenda.
Enchant	Pikat; kong-tauwin.
Enchantment	Pikatan; kong-tauw.
Encompass	Koeroeng.
Encounter.	Pertemoehan; berklaian; bertemoe; berklai.
Encourage	Bikin djadi brani; goembiraken.
Encroach	Tempatin; mendjagoin.
Encumber	Halangin; memberatin.

Encumberance	Halangan.
End	Oedjoeng; tamatnja; kematiannja; abisin; toetoep
Endeavour	Tjoba; berichtiar; pertjobaän; ichtiar haloean.
Endow	Tinggalken.
Endure	Teroesin; tahan.
Enemy	Moesoe·
Energetic	Gaga-brani; bisa berkerdja berat.
Energy	Tenaga; kegagahan.
Enervate	Ilang tenaga.
Enfranchise	Lepas; bri kamerdikaän.
Engage	Berklai; melakoeken; pake; berdjandji sewa; bertoendang.
Engagement	Perklaian; perdjandjian; pertoendangan.
Engine	Machine atawa masin.
Engineer	Ingeneur; pembikin atawa djoeroe moedi dari fabriek, masin dan sebaginja.
Engrave	Oekir.
Engaving	Oekiran.
Engross	Tempatin sampe sesek; toelis dengen letter besar.
Enhance	Angkat; tambahken.
Enigma	Badean.
Enjoin	Prenta; kommandir.
Enlarge	Bikin besar; besarken.
Enlighten	Bikin enteng; kasi adjaran.
Enlist	Tjatet; masoeken dalem lijst.
Enliven	Bikin hidoep; bikin girang.
Enmity	Kabentjian.
Enormity	Dosa jang tiada bisa dibebasken.
Enormous	Besar; terlaloe djahat.
Enough	Tjoekoep; katjoekoepan; dengen tjoekoep.
Enquire	Tanja; tilik.
Enrage	Bikin mara; djengekin.
Enrol	Masoeken dalem register atwa lijst.

Ensample	Tjonto.
Ensconce	Lindoengin; djaga.
Ensign	Bendera; soldadoe pembawa bendera.
Ensue	Ikoet.
Entangle	Bikin bingoeng; bikin koesoet.
Enter	Masoek; toesoek.
Enteric	Termasoek dalem bilangan oesoes.
Enterprise	Haloean; toedjoehan.
Entertain	Rawatin; bikin senang.
Entertainer	Djoeroe-rawat tetamoe.
Enthusiasm	Kagoembirahan; kagiatan.
Entice	Boedjoek; pikat.
Entire	Sama sekali; antero.
Entitle	Bri hak pada.
Entrails	Peroet.
Entrance	Pintoe; djalanan masoek.
Entrance	Kasoekahan; kagirangan,
Entreat	Minta dengan sanget.
Entreaty	Sembajangan jang soedjoet.
Entrust	Pertjaiaken.
Entry	Entree; ongkos boeat masoek dalem satoe pakoempoelan.
Enumerate	Reken atawa itoeng.
Enunciate	Kata; oetjapken.
Envelop	Toetoep; boengkoes; semoeniken.
Envelope	Envelop; toetoepan soerat; sin-hong.
Enviable	Mempoenjai rasa mengiri.
Envious	Mengiri.
Environ	Koeroeng; kiterin.
Environs	Tempat-tempat jang berdamping.
Envoy	Soeroehan.
Envy	Pengrasaän mengiri; iri-in.
Epaulet, Epaulette	Epaulet; aboeran roentje-roentje jang di pake di atas poendak badjoe.
Epic	Sairan dari orang gaga; termasoek dalem golongan orang-orang gaga.

Epidemic	Penjakit jang menoelarin.
Epigram	Sairan jang pendek tapi bersari.
Epilogue	Katetepan hati.
Episcopacy	Pamerentahan jang dioeroes oleh bisschop atawa padri kepala.
Episcopal	Termasoek dalem bilangan pamerentahan jang dioeroes oleh bisschop atawa padri kepala.
Episode	Tjerita jang betoel soeda kedjadian.
Epistle	Soerat.
Epitaph	Toelisan di atas batoe koeboeran; bongpay.
Epitome	Tjerita ringkes.
Epoch	Masa; djeman.
Equable	Litjin; tida mengkeroet.
Equal	Pantaran; sama rata.
Equality	Qualiteit atawa matjem jang sama.
Equally	Dengen keadaän jang sama.
Equator	Djalanan mata-hari; garisan jang diteeken tenga-tenga bola doenia.
Equestrian	Termasoek dalem golongan koeda.
Equidistant	Sama djaoenja.
Equilateral	Mempoenjai semoea pinggiran sama.
Equilibrum	Keadaän diam.
Equip	Lengkepin; pakein.
Equipage	Penganter; kreta.
Equipment	Kalengkepan jang perloe; pakean.
Equitable	Adil; hati lempeng.
Equity	Keadilan; kabeneran.
Equivalent	Sama rata; sama berat, dan harganja
Era	Djeman; masa.
Erase	Gosok; bikin ilang.
Eraser	Gosokan; sapoean papan-boord.
Ere	Seblonnja; lebi doeloe.
Ergo	Dari itoe sebab; dari lantaran begitoe.
Erect	Lempeng; angkat; bikin atawa berdiriken.

Erection	Pendirian atawa pembikinan; gedong.
Err	Sala; kliroe; kesasar.
Errand	Soeroehan.
Errant	Djalan-djalan; mengoembara; mengglandangan.
Erratic	Mengglandangan; mengoembara.
Erratum	Kesalaän dalem pertjitakan.
Erroneous	Sala; palsoe.
Error	Kasalaän kadosahan.
Erst	Doeloe; satoe kali.
Eruption	Petjanja goenoeng api.
Escape	Pemboeronan; boeron.
Eschew	Djaoeken; singkirken.
Escort	Pelindoeng; pendjaga.
Escort	Toenggöein dan djaga.
Esculent	Barang makanan; boleh dimakan.
Esparto	Roempoet jang kasar.
Especial	Teroetama; oetama.
Especially	Teroetama; apa poela.
Esperanto	Bahasa doenia.
Espouse	Kawin; menika; poengoet anak.
Espy	Liat; saksiken.
Esquire	Pangkat di bawa ridder
Essay	Pertjobaän; karangan jang pendek.
Essay	Tjoba.
Essence	Tabiatnja barang; aer wangi.
Essential	Punt atawa pembitjarahan jang oetama; perloe.
Establish	Berdiriken; boeka.
Estate	Harta banda; tana.
Esteem	Kahargaän besar; hargaken.
Estimable	Boleh dihargaken.
Estimate	Hargaken; taksir harga.
Estimation	Taksiran harga.
Etcetera	Dan laen-laen; dan sebaginja; enz.
Eternal	Tahan lama; selama-lamanja.

Eternity	Tempo selama-selamanja.
Ethics	Ilmoe peladjaran tentang pri-boedi kabe-djikan; sioe-sin.
Etiquette	Kasopanan; atoeran bergaoelan.
Ethnology	Peladjaran dari bangsa manoesia.
Evacuate	Bikin kosong; tinggalken.
Evacuation	Pembikinan kosong; penarikan.
Evangelical	Berhoeboeng dengen pakerdjahan soetji jang termasoek dalem agama Kristen.
Evangelist	Toekang bikin lezing atawa yan-swat tentang pembitjarahan agama.
Eve	sore.
Even	Sore; rata; litjin; bikin rata; begitoe poen djoega.
Evening	Sore.
Event	Kedjadian; ketjilakaän.
Eventful	Penoe kedjadian atawa ketjilakaän.
Ever	Selaloe; selamanja.
Evergreen	Selamanja idjo; poehoen jang selamanja ada mempoenjai daon.
Everlasting	Tahan selama-selamanja; sampe di achir djeman.
Every	Segala; semoea; sembarang;
Evidence	Boekti; alesan; ketrangan; kenjatahan.
Evident	Berboekti; beralesan terang atawa njata.
Evil	Kedjahatan; djahat.
Evince	Bikin terang atawa njata.
Evolution	Pemboekaän; evolutie.
Ewe	Kambing Blanda prempoean.
Ewer	Kendi jang besar.
Exact	Betoel; tjotjok.
Exaggerate	Melebiïn dari sabeneruja; ngobrolin.
Exalt	Angkat; bikin tinggi atawa agoeng.
Exalted	Tinggi atawa agoeng.
Examination	Examen; papreksahan; penilikan.
Examine	Preksa; tilik.

EXAMPLE — 125 — EXEMPLAR

Example   Tjonto; monsters; toeladan.
Excavate   Gali.
Exceed   Meliwatin; melebiïn.
Exceeding   Amat besar; melebiïn wates.
Excel   Meliwatin; melebiïn; menangin.
Excellence   Kabagoesan; kabaean.
Excellent   Paling bagoes; no. satoe.
Excelsior   Mempoenjai haloean atawa toedjoehan jang lebi tinggi.
Except   Melaenken; katjoewali.
Exception   Katjoewalian.
Excess   Keadaän lebi dari banjak atawa tjoekoep; melebiïn wates.
Excessive   Kliwat banjak; banjak melebiïn wates.
Exchange   Toekar-menoekar; toekaran,
Exchequer   Kas oewang.
Excise   Bea atas barang-barang.
Excite   Bikin mendoesin atawa bangoen; goembiraken.
Excitement   Mendoesin atawa bangoenan; goembirahan.
Exclaim   Bertreak; berseroe.
Exclamation   Soeara treakan atawa seroean; tanda kaget (!).
Exclude   Katjoewaliken; bedaken larang.
Exclusion   Katjoewalian; bedahan; larangan.
Excommunicate   Poetoesken perhoeboengan.
Excrement   Kotoran; nadjis.
Excursion   Melantjongan. pasiaran.
Excursive   Jang pasiar.
Excuse   Minta maäf atawa ampoen; maäfan atawa keampoenan.
Execute   Lakoeken; djatoken hoekoeman mati.
Executive   Raad jang mendjalanken pamerentahan.
Executor   Algodjo.
Exemplar   Tjonto; exemplaar.

Exemplary	Boeat tjonto.
Exemplify	Kasi ketrangan dengen tjonto.
Exempt	Merdika.
Exemption	Kamerdikaän.
Exercise	Gerakan badan; the-tjauw; peladjaran; ja-kinken atawa apalken.
Exert	Kaloearken tenaga; tjoba.
Exertion	Tenaga; pertjobahan.
Exhalation	Hawa jang kaloear dari napas.
Exhale	Kaloearken hawa napas.
Exhaust	Tjapein; bikin tjape.
Exhibit	Pertoendjoeken.
Exhibition	Pertoendjoekan; tentoonstelling.
Exhilarate	Bikin girang.
Exile	Orang jang dihoekoem boewang, hoekoeman boewang; hoekoem boewang.
Exigent	Perloe sekali.
Exist	Ada; hidoep; tinggal.
Existence	Adanja; penghidoepan; djiwa.
Exorbitant	Melebiïn; wates tida boleh di kasi mengarti.
Exorcise	Oesir setan.
Expand	Melar; djadi besar.
Expance	Kamelaran.
Expatriate	Boewang dari tana kelahirannja.
Expect	Pengharepan; penoenggoehan.
Expectation	Harep; mengharep.
Expectation	Pengharepan boeat dapet boedel.
Expectorate	Batok dan berloeda.
Expedient	Tipoe-daja; satoedjoe; perloe.
Expedition	Kaboeroe-boeroehan; haloean; expeditie.
Expel	Omslag; oesir.
Expend	Kaloearken; pake.
Expenditure	Ongkos.
Expense	Ongkos; harga.
Expensive	Mahal; rojaal atawa boros.
Experience	Pengatahoean; practyk atawa apalan; apalin.

Experiment	Pertjobahan; bikin pertjobahan.
Expert	Pande; orang jang pande.
Expire	Mati; abis.
Explain	Kasi mengarti.
Explanation	Ketrangan.
Explicit	Terang; teges.
Explode	Meledak.
Exploit	Pahala; djasa; kong-lo.
Exploration	Pamereksaän ; tilikan,
Explore	Tjari ketrangan; tilik atawa preksa.
Explosion	Soeara meledak; meledaknja.
Exponent	Wakilnja.
Export	Barang kaloearan negri ; kaloearken dari negri.
Exportation	Pengangkoetan barang aken dikasi kaloear negri.
Expose	Reba; telandjang; masoek atawa terdjoem dalem katjilakaän.
Expound	Kasi mengarti; kasi ketrangan.
Express	Express atawa kreta api spoed; soeroehan loear biasa; njata; kata atawa seboet.
Expression	Seboetan.
Expressly	Dengen njata; dengen terang atawa teges,
Expulsion	Oesiran.
Expunge	Seka; tjit.
Expurgate	Bikin bersi; bersiken.
Exquisite	Paling bagoes; jang terpili,
Extant	Jang sekarang ada,
Extend	Londjorin; sampeken; melar.
Extension	Londjoran; pembikinan besar; kemelaran,
Extensive	Besar; loewas,
Extent	Besarnja; loewasnja.
Exterior	Loewarnja; di sebla loewar.
Exterminate	Roesakin sama sekali,
External	Di bagian loewar.
Extinct	Binasaken; mati-in; pademken,

Extinguish	Mati-in ; pademken.
Extol	Oempak.
Extort	Tindi ; pidjit.
Extortion	Tindian ; pidjitan.
Extra	Penamba.
Extract	Tarikan ; pilihan.
Extract	Tarik ; pili.
Extraction	Kelahiran ; persamaän dara.
Extraneous	Asing.
Extraordinary	Loear-biasa.
Extravagance	Karojaalan ; kaborosan.
Extravagant	Rojaal ; boros.
Extreme	Paling ; terlaloe banjak.
Extremity	Oedjoeng jang paling djaoe ; kaperloean ; anggota ; kaki-tangan.
Extude	Kasi kaloear aer.
Exult	Bergirang dengen sanget.
Exultation	Kagirangan besar.
Eye	Mata ; djaga dengen teliti.
Eyeball	Bidji mata.
Eyebrow	Alis.
Eyedrop	Aer mata.
Eyeglass	Katja mata.
Eyelash	Boeloe mata.
Eyelet,	
Eyelethole	Lobang mata.
Eyeliad	Mata krandjang.
Eyelid	Koelit mata.
Eyeshot	Pengliatan.
Eyesore	Barang jang bikin mata sakit.
Eyre	Pasiar ; ngoembara ; ambtenaar jang djalan-menilik.
Eyry, Eyrie	Sarang boeroeng arend ; sarang boeroeng alap-alap.

F.

Fable	Tjerita dongeng ; blaga atawa poera-poera.
Fabric	Gedong ; kaen.
Fabricate	Tjari taoe ; bikin.
Fabulous	Belaga ; kosong belaka.
Face	Moeka ; ketemoe ; bantah.
Facetious	Banjol ; membadoet.
Facilitate	Bikin lebi gampang.
Facility	Kamerdikaän aken berboeat.
Facing	Toetoepan jang djarang atawa tipis.
Fact	Kedjadian ; kabeneran.
Faction	Party atawa kaoem jang berbantah.
Factious	Soeka membagi party atawa kaoem ; soeka berbantah.
Factor.	Agent ; nummer jang memkali (×).
Factory	Fabriek ; tempat pembikinan barang.
Faculty	Kepandean dalem pakerdjahan.
Fad	Edan ; gila ; gendeng.
Fade	Lajoe ; ilang warna.
Fag	Orang jang bekerdja tjape ; paksa bekerdja tjape.
Fag	Kaen poenja samboengan benang atawa broentoesan.
Fagot	Saiketan kajoe, Djoega ditoelis *Faggot*.
Fail	Sala ; teledorin ; sial.
Failing	Kesalaän ; kekliroean.
Failure	Kesialan ; kegagalan.
Fain	Girang ; dengen girang.
Faint	Lema ; lemes djadi lema atawa lemes.
Fair	Pasar ; bagoes ; adil ; sedeng.
Fairly	Dengen adil ; dengen sedeng.
Fairy	Peri kajangan ; maleikat.
Faith	Kapertjaiaän.
Faithful	Setia ; boleh dipertjaia.

Fake	Belaga ; poera-poera.
Falchion	Pedang ketjil.
Fallow	Tana jang tida dipake ; samatjem men_djangan ; warna mera atawa koening poe-tjet.
False	Palsoe ; tida berhati djoedjoer.
Falsehood	Kepalsoean ; kedjoestaän.
Falter	Mandek atawa brenti dalem pembitjaraän.
Fame	Nama termashoer.
Familiar	Iblis djahat ; terkenal ; disoekai.
Familiarity	Kesoekahan ; kenalan.
Family	Familie ; kaloewarga.
Famine	Bahaja lapar.
Famish	Kelaparan.
Famous	Termashoer ; terkenal.
Fan	Kipas.
Fanatic	Orang jang giat ; giat dalem pikiran.
Fanaticism	Kagiatan dalem pikiran.
Fanciful	Sebagi mengimpi ; lapat-lapat.
Fancy	Pikiran jang lapat-lapat ; rasa lapat-lapat atawa sebagi mengimpi.
Fane	Gredja ; klenteng.
Fang	Gigi jang tadjem.
Fantastic	Sebagi orang jang mengimpi ; sebagi la-pat-lapat.
Far	Djaoe.
Farce	Permaenan jang boleh bikin orang djadi tertawa.
Fare	Pembajaran kandaran ; passigier ; maka-nan.
Fare	Berada ; oempanin.
Farinaceous	Terbikin dari tepoeng.
Farm	Kebon ; tana peroesahan , peroesahin.
Farmer	Toekang kebon ; orang tani.
Farrier	Doktor koeda ; toekang bikin besi koeda.

Farrow	Pembaringan boeat babi ; melahirken binatang babi.
Farther	Lebi djaoe.
Farthing	Oewang inggris jang ada djadi $^1/_4$ penny kira-kira sama oewang disini $1^1/_4$ cent.
Fascinate	Kagoemin ; bikin orang djadi soeka atawa gilain.
Fashion	Matjem ; roman ; atoeran ; tjitakan.
Fast	Poeasa ; kentjeng ; lekas.
Fasten	Bikin kentjeng atawa lekas.
Fastness	Kakentjengan ; kalekasan ; benteng jang tegoe.
Fat	Minjak ; gemoek.
Fatal	Membawaken kematian.
Fate	Peroentoengan ; kaperloean jang tiada bisa disingkirken.
Father	Ajah ; bapa. .
Fathom	Oekoeran dari anem kaki ; djakdjakin.
Fathomless	Tida bisa kedjakdjak.
Fatigue	Lela ; tjape ; bikin lela ; bikin tjape.
Fatten	Bikin gemoek.
Fatuity	Kebodohan.
Fault	Kesalahan.
Faulty	Sala ; tiada betoel.
Favour	Kabaean ; pengasian ; soerat; bantoe.
Favourable	Baek satjara sobat.
Favourite	Orang jang tersajang ; goela-goela ; paling disoekai.
Fawn	Anak mendjangan ; mengoempak.
Fay	Maleikat ; pri kajangan.
Fealty	Kapertjaiaän ; kedjoedjoeran.
Fear	Takoet ; ketakoetan.
Fearful	Ketakoetan ; pengetjoet.
Feasible	Boleh diberboeat.
Feast	Pesta ; perdjamoean ; lajanin tetamoe.
Feather	Boeloe boeroeng.

Feature	Moeka; bagian jang nondjol.
Fecundity	Berboea banjak; kesaratan.
Federal	Berhoeboeng dengen persariketan atawa kontract.
Federation	Persariketan; pakoempoelan.
Fee	Pembajaran.
Feeble	Lema; tida koewat.
Feed	Makanan; lapangan roempoet; kasi makan atawa oempanin.
Feel	Rasa.
Feeling	Pengrasaän.
Feign.	Belaga; poera-poera.
Feint	Belagaän; poera-poeraän.
Felicity	Kasenangan jang tida terhingga·
Feline	Termasoek dalem bangsa koetjing.
Fell	Soeda djato; bengis potong atawa tebang.
Fellow	Machloek; orang; temen.
Fellowship	Pertemenan; persobatan.
Felly	Rim atawa pinggir roda.
Felon	Berdosa; bengis.
Felony	Dosa jang berat.
Felt	Tricoe; soeda rasa.
Female	Prempoean; betina.
Feminine	Termasoek dalem fihak prempoean.
Fen	Tempat loempoer.
Fence	Pager; pagerin; djagain; pake pedang.
Fend	Tjega; loepoetken; singkirken.
Fender	Besi anglo.
Ferment	Mendjadi melar atawa jang orang Tionghoa bilang *hwat* sebagi dek pranti bikin koewe; kemoerkaän.
Fern	Samatjem poehoen.
Ferocious	Biadab; galak.
Ferosity	Kegalakan jang biadab.
Ferret	Samatjem binatang sebagi marmoet; tjari

Ferrule	Tjintjin tembaga di oedjoeng toengket atawa rotan.
Ferry	Perdjalanan di atas aer; angkat aer.
Fertile	Gemoek; banjak kaloearken hasil.
Fervent	Asik; goembira.
Fervour	Keasikan; kegoembiralian.
Festival	Pesta; perdjamoean; termasoek dalem pesta atawa perdjamoean.
Festoon	Boeket kembang.
Fetch	Pergi ambil.
Fete	Pesta; hari raja.
Fetid	Baoe engas.
Fetter	Rante; iket.
Feud	Pertengkaran jang tiada brentinja.
Feudal	Termasoek dalem bilangan atoeran mengambil tana dengen pengaroenja balatentara.
Fever	Meriang; demem.
Few	Sedikit; bebrapa.
Fez	Samatjem topi bangsa Toerki.
Fib	Kapalsoean.
Fibre	Benang papoehoenan atawa raroempoetan.
Fickle	Bisa ditoekar-toekar; boleh diroba-roba.
Fictile	Terbikin dari tana lempoeng.
Fiction	Barang jang tida boleh mendjadi; pakerdjahan orang mengimpi.
Fiddle	Viool; biola.
Fidelity	Kesetiaän hati.
Field	Lapangan; sawa.
Fierce	Galak; biadab.
Fiery	Sebagi api; panas; brangasan.
Fife	Samatjem soeling ketjil.
Fight.	Berklai; perklaian; paprengan.
Figment	Pendapetan baroe.
Figurative	Tertjitak.
Figure	Roman; nummer.

File	Kikir ; mengikir ; djalan bebaris.
Filial	Berbakti ; oehauw.
Fill	Isi ; kapenoean.
Filly	Anak koeda prempoean.
Film	Film gambar idoep ; koelit tipis.
Filter	Saringan aer ; saring.
Filth	Kekotoran ; kemesoeman.
Filthy	Kotor ; mesoem.
Fin	Kiplik ikan
Final	Pengabisan ; achir.
Finance	Financie ; oewang.
Find	Tjari ; dapet.
Fine	Hoekoem denda ; hoekoeman denda ; ba goes ; aloes.
Finery	Pakean jang rébo atawa perlente.
Finger	Djeridji.
Finish	Abis ; abisin.
Finite	Ada watesnja ; berwates.
Fir	Poehoen tjemara; siong.
Fire	Api ; bakar.
Firkin	Takeran dari 8 atawa 9 gallon.
Firm	Toko ; perseroan ; kekel ; tegoe.
Fiamness	Kakekelan ; kategoehan.
First	Ka satoe ; pertama ; oetama.
Fish	Ikan ; pantjing ikan.
Fishery	Tempat pranti taro ikan.
Fist	Kepelan.
Fit	Satoedjoe ; sedeng ; hanteman atawa la- brakan.
Fitly	Dengen satoedjoe ; dengen sedeng.
Fix	Kentjengin ; sangkoetin.
Fixture	Barang sangkoetan.
Flabby	Lembek ; lemes.
Flag	Saroepa tetaneman ; batoe ; bendera.
Flake	Potongan saldjoe ; timbangan ; koepas.
Flame	Njalanja ; kebrangasan ; menjala.

Flank	Labrak dari sampingnja ; bentoer.
Flannel	Kaen flanel.
Flash	Berkilat ; mengkredep ; kilat ; kredepan.
Flask	Botol atawa fles.
Flat	Rata; litjin; tana rata; noot dalem permaenan muziek; tingkatan roema.
Flatten	Bikin rata.
Flatter	Oempak ; poedji.
Flattery	Oempakan ; poedji-poedjian.
Flaunt	Banggaken ; oewarken.
Flavour	Rasa ; baoe ; kasi rasa.
Flax	Tetaneman jang boleh di bikin kaen linen.
Flea	Koetoe.
Fledge	Melengkepin dengen boeloe.
FFlee	Lari ; boeron.
FFleece	Boeloe kambing ; wool.
Fleet	Pasoekan kapal prang ; tjepet ; ladjoe.
Fleeting	Tiada tahan lama.
Fleetness	Tjepetnja; katjepetan ; keladjoean.
Flesh	Daging.
Fleshy	Berdaging ; montok ; gemoek.
Flexible	Gampang dieloek ; gampang di bengkokin.
Flicker	Mengkredep sebagi api.
Flight	Pemboeronan ; penglarian ; sakawanan boeroeng.
Flighty	Adjaib ; tjepet; tida tetep.
Flinch	Moendoer ; mengkeret.
Fling	Lempar ; sambit; boewang.
Flint	Batoe api.
Flit	Menerobos ; pinda.
Float	Ngambang ; pelampoeng.
Flock	Sakawanan kambing ; berkoempoel atawa berkawan.
Floe	Ys atawa aer batoe jang ngambang.
Flog	Tjamboek ; petjoet.
Flood	Bandjir ; aer bandjir.

Floor	Lante ; batoe ; djoebin ; tingkatan.
Florid	Bewarna trang.
Florin	Oewang 2 shillings, djadi oewang disini f 1.20
Florist	Toekang tanem kembang atawa boenga.
Flounce	Bersi-in pakean ; sentak atawa gentak.
Flounder	Berkoetet-koetetan di loempoer.
Flour	Tepoeng; trigoe.
Flourish	Berswara seperti trompet ; gerakan jang tjepet; madjoe; soeboer; gojang.
Flow	Ngaliran aer ; ngalir ; anjoet.
Flower	Kembang atawa boenga.
Flue	Djalanan atawa semprong asep.
Fluent	Tetes dalem omongan.
Fluid	Barang beraer.
Flurry	Kalang-kaboet ; boeroe-boeroe.
Flush	Moeka mera lantaran maloe.
Flute	Soeling ; menjoeling ; loekoe atawa kasi aer djalan.
Flutter	Tjepet ; sebat ; gerakan jang tida tentoe ; kalang-kaboet; gerakan sajap dengen lekas; kerepekan.
Fly	Laler ; terbang.
Floal	Koeda prempoean moeda.
Foam	Boesa ; berboesa.
Fob	Kantong horloge.
Fodder	Makanan heiwan.
Foe .	Moesoe.
Fog	Halimoen ; emboen jang berasep.
Foil •	Pedang pranti mementja atawa pakkoen ; sakeping logam jang tipis; oeroengken.
Fold	Goeloeng ; lipet ; lepit ;kandang kambing.
Foliage	Daon poehoen.
Folk	Orang bangsa menoesia.
Follow	Ikoet ; boentoetin.
Follower	Pengikoet ; moerid.

Folly	Kalemaän ; kabodohan.
Fond	Soeka ; tjinta.
Fondle	Peloek.
Fondness	Kasoekahan.
Food	Makanan.
Fool	Orang bodo ; tipoe.
Foolish	Bodo ; geblek.
Foolscap	Kertas toelis jang pandjangnja 17 duim dan lebarnja 13½ duim.
Foot	Kaki ; 12 duim ; indjek.
Footman	Boedjang ; jongos.
Foetstep	Djalanan.
For	Boeat ; sebab ; oleh kerna.
Forbear	Tahan ; djaoeken.
Forbearance	Tahanan sakit jang lama.
Forbid	Larang.
Force	Kekoewatan ; angkatan prang ; paksa.
Forcible	Koewat ; tegoe ; berat.
Ford	Begian jang tjetek dari satoe kali atawa soengei.
Fore	Di hadepan ; lebi doeloe.
Forecast	Doegahan lebi doeloe.
Forecastle	Moeka kapal ; bagian depan dari satoe kapal.
Forehead	Djidat.
Foreign	Asing ; laen negri.
Foreigner.	Orang asing ; orang dari laen negri.
Foreland	Tandjoeng ; oedjoeng tana.
Foreman	Pemimpin ; kepala.
Foremost	Pertama ; paling depan.
Forest	Oetan besar.
Forester	Pendjaga oetan.
Forewarn	Bri nasehat lebi doeloe.
Forfeit	Dendahan oewang ; hoekoeman denda ; ilang lantaran sala sendiri.
Forge	Bengkel toekang besi; poekoel besi panas ; tiroe.

Forgery	Tiroean dari toelisan, pembikinan oewang dan sebaginja.
Forget	Loepa ; tiada perhatiken
Forgive	Ampoenken ; maäfken.
Fork	Garpoe.
Forlorn	Sepi ; di tinggal saorang diri.
Form	Roman ; matjem ; peradatan ; bangkoe pandjang ; berichtiar ; bikin.
Formal	Betoel ; toelen ; sah.
Formation	Ichtiar ; pembikinan ; roman.
Former	Lebi doeloe ; lebi depan.
Formidable	Bikin orang takoet ; menakoetin.
Forsake	Tinggalken ; lakoeken.
Forsooth	Dalem kabeneren.
Fort	Benteng.
Forth	Ka depan ; madjoe.
Forthwith	Lantes ; dengen sigra.
Fortification	Pakerdjahan atawa ilmoe boeat mendjaga.
Fortify	Bikin tegoe.
Fortnight	Doea minggoe ; 14 hari.
Fortress	Benteng ; tempat jang di bikin tegoe.
Fortunate	Broentoeng ; bernasib bagoes.
Fortune	Peroentoengan atawa nasib bagoes.
Forward	Madjoe ; ka depan ; di depan.
Foster	Piara ; rawatin ; kweepang.
Foster-child	Anak piara ; anak kweepang.
Foster-mother	Mah piara ; iboe kweepang.
Foul	Tjoerang ; kotor.
Found	Soeda dapet ; berdiriken ; djadi logam.
Foundation	Fondament ; tee-ki ; tatakan ; dasarnja.
Foundling	Anak jang disia-sia.
Fondry	Tempat atawa ilmoe boeat bikin logam.
Fountain	Mantjoeran aer ; mata aer.
Fowl	Ajam-ajam ; boeroeng.
Fowler	Pemboeroe ajam oetan.
Fox	Rase.

Fraction	Petjahan ; pentjaran ; namanja dari saroepa itoengan.
Fractious	Soeka bertengkar ; bawel.
Fracture	Petjaken ; pentjar.
Fragile	Gampang petja.
Fragment	Petja-petjahan.
Frail	Lema; tiada koewat.
Frame	Arkoe ; lijst portret ; keng gambar.
Franchise	Hak boeat kasi swara dalem madjelis. Parlement.
Frank.	Teroes-trang ; hati lempeng.
Frantic	Hilap ; laplapan.
Fratcicide	Pemboenoehan atawa pemboenoe dari soedara.
Fraud	Tipoe ; daja.
Fraudulent	Tida setia ; soeka menipoe.
Fray	Pertengkaran ; berklaian.
Freckle	Tjeroetoean di atas koelit.
Free	Vrij ; merdika.
Freebooter	Perampok ; penjamoen.
Freedom	Kamerdikaän.
Freehold	Tana jang dioeroes dengen zondor pembajaran.
Freeman	Orang atawa rahajat jang merdika.
Freeze	Djadi keras ; djadi aer batoe ; kiat.
Freight	Ongkos kapal , moewatan kapal.
Frenzy	Kagilaän ; kagendengan.
Frequent	Sringkali.
Frequent	Koendjoengin atawa melantjongin sering-sering.
Fresh	Seger ; baroe.
Fret	Mara pikiran ; bikin mara.
Fretwork	Pakerdjahan mengoekir.
Friar	Padri ; wesio.
Friction	Gosokan ; sangkoetan.
Friend	Sobat ; temen.

Friendship	Persobatan ; pertemenan.
Frigate	Kapal prang.
Fright	Kaget ; ketakoetan.
Frighten	Bikin kaget ; bikin takoet.
Frigid	Dingin ; tiada mempoenjai hati tjinta.
Fringe	Pinggiran ; ploeian.
Frisk	Lontjat-lontjat ; dansa.
Frisky	Gesit ; soeka lontjat-lontjat ; tiada bisa diam.
Frock	Badjoe roki.
Frog	Kodok ; tenganja telapakan kaki koeda.
Frolic	Keloetjoean ; tipoe-daja.
Frolicsome	Loetjoe ; mempoenjai banjak tipoe-daja.
From	Dari.
Front	Depan ; hadepan.
Frontage	Bagian depan.
Frontier	Wates negri.
Frontispiece	Gambar jang berhadepan dengen lembaran kalimat boekoe.
Frost	Emboen jang djadi keras ; saldjoe aloes.
Froth	Boesa.
Frown	Moeka asem ; tekoek moeka.
Frugal	Bisa tarik ongkos ; bisa himat.
Fruit	Boea ; hasil.
Fruitful	Berboea banjak ; gemoek.
Frustrate	Oeroengken ; tjega.
Fry	Anak ikan ; goreng.
Fuel	Kajoe bakar.
Fugitive	Pemboeronan ; penglarian.
Fulfil	Penoeken ; kaboelken.
Full	Penoe ; tjoekoep.
Fluminate	Gledek ; goentoer.
Fumble	Pegang dengen likat.
Fume	Asep ; mara ; bikin mara.
Fun	Permaenan ; bebanjolan.
Function	Pakerdjahan ; kewadjiban.

Fund	Kapitaal ; oewang simpenan.
Funeral	Kematian ;. berhoeboeng dengen oeroesan atawa koeboer mait orang.
Fungus	Djamoer.
Funnel	Semprong asep : tjorong.
Funny	Loetjoe ; heran.
Fur	Boeloe binatang.
Furbish	Poles.
Furious	Mara ; hilap.
Furl	Goeloeng : lipet.
Furlong	Saperdelapan dari satoe paal ($^1/_8$ paal).
Furlough	Verlof; permisi boeat berlaloe.
Furnace	Anglo ; tempat api.
Furnish	Lengkepin ; kasiken.
Furniture	Perabot roema-tangga
Furrow	Tana bekas diloekoe ; solokan ; kisoet.
Further	Lebi djaoe ; bantoe ; goembiraken.
Furhest	Paling djaoe.
Fury	Amarah besar ; kehilapan.
Fuse	Loemerin dengen panas.
Fusil	Saroepa senapan jang enteng.
Fusion	Loemeran ; hoeboengan.
Fuss	Kekaloetan ; kalang kaboetan.
Fusty	Sekoan ; berbaoe tida enak.
Futile	Tida bergoena ; boeroek.
Future	Tempo jang bakal dateng ; jang bakal dateng ; blakang hari.
Futurity	Tempo jang bakal dateng ; blakang hari.

G.

Gab	Omongan iseng-iseng.
Gable	Oedjoeng roema.
Gad	djalan moendar-mandir; djalan tida brentinja.
Gag	Soempelan moeloet; soempel moeloet.
Gage	Tanggoengan; gadean.
Gaiety	Kagirangan.
Gain	Kaoentoengan; kafaedahan; oentoeng; dapet.
Gainsay	Bantah; bertengkar.
Gait	Gerakan djalan.
Gaiter	Iketan kaki.
Gala	Pesta; pertoendjoekan.
Gale	Angin besar; angin riboet.
Gallant	Toekang tjinta prempoean; pasang mata atas prempoean.
Gallant	Brani; gaga.
Galleon	Samatjem kapal Spanjol.
Gallery	Djalanan jang pandjang; tempat doedoek jang sebla atas dalem roema komedi.
Galley	Samatjem praoe pandjang; kolek.
Gallon	Satoe takeran dari 4 quarts.
Gallop	Tindakan jang lekas dari satoe koeda; djalan dengen lekas.
Galvanic	Berhoeboeng dengen electris.
Gamble	Maen top.
Game	Permaenan; binatang galak atawa pemboeroean maen.
Gammon	Kaki babi jang diasinin sebagi ham.
Gander	Gangsa lelaki.
Gang	Kawanan; trop.
Gangway	Djalanan di atas kapal.
Gaol	Pendjara; pemboeian.

Gaoler	Cipier boei; pendjaga roema boei.
Gap	Lobang.
Gape	Menganga.
Garage	Istal pranti simpen kreta motor.
Garb	Pakean.
Garden	Kebon; taman.
Gargle	Aer kekoemoer; kekoemoer.
Garland	Boeket kembang.
Garment	Pakean.
Garner	Loemboeng simpen padi.
Garnish	Riasin ; bikin bagoes.
Garret	Kamar di woewoengan roema,
Garrison	Barisan soldadoe pendjaga; lengkepin dengen balatentara.
Garter	Kousband
Gas	Hawa gas.
Gasp	Menganga boeat bernapas ; bernapas dengen soesa
Gastric	Berhoeboeng dengen peroet.
Gate	Pintoe loewar.
Gateway	Djalanan jang teroes ka pintoe loewar.
Gather	Koempoelin ; berkoempoel.
Gathering	Koempoelan orang; ngangkoet nana.
Gaudy	Rébo ; perlente.
Gauge	Oekoeran ; oekoer.
Gauntlet	Saroeng tangan dari besi.
Gauze	Kaen djarang ; tjit gazoline.
Gawky	Djelek ; tiada kroewan bangoen.
Gay	Bagoes ; girang.
Gaze	Awasin.
Gazette	Soerat kabar.
Gazetteer	Kitab logat bagi peladjaran ilmoe boemi.
Gear	Gir sepeda ; pakean koeda.
Gelatine	Ager-ager; tjioh-hwa.
Gem	Batoe pertama.
Gender	Kaoem ; fihak,

Genaraal	Generaal ; panglima prang ; biasa.
Generally	Dengen biasa.
Generate	Toeroenin ; kaloearin. .
Generation	Toeroenan ; anak-tjoetjoe ; bangsa ; kaoem kaloewarga.
Generosity	Karojaalan ; kabaean hati.
Generous	Rojaal ; baek hati.
Genial	Menggirangin.
Genius	Maleikat ; kapinteran ; orang pinter.
Genteel	Taoe adat ; berprilakoe hormat.
Gentle	Baek ; lema-lemboet.
Gentleman	Orang jang lema-lemboet; toean-toean; orang bangsawan.
Gently	Dengen hati-hati ; dengen lema-lemboet.
Genuine	Toelen ; tida palsoe.
Geography	Ilmoe boemi ; tee-li.
Geology	Ilmoe peladjaran dari pembikinan dan tabiat boemi ; tee-sit hak.
Geometry	Ilmoe mengangka ; ilmoe mengitoeng garis-garisan.
Germ	Poentjoek atawa moentjoek ; poko ; koetoe-koetoe aloes.
Germinate	Memoentjoek ; kaloear moentjoek.
Gestation	Boentingnja ; kedoedoekan peroet.
Gesture	Gerakan badan ; banjolan.
Get	Dapet.
Geyser	Mata aer jang kaloearken aer panas.
Ghastly	Sebagi orang mati ; poetjet.
Ghost	Setan ; iblis.
Giant	Djin.
Gibbet	Tiang pegantoengan ; gantoeng.
Gibe	Lewein ; lewean.
Giddy	Mabok.
Gift	Barang pengasihan ; persenan.
Gifted	Dikasi ; disertain.
Gig	Bendi.

Gild	Sepoe emas.
Gill	Takeran dari $1/_4$ pint.
Gill	Angsang ikan.
Gimlet	Poesoet ; bor ketjil.
Gin	Genever atawa pait ; djebakan.
Ginger	Djahe.
Gipsy	Toekang pelantjongan ; toekang-itoengin peroentoengan ; pokkwa senshe.
Giraffe	Saroepa binatang jang paling tinggi di ini doenia.
Gird	Koeroeng ; gesperin.
Girdle	Band ; angkin ; gesper.
Girl	Anak prempoean.
Gist	Maksoed jang oetama.
Give	Kasi ; bri.
Glacier	Lapangan aer batoe.
Glad	Girang.
Glade	Lobang di oetan.
Gladiator	Toekang maen pedang ; orang jang berklai dengen oepahan.
Glance	Tengok.
Gland	Daging.
Glanders	Penjakit koeda.
Glare	Trang jang silo.
Glaring	Terboeka ; trang.
Glass	Glas ; katja ; terbikin dari glas.
Glaze	Lengkepin dengen glas ; lapisin.
Gleam	Sinar tjahia ; bertjahia.
Glee	Kagirangan.
Glen	Lemba jang sempit.
Glide	Anjoet dengen pelahan ; menoeroet.
Glimmer	Trang jang samar-samar.
Glimpse	Pengliatan ; pemandangan.
Glisten	Mengkredep ; mengkilap.
Glister	Mengkredep ; mengkilap.
Glitter	Mengkredep ; bertjahia ; mengkilap.

10.

Gloaming	Menggerip.
Gloat	Awasin ; ngilerin.
Globe	Bola doenia ; barang jang boender.
Glomerate	Djadi boender.
Gloom	Kaglapan ; kadoekaän ; kakeselan.
Gloomy	Glap; doeka kesel.
Glorify	Poedji dengen tinggi ; hormatin.
Glorious	Gaga ; haroes di hormatin.
Glory	Kagagahan ; kahormatan.
Glossy	Litjin dan mengkilap.
Glove	Saroeng tangan.
Glow	Panas jang mengkredep ; mengkredep.
Glow-worm	Kalimaja.
Glue	Gom ; geta.
Glum	Bermoeka asem ; keren.
Glut	Keadaän terlaloe banjak atawa meliwatin wates ; isi terlaloe banjak atawa meliwatin wates.
Glutton	Orang jang kelaparan makan ; namanja saroepa binatang sebagi biroewang.
Glycerine	Minjak ramboet.
Gnarled	Penoe boentelan.
Gnash	Gigit-gigit gigi.
Gnat	Agas.
Gnaw	Mämä atawa koenja,
Go	Pergi.
Goad	Toengket jang tadjem ; bikin mara.
Goal	Pintoe goal seperti dalem permaenan bola.
Goat	Domba.
Goblet	Glas minoem.
Goblin	Iblis ; memedi.
God	Toehan Allah.
Godfather	Bapa akoean pada waktoe satoe anak dinazaraniken (baptize).
Godless,	Tida takoet Toehan-Allah.
Godliness	Kasoetjian jang betoel.

Godly	Soetji; alim.
Gold	Emas
Golden	Terbikin dari emas; sebagi emas.
Goldsmith	Toekang emas.
Golf	Permaenan bola dan roejoeng sebagi rugbij.
Golfer	Jang maen permaenan bola dan roejoeng.
Gondola	Samatjem praoe jang dipake di Venetie.
Good	Baek; kabaean.
Goodly	Bagoes diliatnja; tjakap.
Goodness	Kabagoesan; katjakapan; kabaean.
Goods	Barang.
Goose	Gangsa prempoean; besi strikaän toekang badjoe.
Gorge	Tenggorokan; telen dengen rakoes.
Gorgeous	Bagoes; perlente.
Gosling	Anak gangsa.
Gospel	Kabar baek; pakerdjahan soetji jang ber-hoeboeng dengen agama Kristen.
Gossip	Mengobrol; kong-kouw.
Gout	Sakit di boekoe-boekoe anggota; sakit peroet-kemboeng; boesoeng.
Govern	Prenta; oeroesin.
Government	Gouverneur; pamerenta; atoeran memerenta.
Governor	Gouvernement; orang jang memerenta; hakim besar.
Gown	Pakean.
Grace	Kabagoesan; kabaean; sembajangan jang sabentaran; saderhana; riasin.
Graceful	Bagoes dan saderhana.
Gracious	Baek; moera-hati.
Grade	Tingkatan; pangkat.
Gradual	Dengen tingkatan.
Gradually	Palahan-pelahan.
Grain	Bidji; beras Blanda; djagoeng.

Grammar	Ilmoe menoelis dan mengomong.
Granary	Goedang simpen padi.
Grand	Bagoes ; oetama.
Grandeur	Kabagoesan.
Grange	Roema dan kebon atawa pekarangan,
Grape	Boea anggoer ; mimis.
Grapple	Tanggap ; tjengkerem ; djambret.
Grasp	Tanggapan ; tjengkereman ; djambretan.
Grass	Roempoet.
Grate	Anglo ; tempat api ; gosok dengen keras ; bikin mara.
Grateful	Merasa trima kasi ; oe-tjeng.
Gratification	Pengrasaän trima kasi.
Gratify	Mengoetjap atawa bilang trima kasi.
Gratis	Dengen zonder bajaran; vry.
Gratifude	Pengrasaän trima kasi.
Gratuity	Barang pengasian atawa pesenan.
Grave	Koeboeran ; keren ; oekir.
Gravel	Pasir batoe.
Graver	Perabot atawa pekakas mengoekir.
Gravitate	Selaloe menoedjoe ka tenga.
Gravity	Kakerenan ; kaberatan.
Gravy	Koewa.
Gray, grey	Daoek-daoek ; aboe-aboe.
Graze	Makan roempoet ; gosok dengen plahan.
Grazier	Toekang kasi makan heiwan.
Grease	Minjak ; minjakin.
Great	Besar ; agoeng.
Greatness	Kabesaran ; kaägoengan.
Greedy	Rakoes.
Green	Warna idjoe ; lapangan ; seger ; belon mateng.
Greet	Samboet.
Gridiron	Panggangan
Grief	Kesoesaän ; kadoekaän.
Grievance	Kasoesaän ; kesalaän.

Grieve	Merasa soesa atawa doeka.
Grim	Bengis dan asem.
Grimage	Moeka asem ; moeka jang di-tekoek.
Grime	Kotoran ; tana ; djadi kotor.
Grin	Tjengar-tjengir ; tertawa berkakakan.
Grind	Giling ; gosok.
Grip	Djambret ; tjengkerem.
Gripe	Teken ; tindi ; tjoebit ; penjakit dalem peroet.
Grisly	Menakoëtin ; boleh bikin orang djadi takoet.
Groan	Nangis sesambatan.
Grocer	Toekang waroeng.
Groom	Toekang rawat koeda ; penganten lelaki.
Groove	Tana loekoean.
Grope	Mengoesoet di tempat gelap.
Gross	12 dozen ; 144 ; djoembla ; goemploekan ; kasar ; besar.
Ground	Tana ; berdiriken ; sangkoetin ; kandas.
Groundless	Tida mempoenjai fondament atawa tee-ki.
Group	Koempoelan ; tangke ; berkoempoel ; bertangke.
Grove	Oetan ketjil.
Grovel	Merajap ; merangkang.
Grow	Toemboe ; djadi besar.
Growl	Mengaoeng ; menggrendeng.
Grub	Tjatjing ketjil ; gali.
Grudge	Sakit hati ; kasi dengen tida senáng hati.
Gruel	Boeboer.
Gruff	Keren ; asem.
Grumble	Menggrendeng ; menggroetoe.
Grunt	Soeara babi ; bersoeara seperti babi.
Guarantee	Tanggoeng ; tanggoengan.
Guard	Djaga ; djagaän.
Guardian	Pendjaga ; ahliwaris.
Guess	Tebab ; bade.

Guest	Tetamoe ; toentoen.
Guide	Penoentoen ; toentoen.
Guile	Berakal ; berdaja.
Guileless	Tida berakal ; tida berdaja.
Guillotine	Masin boeat potong kepala orang.
Guilt	Kesalaän ; kadosahan.
Guilty	Bersala ; berdosa.
Guinea	Oewang Inggris dari 21 shillings.
Guise	Pakean ; roman.
Guitar	Hitar ; saroepa perabot muziek.
Gulf	Teloek ketjil.
Gull	Tipoe ; daja ; samatjem boeroeng laoet.
Gullet	Pipa atawa djalanan makanan.
Gum	Isit ; gom ; geta ; taroin gom ; getain.
Gun	Senapan ; meriam.
Gunnery	Ilmoe menembak.
Gurgle	Anjoet dengen riboët.
Gush	Anjoetan jang deres ; menoebroek.
Gust	Tioepan angin.
Gutter	Djalanan aer ; got.
Guzzle	Minoem banjak.
Gymnasium	Sekola dalem mana ada diadjar peladjaran menggeraken badan.
Gyrate	Terpoeter.
Gyroscope	Pekakas jang bisa terpoeter.

H.

Haberdasher	Toekang klontong.
Habit	Adat ; tabiat ; pakean ; berpake.
Habitation	Tempat tinggal ; tempat kadiaman.
Habitual	Biasa ; kabiasaän ; toeman ; katoemànan.
Habituate	Biasa ; toeman.
Hack	Koeda sewahan ; potong ; keset.
Hackle	Djenger ; boeloe leher dari ajam djago.

Hackney	Koeda sewahan; sewaken; pake banjak.
Haft	Gagang piso.
Hag	Prempoean toea jang djelek; kamoerkaän.
Haggard	Galak dan kasar.
Haggle	Tawaran.
Hail	Oedjan aer batoe; samboetan; bertreak atawa berseroe; toeroen oedjan aer batoe.
Hailstone	Oedjan aer batoe.
Hair	Ramboet; boeloe.
Halbert	Samatjem pekakas prang koeno.
Hale	Kasehatan badan; sehat.
Half	Satenga; satoe dari doewa.
Hall	Pertengahan roema.
Hallow	Bikin soetji atawa alim.
Hallucination	Tipoe-daja; kesalaän.
Halo	Boenderan; kalangan.
Halt	Brenti; djalan dengen pintjang-pintjang.
Halter	Tambang; iket dengen tambang.
Halve	Bagi doewa.
Halyard	Tambang lajar.
Ham	Ham; paha babi jang diasinin.
Hamlet	Goemploekan atawa koempoelan dari roema-roema.
Hammer	Martil; poekoel dengen martil.
Hamper	Bakoel jang tertoetoep; gangoe; bikin bingoeng.
Hamstring	Oerat ham; potong oerat paha.
Hand	Tangan; toelisan; orang bekerdja; kasi dengen tangan.
Handicap	Gandahan; apitan.
Handicraft	Pakerdjahan jang dikerdjaken dengen dagangan.
Handkerchief	Sapoe-tangan.
Handle	Gagang; pegangan; pegang.
Handsome	Bagoes; tjakap.

Handy	Bisa menggoenaken ; moengil.
Hang	Gantoeng.
Hank	Sagoeloeng benang.
Hanker	Kapingin dengen sanget ; mengiier.
Hap	Waktoe ; koetika ; djato.
Hapless	Tida broentoeng ; sial.
Haply	Brangkali.
Happiness	Kasenangan.
Happy	Senang.
Harass	Ganggoe ; bikin mara ; tjah-nauw.
Harbinger	Orang jang diprenta djalan lebi doeloe ; pemboeka djalan ; sian-hong.
Harbour	Pelaboean kapal.
Hard	Soesa ; keras ; tertoetoep.
Hardihood	Kabranihan.
Hardly	Ampir belon ; dengen soesa.
Hardship	Kesoesaän ; tindian.
Hardware	Barang besi besi.
Hardy	Brani ; koewat bekerdja.
Hare	Klintji oetan.
Hark	Denger ; pasang koeping.
Harm	Behaja keloekaän ; behajain ; bikin loeka.
Harmonium	Piano jang diboenjiken dengen angin.
Harmony	Keakoeran ; persariketan.
Harness	Pakean koeda ; pakein koeda.
Harpoon	Djemparing.
Harrier	Samatjem andjing jang biasa memboeroe klintji.
Harrow	Garoekan ; garoek tana ; bikin soesa.
Harsh	Bengis ; kasar ; asem.
Hart	Mendjangan lelaki.
Harvest	Moesin potong ; potong padi.
Hash	Daging jang dipotong-potong ; potong daging.
Hassock	Tiker pranti berloetoet atawa berkoewi.
Haste	Boeroe-boeroe ; spoed.

Hasty	Terboeroe-boeroe ; keboeroe napsoe.
Hat	Topi ; kopia.
Hatch	Netesin ; berdaja.
Hatchet	Kampak ketjil.
Hatchway	Lobang di deck kapal.
Hate	Bentji ; kabentjian.
Hatred	Kabentjian.
Haughty	Angkoe ; beradat tinggi.
Haul	Tarik ; djambret.
Haunt	Tempat jang sring dipergi-in ; tempat jang ditoegoerin ; sering pergi-in atawa toegoerin.
Have	Ada poenja ; mempoenjai ; soeda.
Haven	Pelaboean.
Havoc	Ketjilakaän ; pemboenoehan.
Hawk	Boeroeng alap-alap ; tawarin boeat didjoeal.
Hawker	Toekang klontong.
Hawser	Kawat ketjil.
Hay	Roempoet kering.
Hazard	Korban ; korbanken.
Haze	Halimoen.
Hazel	Saroepa boea kenari , warna koening toea.
He	Dia, (lelaki).
Head	Kepala ; kepalain.
Headland	Tandjoeng.
Headlong	Gegabroekan ; dengen lekas.
Headstrong	Bengal ; bandel ; berkepala batoe.
Heal	Obat ; semboein ; djadi semboe atawa baek.
Health	Kasegeran ; kasehatan badan ; kewarasan.
Healthy	Seger ; sehat waras.
Heap	Toemploekan ; toemploekin.
Hear	Denger ; dikasi taoe.
Hearken	Denger ; pasang koeping.
Hearsay	Kabar angin.

Hearse	Kreta mati.
Heart	Hati atawa ati ; kebranian; tenga-tenganja.
Hearth	Dapoer ; anglo ; tempat api.
Heat	Panas jang heibat; bikin panas.
Heath	Raroempoetan; tempat kosong jang tiada bergoena.
Heave	Bangoen ; bengkak.
Heaven	Sorga.
Heavy	Berat.
Hectic	Meriang jang toeman , sakit meriang.
Hedge	Pager ; pagerin.
Hedgehog	Landak.
Heed	Perdoeli ; ; perhatiken ; perdoelian ; perhatian.
Heel	Tjang atawa blakang kaki.
Heifer	Anak sampi.
Height	Tingginja.
Heir	Toeroenan
Hell	Noraka.
Helm	Kamoedi ; kamoedi-in.
Helmet	Topi prang besi.
Help	Toeloeng ; bantoe ; pertoeloengan pembantoean.
Helpmate	Temen pembantoe ; persero.
Hem	Wates ; koeroeng.
Hemisphere	Sabela dari bola doenia.
Hemp	Poehoen jang mengaloearken benang paranti bikin tambang.
Hen	Ajam biang.
Hence	Dari ini tempo ; dari ini tempat.
Henceforth	Dari sekarang ka blakangin.
Henpecked	Di bawa pengaroenja istri.
Heptagon	Roman jang mempoenjai toedjoe pinggir ; tjit kak.
Heptarchy	Pemerentahan jang dioeroes oleh toedjoe radja.

Her	Dia (prempoean) poenja; dia prempoean).
Herald	Orang jang diprenta djalan lebi doeloe; siang-hong; kaloearken tita.
Herb	Raroempoetan.
Herbage	Tana lapang.
Herculean	Seperti Hercules; sanget koewat.
Herd	Kawanan heiwan; angon heiwan.
Herdsman	Toekang angon heiwan.
Here	Disini.
Hereafter	Dalem tempo jang bakalan dateng.
Hereditary	Menoeroet toeroenan; toeroen-menoeroen.
Heresy	Kesalaän atawa kakliroean dalem agama.
Heretic	Orang jang memoedja agama jang sala atawa kliroe.
Heritage	Harta peninggalan; betoel.
Hermit	Orang pertapaän.
Hero	Orang jang gaga-brani.
Heroic	Gaga-brani; agoeng.
Heroine	Orang prempoean jang gaga brani.
Heroism	Kagagahan-brani.
Heron, Hern	Boeroeng bango; boeroeng jang mempoenjai leher panjang.
Hesitate	Brenti mandek.
Hew	Potong; tebang.
Hexagon	Roman jang mempoenjai anam pinggir; lak-kak.
Hiccough	Berbangkes.
Hidden	Tersemoeni; terpendem.
Hide	Koelit mata; semoeniken.
Hideous	Menakoetin.
Hie	Boeroe-boeroe.
Higgler	Orang jang berdagang dalem provisiën atawa barang blik.
High	Tinggi; agoeng.
Highland	Negri jang banjak goenoeng.
Highness	Katinggian; gelaran jang dibri pada anak-radja dan laen-laen orang jang agoeng.

Highway	Djalan besar.
Hil	Boekit.
Hilt	Gagang pedang.
Him	Dia (lelaki) dipake di boentoet omongan.
Hind	Mendjangan prempoean ; blak ung.
Hinder	Di blakang ; tahan.
Hinderance	Barang tahanan atawa tjegatan ; halangan.
Hindermost	Paling blakang.
Hinge	Engsel.
Hint	Voorstelan ; pembitjaraän voorstel ; kasi pembitjaraän.
Hip	Selangkangan.
Hippodrome	Komedi koeda dalem mana ada ditoendjoekin adoean koeda.
Hippopotamus	Koeda aer.
Hire	Sewahan ; sewa.
Hireling	Orang jang bekerdja dengen gadji.
His	Dia (lelaki) poenja.
Hiss	Soeara s-s-s-s-e ; soeara seperti aer mendidi.
Historian	Pengarang hikajat.
History	Hikajat.
Hit	Poekoel ; poekoelan.
Hither	Ka ini tempat ; ka mari.
Hive	Sarang tawon.
Hoard	Barang simpenan jang tersemoeni ; simpen dengen resia.
Hoarse	Kasar ; serak.
Hoary	Daoek ; aboe-aboe.
Hoax	Akal ; maen akal.
Hob	Sampingnja tempat api.
Hobble	Djalan pintjang-pintjang.
Hobby	Pemboeroean jang disoekai.
Hockey	Saroepa permaenan bola.
Hod	Tempat ter.
Hoe	Patjoel ; skop

Hog	Babi oetan ; bengkokin.
Hogshead	Satoe tong dari 63 gallons.
Hoist	Naekeu.
Hold	Pegangan ;, pengaroe ; tahanan dalem pendjara ; bagian dalem dari satoe kapal ; pegang , djaga.
Hole	Lobang.
Holiday	Hari besar ; hari raja.
Holiness	Kasoetjian.
Hollow	Berlobang ; tida berhati djoedjoer ; gali.
Holster	Saroeng pistol.
Holy	Alim ; soetji.
Homage	Kasoetjian.
Home	Tempat tinggal ; roema ; negri tana aer.
Homely	Saderhana ; sebagi di roema sendiri.
Homicide	Pemboenoehan dari saorang lelaki.
Hone	Batoe gosok.
Honest	Djoedjoer ; berhati lempeng.
Honey	Madoe tawon.
Honeymoon	Boelan ka satoe dari tempo kawin.
Honour	Kahormatan ; kaägoengan ; hormatin.
Honourable	Boleh dihormatin.
Hood	Topi ; kopia.
Hood-wink	Tipoe.
Hoof	Koekoe koeda, sampi, kerbo dan sebaginja.
Hook	Pantjing.
Hoop	Besi boenderan ; soempe besi.
Hoot	Menggroetoe ; berboenjinja boeroeng kokokbloek.
Hop	Lompat ; samatjem poehoen jang dipake pranti bikin bier.
Hope	Harep ; pengharepan.
Hopper	Tempat kaloear beras dalem penggilingan ; Toekang lompat atawa lontjat ; praoe pranti angkoet loempoer jang soeda dikeroek.

Horde	Kaoem jang mengglandangan.
Horizon	Tempat ketemoenja langit dengen aer.
Horizontal	Mandjang ; rata.
Horn	Tandoek ; mangkok ; trompet.
Hornet	Tawon tjeking.
Hornpipe	Saroepa pekakas muziek.
Horrible	Menakoetin.
Horrid	Gelap ; serem ; menakoetin.
Horror	Ketakoetan ; kesereman.
Horse	Koeda ; soldadoe koeda ; kajoe gantoengan.
Horseplay	Permaenan jang kasar; permaenan jang tiada menoeroet atoeran.
Hosanna	Poedjian pada Toehan-Allah.
Hose	Kous kaki; pipa jang terbikin dari koelit.
Hosier	Toekang djoewal kous kaki.
Hopitable	Baek maski pada orang jang tiada dikenal ; ko-ie.
Hospital	Hospitaal ; roema sakit.
Host	Toean-roema; balatentara.
Hostage	Orang jang dikasi sebagi tanggoengan.
Hostess	Njonja-roema.
Hostile	Biadab ; sebagi orang paprangan ; kedjem ; bertentangan.
Hostler	Pengrawat koeda dalem satoe roema menginep.
Hot	Panas ; pedes ; ingin dengen sanget.
Hotel	Hotel ; roema menginep.
Hotly	Dengen hati jang kepingin ; dengen heibat.
Hound	Andjing pemboeroe.
Hour	Djam ; 60 minuut.
House	Roema; kaoem-kaloewarga ; kekel.
Household	Kaoem-kaloewarga ; familie.
Housewife	Pengoeroes roema.
Hovel	Atep ; roema atep.
Hover	Ngelaksapan ; terbang ; liwat.
How	Begimana ; tjara begimana.

Howbeit	Begimana djoega.
However	Begimana djoega ; toch.
Howl	Mengaoeng; soeara mengaoeng.
Hub	Poeser roda.
Huckster	Toekang djoewal barang ketjil-ketjil.
Huddle	Pake atawa taro boeroe-boeroe ; rapetin sama-sama.
Hue	Warna; bertreakan.
Huff	Toedoehan sala jang koenjoeng-koenjoeng toedoe sala atawa kasi sala.
Hug	Peloekan jang rapet ; peloek; berdamping ber-sama-sama.
Huge	Besar; bangkotan.
Hulk	Badannja kapal atawa praoe jang soeda toea.
Hull	Badannja kapal atawa praoe: koelit ke-nari.
Hum	Soeara mengaoeng dari tawon ; njanji dengen zonder perkataän.
Human	Menoesia; berhoeboeng dengen menoesia.
Humane	Baek boedi; moera hati.
Humanity	Tabiat menoesia; kabaéan boedi ; kamoera-han hati.
Humble	Renda ; merenda.
Humbug	Djoesta; djoestaken.
Humid	Basa; semek atawa demek.
Humilate	Merendain ; rendain.
Humility	Adat jang tiada soeka menjombong; adat jang saderhana.
Humorous	Berakal; berdaja.
Humour	Akal-boedi; daja.
Hump	Bongkok; barang nondjol di bagian bla-kang.
Hunger	Kelaparan ; rasa lapar.
Hungry	Lapar.
Hunt	Memboeroe,

Hurdle	Soempe kajoe.
Hurl	Lemparken ; boewang.
Hurra, Hurrah	Soeara soerakan.
Hurricane	Angin riboet jang heibat.
Hurry	Boeroe-boeroe.
Hurt	Loeka ; bikin loeka.
Husband	Laki ; soeami.
Husbandman	Toekang rawat atawa loekoe tana.
Hasbandry	Rawatan atawa loekoean dari tana.
Hush	Diam ; soenji.
Husk	Koelit boewa-boewahan.
Huskiness	Kakeringan ; kaserakan.
Hussar	Soldadoe hussar ; soldadoe koeda jang tje- pet.
Hustle	Toelak ; soeroeng : mereboet.
Hut	Pondok ; roema atep.
Hutch	Peti ; kas.
Huzza	Treakan girang.
Hydrant	Pompa aer ; pipa aer.
Hydrogen	Saroepa hawa gas jang enteng dan gampang menjala.
Hygiene	Ilmoe peladjaran jang menjeritaken atoe- ran boeat mendjaga pri-kesehatan toe- boe.
Hydrophobia	Sakit lantaran digigit andjiug gila ; takoet aer.
Hymn	Njanjian poedji poedjian.
Hyphen	Tanda(-) jang digoenaken beeat samboeng perkataän.
Hypocrisy	Belagahan ; poera-poerahan ; bertingka- han.
Hypocrite	Orang jang belaga-laga, poera-poera atawa bertingka-tingka.
Hypothesis	Andean ; doegahan.

I.

I	Saja ; akoe ; perkataän menoendjoeken orang jang mengomong.
Ibis	Sabangsa boeroeng soetji di negri Mitsir (Egypt).
Ice	Aer batoe ; ijs.
Iceberg	Goemploekan aer batoe jang mengambang di moeka aer.
Icicle	Goemploekan aer batoe jang tergantoeng.
Idea	Pikiran.
Ideal	Sebagi orang mengimpi ; lapat-lapat terkandoeng dalem pikiran.
Identical	Sama ; mirip.
Identify	Menoendjoeken kesamaännja atawa miripnja.
Idiocy	Kalemahannja pikiran.
Idiom	Atoeran mengomong dengen menoeroet tjara kabiasahan.
Idiot	Orang jang kliwat bodo.
Idle	Males ; tida soeka bekerdja ; tida beharga.
Idleness	Kemalesan ; kenganggoeran,
Idol	Dato.
Idolatry	Pemoedjahan dato.
Idolize	Kagoemin ; tjintahin dengen sanget.
If	Djikaloe ; manakala.
Ignite	Pasang ; taroken api.
Ignoble	Renda ; hina ; boekan toeroenan baek-baek.
Ignominy	Pengrasaän maloe ; kehinaän.
Ignorance	Kabodohan ; kagoblokan.
Ignorant	Bodo ; goblok.
Ignore	Melaenken ; tinggalken.
Ill	Kedjahatan ; bahaja ; djahat ; sakit ; tiada sehat.
Illbred	Boekan toeroenan orang baek-baek ; kasar.

11

Illegal	Melanggar atoeran atawa wet.
Illegible	Jang ·tiada bisa dibatja.
Illiberal	Djahat ; pelit.
Illicit	Tida menoeroet wet; bertentangan dengen wet atawa oendang-oendang negri.
Illiterate	Tida terpladjar
Illness	Penjakit.
Illude	Lewein atawa djengekin ; tipoe atawa akalin.
Illuminate	Pasang penerangan ; riasin.
Illumine	Bikin terang ; bikin enteng.
Illusion	Pertoendjoekan jang palsoe.
Illustrate	Kasi ketrangan.
Illustration	Ketrangan ; gambar.
Illustrious	Termashoer ; terkenal bagoesnja.
Image	Gambar ; bajangan ; boneka.
Imaginary	Sebagi orang mengimpi ; lapat-lapat ; boekan sewadjarnja ada.
Imagination	Peta dalem pikiran ; pikiran jang lapat-lapat.
Imagine	Pikir ; timbang.
Imbecile	Lema ; kenji.
Imbibe	Minoem.
Imbrue	Djoerang ; basaken.
Imbue	Tjelep dalem warna.
Imitate	Tiroe ; toeroet toeladan.
Imitation	Tiroean ; imitatie.
Immaculate	Tida bernoda ; poeti bersi.
Immaterial	Tida perloe ; tiada sangkoetan ; tiada djahatnja.
Immature	Tiada mateng ; menta.
Immediate	Lantes ; sigra.
Immediately	Dengen lantes ; dengen sigra.
Immemorial	Tiada bisa diïnget.
Immense	Besar.
Immerge	Lompat atawa toeroen ka dalem aer.
Immerse	Lompat atawa toeroen ka dalem aer ; bekerdja dengen ripoe.

Immigrate	Dateng pinda ka satoe negri.
Imminent	Jang berlengket ; jang tiada berapa lama.
Immoderate	Lebi dari tjoekoep ; tertawa banjak.
Immodest	Tiada beradat aloes ; tiada sopan.
Immoral	Tiada mempoenjai pri-boedi kebedjikan atawa kabaean.
Immorality	Perdjalanan jang tiada baek ; hati jang tiada mempoenjai pri-boedi kebedjikan.
Immortal	Jang tiada bisa mati ; jang bisa selamanja hidoep.
Immortality	Djiwa atawa penghidoepan jang tiada mati atawa bisa selamanja hidoep.
Immovable	Jang tiada bisa digeraken atawa dipinda-pindaken.
Immure	Koeroeng dalem tembok.
Immutable	Jang tiada bisa ditoekar atawa diroba.
Imp	Anak baji ; iblis ketjil.
Impair	Bikin djadi lebi djelek atawa roesak.
Impale	Toesoek dengen kajoe.
Impart	Bagi ; kasi berhoeboeng dengen soerat.
Impartial	Jang tiada berat ka sana ka mari ; berdiri sama tenga.
Impassable	Jang tiada bisa diliwatin.
Impassible	Jang tiada bisa merasaken kesoesaän atawa kasengsaraän.
Impatience	Adat jang tiada sabar.
Impatient	Tiada sabar ; tjerewet.
Impeach	Toedoe berdosa.
Impeachment	Toedoehan dan hoekoeman.
Impeccable	Tiada berdosa ; terbebas dari kadosahan.
Impede	Tjega ; halangin.
Impediment	Tjegahan ; halangan.
Impel	Soeroeng ; toelak.
Impend	Antjem ; bikin takoet.
Impenetrable	Jang tiada bisa dikasi masoek atawa ditoesoek.
Impenitence	Kakerasan hati.

Impenitent	Tiada menjesel; tiada kedoehoeng.
Imperative	Dengen pengaroe atawa kekwasaän.
Imperfect	Tiada tjoekoep atawa lengkep.
Imperfection	Keadaän jang koerang tjoekoep atawa lengkep.
Imperial	Berhoeboeng dengen keradjaän atawa negri jang terprenta oleh keizer ; keizer poenja.
Imperil	Bikin tjilaka.
Imperious	Jang mendjagoin ; jang berkwasa besar.
Imperishable	Jang tiada bisa mati.
Imperitence	Kekasaran; prilakoe jang koerang adjar atawa bentahan.'
Impertinent	Djail ; nakal ; bentahan ; koerang adjar.
Impetuosity	Kakerasan ; kebrangasan.
Impetious	Brangasan ; berhati keras.
Impetus	Kakoewatan dari gerakan
Impiety	Kelakoean jang melanggar tita Allah.
Impious	Tiada soetji ; tiada alim.
Impish	Sebagi satoe anak baji atawa iblis ketjil.
Implacable	Jang tiada soeka dami ; jang tiada soeka bri ampoen atas kesalaännja laen orang.
Implant	Tanem ; oesahain.
Implement	Pekakas ; perabot,
Implicate	Hoeboengken ; rangkepin.
Implicit	Jang soeda ditrangin maksoednja.
Implore	Minta dengen sanget.
Imply	Kandoeng ; maksoedi.
Impolitic	Tiada tjerdik ; bodo.
Import	Dari laen negri ; maksoedi.
Import	Barang-barang jang dateng dari laen negri maksoed.
Importance	Kaperloean ; kapentingan ; kedjadian.
Important	Perloe ; penting.
Importunate	Penting ; memaksa.
Importune	Minta dengen paksa.
Impose	Tipoe ; akalin ; taro,

Imposition	Tipoe-daja ; akal-bangsat ; padjek ; perta-rohan.
Impossible	Tiada boleh djadi; moestail.
Impost	Bae atas barang-barang.
Impostor	Penipoe.
Imposture	Tipoe daja ; akal-bangsat.
Impotence	Kalemahan ; kakenjian.
Impotent	Lema ; kenji.
Impound	Tjega ; toetoep.
Impoverish	Bikin djadi miskin ; djato sengsara.
Impracticible	Jang tiada bisa dikerdjaken atawa dilakoeken.
Imprecate	Toedoe dengen perboewatan djahat.
Impregnable	Jang tiada boleh diambil dengen paksa.
Impregnate	Bikin djadi hamil ; sebar bibit.
Impress	Tjap ; tjitak.
Impression	Tanda ; tjapan atawa tjitakan ; pengaroe ; kedjadian.
Impressive	Keren ; bisa menggerakin hati orang.
Imprint	Tandain dengen teekenan.
Imprison	Masoeken dalem pendjara ; boei.
Improbable	Tiada boleh djadi ; brangkali tiada.
Improper	Tiada betoel ; tiada begitoe.
Impropriety	Keadaän jang tiada satoedjoe.
Improve	Memperbaiki ; bikin djadi lebi baek.
Improvement	Haloean memperbaiki ; pembikinan djadi lebi baek ; kemadjoean.
Improvident	Tiada perhatiken tentang hal-hal jang soeda terdjadi.
Imprudence	Kabodohan ; keadaän koerang tjerdik ; ka-tjongpongan atawa katjeroboan.
Imprudent	Tjongpong ; atawa tjerobo ; tiada ati-ati.
Impudent	Koerang adjar ; tiada taoe adat.
Impudence	Prilakoe jang koerang adjar atawa tiada taoe adat.
Impugn	Poekoel atawa hantem dengen perkataän.

Impulse	Paksahan.
Impure	Tiada bersi ; kotor ; mesoem.
Impurity	Kakotorän ; kamesoeman.
Imputation	Toedoehan atas kedosahan.
Impute	Toedoe ; terka.
In	Didalem ; dipake sebagi soerat tambahan di hadepan perkataän dan bermaksoed *tiada*.
Inability	Kakoerangan kapandean.
Inaccessible	Tiada bisa disampeken.
Inaccurate	Tiada tjotjok ; tiada betoel.
Inaction	Kenganggoeran ; kemalesan.
Inactice	Menganggoer ; males.
Inadequate	Tiada tjoekoep ; tiada setimpal.
Inadvertence	Kesalaän jang dibikin lantaran koerang pikir lebih doeloe.
Inadvertent	Teledor ; koerang pikir.
Inane	Kosong.
Inanimate	Tiada berdjiwa atawa bernjawa.
Inanition	Kekosongan.
Inapplicable	Tiada tjoekoep ; tiada satoedjoe.
Inappropriate	Tiada sedeng ; tiada satoedjoe,
Inaptitude	Keadaän jang tiada senang atawa satoedjoe.
Inasmush	Menimbang atawa menilik.
Inattention	Kateledoran ; koerang perhatian.
Inaudible	Jang tiada bisa didenger.
Inaugurate	Masoek bekerdja.
Inauspicious	Tiada broentoeng ; sial.
Inborn	Memang seeda dasarnja.
Inbred	Terdjadi dengen kamaoehan Allah.
Incalcuable	Jang tiada bisa di-itoeng abis.
Incandescent	Poeti lantaran kapanasan.
Incapable	Tiada setimpel ; tiada sanggoep.
Incapacity	Keadaän tiada sanggoep ; koerang kapandean.
Incarcerate	Pendjara ; boei.
Incarnate	Lapisin dengen isi atawa daging.

Incautious	Koerang ati-ati ; teledor.
Incendiary	Pengasoet ; orang jang membakar roema.
Incense	Menjan ; setanggi.
Incense	Bikin mara; asoet.
Incentive	Gerakan; bikin bergerak.
Inception	Permoelaän.
Incessant	Tiada brentinja ; berdjalan teroes.
Inch	Duim ; $1/_{12}$ dari satoe kaki.
Incident	Ketjilakaän ; kedjadian.
Incidental	Di loewar doegahan ; koenjoeng-koenjoeng, terdjadi.
Incipient	Moelain.
Incision	Loeka.
Incisor	Gigi depan.
Incite	Goembiraken ; gerakan hati.
Incitement	Kagoembirahan ; gerakan hati.
Incivility	Kakoerangan adat atawa prilakoe hormat.
Inclement	Kasar ; berombak ; toeroen angin besar.
Inclination	Dojongnja ; kainginan.
Incline	Dojong ; ingin.
Include	Berikoet ; termasoek dalem golongan.
Inclusive	Jang berikoet ; jang termasoek dalem go-longan ; penoetoepnja.
Incognito	Menjaroe ; semoeni.
Incoherent	Tiada berhoeboeng.
Incombustible	Jang tiada memakan api.
Income	Gadji ; pendapetan ; pentjarian.
Incommode	Bikin soesa ; ganggoe.
Incomparable	Jang tiada ada bandingannja.
Incompetence	Keerang daja; koerang kepandean.
Incompetent	Koerang satoedjoe.
Incomplete	Tiada tjoekoep ; tiada lengkep ; belon abis.
Incomprehensible	Jang tiada bisa diarti-in.
Inconceivable	Jang tiada bisa ditimbang atawa dipoetoesken.
Incongruous	Tiada satoedjoe ; tiada sedeng.

Inconsisten	Tiada saroepa ; boekan satoe matjem.
Inconsolable	Tiada bisa dihiboerin.
Inconstant	Tiada tetep ; tiada tentoe.
Incovenience	Ganggoean.
Incovenient	Tiada satoedjoe ; tiada tjoekoep.
Incorrect	Tiada betoel ; sala.
Incorrigible	Jang tiada bisa dibetoelin.
Incorrupt	Setia ; berhati bersi
Incorruptible	Tiada bisa djadi boesoek ; tiada bisa di-sogok.
Incorruption	Keadaän jang tiada bisa djadi boesoek atawa disogok.
Increase	Tamba ; toemboe.
Increase	Tambahan ; toemboenja.
Incredible	Tiada boleh dipertjaia.
Incredulous	Menerbitken sangkahan atawa katjoerigaän.
Increment	Hasil ; tambahan.
Inculcate	Geraken hati orang dengen kasi pengadjaran.
Incumbency	Pangkoean djabatan atawa pakerdjahan.
Incumbent	Orang jang memangkoe djabatan atawa pe-gang pekerdjahan ; jang memang djadi kewadjibannja ; jang haroes diboewat.
Incur	Terdjadi.
Incurable	Tiada bisa diobatin ; tiada bisa ditoeloeng dengen obat.
Incursion	Labrakan ; hanteman.
Indebtedness	Dalem keadaän mengoetang.
Indecency	Prilakoe jang koerang hormat atawa adat.
Indecent	Tiada berlakoe hormat atawa aloes.
Indeed	Betoel-betoel ; sasoenggoenja.
Indefatigable	Tiada bisa dibikin tjape.
Indefinite	Tiada pasti.
Indelicate	Tiada berlakoe aloes ; kasar ; koerang adjar.
Indemnify	Ganti karoegian,
Indemnity	Gantihan karoegian.
Independence	Kamerdikaän ; kelonggaran.

Independent	Merdika ; tiada terprenta.
Index	Klapper ; penoendjoek ; bikin sama.
Indicate	Hoendjoek ; trangin.
Indication	Tanda.
Indict	Toedoe berboeat dosa.
Indictment	Toedoehan satjara officieel ; toedoehan jang sah.
Indifferent	Teledor ; boleh diliwatin.
Indigenous	Terpranak di satoe negri ; djadi boemipoetra jang aseli.
Indigent	Miskin ; sengsara.
Indigestible	Tiada bisa diantjoerin atawa dipentjernaken didalem peroet.
Indigestion	Penjakit peroet ,koerang koewat antjoerken barang makanan ; sakit pentjernaän makanan ; tjiah-bee siauw.
Indignant	Hati jang mendongkol ; mara.
Indignity	Mendongkolan ; rasa amarah.
Indigo	Nila.
Indiscreet	Tiada tjerdik ; tiada ati-ati ; tjongpong,
Indiscretion	Katjongpongan ; keadaän koerang ati-ati.
Indispensable	Perloe ; pinting.
Indisposition	Koerang kemaoehan ; kalang-kaboetan.
Indisputable	Tiada bisa dibantah atawa disangkal.
Indistinct	Tiada terang; tersemoeni.
Individual	Satoe orang ; saorang diri.
Indocile	Tiada djinek ; tiada gampang diadjar.
Indolence	Kemalesan ; kenanggoeran.
Indolent	Males ; soeka menganggoer.
Indomitable	Tiada bisa dibikin djinek.
Indorse	Toelis di blakangnja.
Indubitable	Tiada bisa dibantah atawa disangkal.
Induce.	Boedjoek ; pikat.
Inducement	Boedjoekan ; pikatan ; gerakan.
Indue	Pakein ; lengkepin.
Indulge	Bersoekoer ; senangin ; idjinken ; berlakoe sembarangan.

Indulgence	Idjinja ; kelakoean jang sembarangan.
Indulgent	Jang di-idjinken ; jang berlakoe dengen sembarangan.
Industrious	Bisa bekerdja keras ; radjin.
Industry	Keradjinan ; ilmoe pertoekangan.
Inebriate	Pemabokan jang soeda kawakan.
Ineffable	Jang tiada bisa dioetjapken dengen perkataän.
Ineffectual	Pertjoema-tjoema sia-sia ; tiada berhasil.
Inefficacy	Keadaän koerang pengaroe atawa kekwasaän.
Inefficient	Tiada sanggoep lakoeken.
Inelligible	Tiada tjoekoep ; tiada haroes.
Inept	Tiada satoedjoe ; tiada betoel.
Inert	Lambat ; geremet.
Inestimable	Di atas harga.
Inevitable	Tiada bisa disingkirken atawa dilaloei.
Inexact	Tiaha betoel ; diada tjotjok ; sala.
Inexpedint	Tiada perloe ; bole traoesa.
Inexpert	Tiada mempoenjai kapandean ; tiada gesit.
Inexpressible	Tiada bisa diseboet dengen perkataän.
Infallible	Jang tiada bisa berboeat sala.
Infamous	Ternama tiada baek ; tiada terkenal.
Infamy, infamousness	Kedjahatan atawa kaboesoekan jang meliwatin wates.
Infancy	Waktoe ketjil ; waktoe jang paling slang ; permoelaän.
Infant	Anak baji ; anak orok.
Infanticide	Pemboenoehan atawa pemboenoenja anak baji.
Infantry	Barisan soldadoe djalan kaki.
Infatuated	Tjaboel ; genit.
Infatuation	Ketjaboelan ; kagenitan ; kabodohan.
Infect	Toelarin penjakit.
Infection	Toelarannja penjakit.

Infelicity	Keadaän jang tiada senang,
Inter	Rampas ; tarik ; potong.
Inference	Rampasan ; tarikan ; potongan.
Inferior	Orang sebawahan ; sebawahan ; lebi renda.
Infernal	Termasoek dalam bilangan noraka.
Infest	Bikin soesa sanget.
Infidel	Orang jang tiada menaro kapertjaiaän dalem agama.
Infidelity	Tiada menaro kapertjaiaän dalem agama,
Infiltrate	Masoek dari lobang kringet.
Infinite	Tiada berwates,
Infinity	Keadaän jang tiada ada watesnja.
Infirm	Kenji ; sakitan.
Infirmary	Roema sakit.
Infirmity	Kakenjian ; kalemahan.
Inflame	Djengekin atawa lewein ; bikin mara.
Inflammation	Pembakaran ; warna mera dan hawa panas.
Inflate	Djadi bengkak atawa kemboeng dengen angin.
Inflated	Sombong ; beradat tinggi.
Inflect	Roba ; toekar.
Inflection	Perobahan ; penoekaran.
Inflexible	Kakoe ; tiada lemes.
Inflict	Taro ; tipoe ; persakiti.
Infliction	Hoekoeman.
Influence	Kekwasaän ; pengaroe ; bergerak ; pimpin.
Influenza	Sakit batok pilek.
Inform	Bri kabar ; kasi taoe.
Informal	Tiada tetep ; tiada tentoe.
Information	Kabaran.
Infraction	Pelanggaran.
Infrequent	Djarang ; tiada loemrah atawa biasa.
Infringe	Petjaken ; roesakin.
Infuriate	Bikin mara ; gosok-gosok ; àsoet.
Infuse	Tjelep ; toewang ; bernapas.
Intusion	Tjelepan ; minoeman jang terbikin dengen ditjelep.

Ingenious	Pinter ; mempoenjai kapandean.
Ingeniuty	Kapinteran ; kapandean.
Ingenuous	Teroes-trang ; berhati lempeng.
Ingot	Palangan besi.
Ingratiate	Dapet kasoekahan orang.
Ingratitude	Adat jang koerang trima ; bo-tjeng.
Ingredient	Boemboe.
Ingress	Djalanan masoek.
Ingulf	Telen.
Inhabit	Tempatin ; berdiam.
Inhabitant	Pendoedoek negri.
Inhale	Sedot ; tarik ka dalem paroe.
Inherent	Tinggal di dalem ; jang memangnja ada.
Inherit	Toeroenin.
Inheritance	Toeroenan ; peninggalan harta-banda.
Inhuman	Tiada mempoenjai hati menoesia ; kedjem··
Inimical	Tiada satjara sobat ; biadab.
Inipuitious	Djahat.
Iniquity	Kedjahatan ; kedosahan.
Initial	Potong letter ; pertama.
Inject	Djebloesin ; lemparken.
Injudicious	Tiada berlakoe aloes ; kasar.
Injunction	Prentahan ; tita.
Injure	Bikin loeka ; persakiti.
Injury	Pembikinan loeka.
Injustice	Kesalahan jang telah diperboeat; keadaän koerang adil.
Ink	Tinta.
Inland	Didalem negri; djaoe dari laoet.
Inlet	Djalanan masoek ; gang.
Inmate	Orang jang tinggal bersama-sama dalem satoe roema ; temen-tinggal.
Inmost	Paling dalem.
Inn	Tempat menginep ; roema makan.
Innate	Memang soeda dasarnja ; memang terlahir begitoe.

Inner	Lebi dalem.
Innermost	Paling dalem.
Innocence	Keadaän poeti-bersi keadaän tiada bersala.
Innocent	Poeti-bersi ; tiada bersala ; bisa menerbitken hati kesian.
Innocuosus	Tiàda berbahaja.
Innoxious	Tiada berbahanja ; slamat.
Innuendo	Pembitjaraän atawa sindiran jang menjimpang.
Innummerable	Jang tiada bisa direken atawa di-itoeng.
Inoculate	Masoeken aer obat dari tenga blakang toeboe.
Inodorous	Tiada mempoenjai baoe.
Inoffensive	Tiada berbahaja ; tiada besala.
Inopportune	Tiada setoedjoe ; tiada biasa dengen hawa.
Inordinate	Kliwat banjak.
Inorganic	Zonder atawa tiada mempoenjai anggota badan.
Inquest	Pertanjaän tentang meninggalnja satoe orang.
Inquietude	Keadaän tiada bisa diam.
Inquire	Tanja ; tjari ketrangan ; sediki.
Inquiry	Pertanjaän ; selidikan.
Inquisitive	Gegetoen ; apa sadja maoe taoe.
Inroad	Labrakan jang koenjoeng-koenjoeng;
Insalubrious	Tiada sehat ; tiada seger.
Insane	Gelo ; edan ; gila ; angin-anginan.
Insanity	Kegeloan ; kaedanan ; kegilaän.
Insatiable	Tiada bisa dipoewasken.
Inscribe	Toelis.
Inscription	Toelisan.
Inscrutable	Tiada bisa ditjari atawa didapetin.
Insect	Koetoe.
Insectivorous	Makan koetoe-koetoe ; hidoep dengen dahar koetoe-koetoe.
Insecure	Berbahaja ; tiada slamat.
Insecurity	Behaja ; ketjilakaän.

Insensate	Tiada mempoenjai pengrasaän
Insensible	Tiada terasa.
Insensibly	Dengen tiada terasa.
Insert	Masoeken.
Inside	Dalemnja ; di dalem.
Insight	Pengatahoean jang loewas.
Insignia	Tanda perbedahan.
Insignificant	Tiada beharga ; tiada perloe.
Insincere	Tiada djoedjoer ; berhati palsoe.
Insinuate	Sindirin.
Insinuation	Sindiran.
Insipid	Tawar ; tiada rasa apa-apa.
Insist	Bentahan ; berkeras.
Insnare	Oempanin ; djebak.
Insobriety	Kemabokan.
Insolence	Kelakoean jang djoemawa atawa sombong.
Insolent	Djoemawa ; sombong.
Insolvent	Tiada bisa membajar.
Insomuch	Soepaja ; dengen tjara begitoe.
Inspect	Preksa ; tilik.
Inspection	Preksahan ; tilikan.
Inspector	Inspecteur; toekang atawa orang jang pereksai mandoor.
Inspiration	Tarik panas ; pengaroe jang soetji.
Inspire	Tarik napas ; bernapas.
Install	Angkat dalem pekerdjahan.
Installation	Keangkatan dalem pekerdjahan.
Instalment ·	Mendering ; termin ; pembajaran dengen menjitjil.
Inatence	Tjonto ; tjontoin.
Instant	Tempo ; lantas ; sigra ; perloe.
Instantaneous	Dilakoeken dengen koenjoeng-koenjoeng.
Instead	Gantinja ; boekannja.
Instep	Bagian sebla atas dari kaki.
Instigate	Asoet ; boedjoek.
Instinct	Kapandean jang soeda didjadiken oleh natuur atawa Allah

Institute	Pakoempoelan dari penjoeratan ; roema sekola ; berdiriken.
Institution	Atoeran ; pakoempoelan ; roema sekola ; pendirian.
Instruct	Adjar ; toetoen.
Instruction	Pengadjaran; toentoenan.
Instrument	Pekakas ; perabot.
Instubordination	Kamoengkiran boeat menjera pada kekwasaän.
Insufferable	Tiada bisa dirasa.
Insufficient	Tiada tjoekoep ; tiada satoedjoe.
Insular	Terkoeroeng dengen aer ; poelo.
Insulate	Taro sendirian.
Insult	Tjomelan ; makian.
Insult	Lombongken ; agoengken.
Insurance	Assurance ; pertanggoengan atas keroegian.
Insure	Kasi tanggoengan atas keroegian.
Insurgent	Hoeroe-hara ; gerakan hoeroe-hara.
Insurrection	Bangoennja lagi dari koeboeran ; hoeroe-hara.
Intact	Tiada dioesik-oesik ; tiada dioesil-oesil.
Integer	Nummer besar ; angka jang penoe.
Integrity	Kasampoernaän ; kadjoedjoeran.
Integument	Barang jang menoetoepin.
Intellect	Pengartian.
Intelligence	Pengartian ; kabaran.
Intelligent	Mempoenjai pengartian ; radjin ; mempoenjai ketrangan tjoekoep.
Intemperance	Keadaän lebi dari tjoekoep atawa terlaloe banjak.
Intemperate	Dikasi terlaloe banjak ; keras.
Intend	Ingin ; maoe.
Intense	Terlaloe banjak.
Intensity	Keadaän terlaloe banjak.
Intention	Kemaoehan ; kainginan.
Inter	Teman ; koeboer.

Intercede	Minta boeat kabaean.
Intercept	Tangkep di djalanan.
Intercessor	Pemisa ; orang jang bikin dami.
Intercourse	Haloean ; hoeboengan dengen dagangan.
Interdict	Larang.
Interdict	Soerat mahloemat dalem maña ada dikasi larangan.
Interest	Kabaean ; bagian ; rente atawa boenga.
Interfere	Ganggoe.
Interference	Ganggoean,
Interior	Bagian sebla dalem ; oedik.
Interjection	Perkatän jang menjataken rasa kaget, heran dan sebaginja.
Interleave	Taro lembaran antara.
Interloper	Orang jang tjampoer tangan.
Intermediate	Antara.
Interment	Berhoeboeng dengen pengoeboeran.
Interminable	Tiada ada oedjoengnja atawa abisnja.
Intermission	Pembrentian boeat samentara waktoe ; toendahan.
Intermit	Brenti boeat samentara waktoe ; toenda.
Intermitten	Let-lèt ; satoe hari dateng dan satoe hari tiada.
Internal	Bagian sebla dalam ; roemahan poenja.
International	Diantara semoea bangsa,
Interpolate	Masoeken.
Interpose	Taro diantaranja.
Interpret	Salin ; kasi ketrangan.
Interpreter	Djoeroe penjalin.
Interrogate	Tanja.
Interrogation	Pertanjaän.
Interrupt	Potong ; petjaken ; tjega ; halangan.
Interruption	Tjegahan ; halangin.
Intersect	Bagi doea.
Intersperse	Pentjarken disana sini.
Interstice	Tempat kosong antara.

Interval	Djaoenja antara.
Intervene	Dateng antara ; tjampoer tangan.
Intervention	Pembikinan dami.
Interview	Pertemoehan dengen tjara officieel.
Intestate	Orang jang mati boekan atas kemaoehannja sendiri ; mati boekan atas kemaoehan sendiri.
Intestine	Di sebla dalem.
Intestines	Oesoes atawa oetjoes.
Intimacy	Pesobatan.
Intimate	Sobat jang rapet ; rapet; kasi pikiran; kata.
Intimation	Pembitjaraän; pengasihan pikiran; pembrian taoe.
Intimidate	Bikin djadi takoet.
Into	Ka dalem.
Intolerable	Jang tiada bisa ditoendjang atawa tahan.
Intolerance	Keadaän tiada tahan aken meliat.
Intoxication	Kemabokan.
Intractable	Bandel; bengal.
Intransitive	Jang bergerak sendiri.
Intrench	Bikin tegoe dengen gali.solok-solokan dan berdiriken tembok-tembok.
Intrepid	Brani ; tiada pengetjoet.
Intricate	Tertjampoer.
Intrigue	Tipoe-daja; akal.
Intrinsic	Toelen; tiada palsoe.
Introduce	Kasi kenal; anter.
Introduction	Pengasihan kenal; peranteran.
Intrude	Masoek dengen zonder idjin.
Intrusion	Pemasoekan dengen zonder idjin.
Intrust	Pertjaiaken.
Inundate	Meloewapin dengen aer.
Inundation	Bandjir.
Inure	Biasa.
Invade	Labrak; hantem.
Invalid	Tiada mempoenjai kekoewatan; kosong.

Invalid	Orang sakit.
Invalidate	Koerangken tenaganja.
Invaluable	Amat bergoena.
Invariable	Tetep ; tentoe.
Invasion	Labrakan ; hanteman.
Invective	Makian.
Invent	Dapet taoe ; pertama kali dapetken.
Invention	Ilmoe pendapetan baroe,
Inventory	Lijst atawa tjatetan dari barang-barang.
Invert	Terbalikin ; toekar haloean.
Invertebrate	Machloek atawa binatang jang tiada mempoenjai toelang blakang.
Invest	Tinggalken harta ; pakein ; koeroeng ; taro oewang.
Investigate	Preksa ; tilik.
Investigation	Pemereksaän ; tilikan.
Inveterate	Terdoedoek dalem.
Indivious	Menerbitken pikiran djelek.
Invigorate	Bikin koewat.
Invincible	Jang tiada bisa dikalaken.
Inviolate	Tiada loeka.
Invisible	Tiada bisa diliat.
Invitation	Oendangan.
Invite	Oendang.
Invocation	Panggilan boeat bri pertoeloengan.
Invoice	Factuur ; nota barang-barang.
Invoke	Panggil dengen sanget.
Involve	Kandoeng ; masoeken.
Ire	Kegoesaran hati ; kamoerkaän.
Iris	Boenderan koeliling anak-anakan mata ; kembang-bandera.
Irksome	Menjapein.
Iron	Besi ; besi strikaän ; terbikin dari besi ; keras ; strika.
Ironclad	Kapal prang jang dilapis wadja,
Irradiate	Riasin dengen tjahia terang,

Irrational	Tiada mempoenjai pikiran; tiada mempoenjai pengartian.
Irregular	Tiada menoeroet atoeran; tiada tentoe.
Irrelevant	Boekan atas kemaoehan.
Irreparable	Tiada bisa dibikin betoel atawa baek.
Irrepressible	Tiada bisa ditindi.
Irresistible	Tiada bisa ditahan atawa ditjega.
Irresolute	Bergojang.
Irrespective	Tiada perdoeli.
Irreverence	Koerang kahormatan.
Irrevocable	Tiada bakalan dipanggil lagi.
Irritable	Gampang dibikin mara.
Irritate	Bikin mara.
Irritation	Kebrangasan; amarah.
Irruption	Labrakan jang koenjoeng-koenjoeng.
Is	Ada.
Islam	Agama Moehamad; bangsa Islam.
Island	Poelo.
Isle	Poelo ketjil.
Isolate	Ditaro sendirian.
Issue	Kaloearan; toeroenan; achirnja; kaloearken; terbitken.
Isthmus	Samboengan tana.
It	Itoe; dia.
Italics	Cursief; *tjitakan miring sebagi ini*.
Itch	Rasa gatel.
Itchy	Gatel.
Item	Oeroesan jang dipisa-pisa.
Iterate	Kata lagi.
Itinerant	Berdjalan sana-sini; mengglandangan.
Itself	Dia sendiri.
Ivory	Gading; tjaling gadja.
Ivy	Saroepa poehoen idjo jang merembet.

J.

Jabber	Omong tjeretjetan,
· Jack	Masin ; bendera ; nama anak lelaki.
Jack-ass	Kalde lelaki.
Jack-boot	Sepatoe botin jang besar.
Jackdaw	Samatjem boeroeng jang mirip dengen gowak.
Jacket	Djas pendek.
Jade	Prempoean jang berderadjat renda ; batoe giok ; koeda jang soeda tjape.
Jag	Lobang ; barang jang terpotong.
Jail	Pemboeian ; pendjara.
Jailer	Cipir boei,
Jam	Gelei (sale) ; manisan.
Jamb	Samping semprong atawa pintoe
Japan	Tjat Japan ; nama negri.
Jar	Tempajan ; kendi ; gojang.
Jargon	Omongan atawa pembitjaraän jang kalang-kaboet.
Jaunt	Pasiar ; perdjalanan.
Javelin	Toembak jang enteng.
Jaw	Toelang pipi jang memegang gigi,
Jay	Boeroeng dengen boeloe jang bagoes.
Jealous	Tjoeriga tjemboeroean.
Jealousy	Ketjoerigaän ; ketjemboeroean.
Jeer	Lewein ; bikin maloe
Jehovah	Toehan Allah.
Jelly	Ager-ager ; tjah-jan.
Jennet	Koeda Spanjol jang ketjil.
Jeopardy	Ketjilakaän ; bahaja.
Jerk	Sentak atawa gentak.
Jest	Kaloetjoean ; badoetan,
Jester	Orang jang loetjoe ; badoet,

Jet	Areng batoe jang bagoes ; mantjoeran aer ; tjabang-gas.
Jetty	Boom ketjil ; tempat praoe berlaboe.
Jewel	Batoe permata.
Jewelry	Mas inten.
Jib	Bagian depan dari lajar kapal ; moengkir.
Jilt	Prempoean jang poera-poera tjinta pada sa- toe lelaki ; poera-poera tjinta ; moengkir.
Jingle	Bikin berboenji ; bikin njaring.
Job	Pakerdjahan ketjil.
Jockey	Menoenggang koeda adoean.
Jocose	Berbanjol ; membadoet.
Jocular	Berbanjol ; membadoet.
Jocund	Selaloe senang ; tiada mempoenjai pikiran.
Jog	Soeroeng pelahan-pelahan.
Join	Samboeng ; samboengan.
Joiner	Toekang kajoe.
Joint	Samboengan ; persariketan ; samboeng.
Jointure	Harta peninggalan boeat istri.
Joke	Banjolan ; badoetan.
Jolly	Girang ; loetjoe,
Jolt	Gojang ; gentak.
Jorum	Glas minoem jang besar.
Jostle	Soeroeng atawa toelak dengen perkoso ; djo- rokin.
Jot	Barang jang ketjil ; barang saboetir ; tjatet.
Journal	Tjatetan sahari-hari.
Journey	Perdjalanan ; pelantjongan.
Journeyman	Orang jang bekerdja ; koeli.
Jovial	Senang ; bagoes ; inda.
Joy	Kagirangan ; girang.
Joyous	Girang ; merasa girang.
Jubilant	Kliwat girang ; girang tiada terhingga,
Jubilee	Pesta atawa kerajahan besar.
Judaic	Termasoek dalem bilangan bangsa Jood ata- wa Jahoedi.

Judge	Hakim ; pikir dan poetoesin satoe perkara.
Judgement	Pikiran dan kapoetoesan tentang satoe perkara.
Judicature	Kekwasaän dari pengadilan.
Judicial	Termasoek dalem bilangan pengadilan.
Judicious	Pinter ; berdaja.
Jug	Kendi atawa goblet aer.
Juggle	Maen soenglap.
Juggler	Toekang maen soenglap.
Jugular	Termasoek dalem bilangan tenggorokan.
Juice	Pati atawa sari boewa-boewahan atawa sajoeran.
Jumble	Adoek ; tjampoer kalang-kaboet ; adoekan atawa tjampoeran kalang-kaboet.
Jump	Lompat.
Junction	Samboengan ; hoeboengan.
Juncture	Tempo jang berbahaja ; waktoe jang penting.
Jungle	Oetan besar.
Junior	Lebi moeda.
Jurisdiction	Kekwasaän aken membikin keadilan ; wates dari kekwasaän.
Juror	Hakim jang bri poetoesan.
Jury	Sakoempoelan orang atawa saorang jang soeda diambil soempanja boeat memoetoesken satoe perkara atawa oeroesan.
Just	Betoel ; baroe ; hati djoedjoer.
Justice	Keadilan.
Justification	Pembelaän diri ; loepoetken diri dari toedoehan.
Justify	Boektiken boeat dapet kabeneran.
Justiy	Dengen betoel ; dengen adil.
Justness	Keadilan ; kadjoedjoeran.
Jut	Nondjol kaloear,
Jute	Samatjem benang poehoen.
Juxtaposition	Deketnja tempat,
Juvenile	Moeda ; orang moeda poenja.

K.

Kail	Samatjem kol (namanja sajoëran).
Kaleidoscope	Keker dari gambar-gambar.
Kangaroo	Saroepa binatang Australie jang mempoenjai kantong anak.
Kaolin	Saroepa porcelein jang paling bagoes.
Kedge	Djangkar ketjil.
Keel	Pantat praoe ; praoe poenja bagian bawa.
Keelhaul	Seret praoe dari pantatnja.
Keen	Tadjem.
Keep	Simpen ; djaga.
Keep	Benteng ; pendjagaän ; ongkost menoempang.
Keeper	Pendjaga ; pengawal.
Keeping	Pendjagaän ; pendjara.
Keepsake	Tanda peringetan.
Keg	Tahang ketjil.
Kelp	Boeboek roempoet laoet boeat bikin glas.
Kennel	Kandang andjing.
Kept	Soeda simpen ; soeda djaga.
Kerb	Liat *Curb*.
Kerchief	Sapoetangan.
Kernel	Isi atawa daging dari soeatoe boea keras, oepama kenari.
Kersey	Kaen wool.
Ketch	Kapal bertiang doea.
Kettle	Teko.
Key	Koentji.
Keyhole	Lobang koentji.
Kibe	Sakit meleka atawa petja di tangan.
Kick	Tendang.
Kid	Anak domba.
Kidnap	Tjoelikin ; bawa lari orang.
Kidney	Kantong kentjing.
Kilderkin	Tahang atawa tong ketjil.

Kill	Boenoe.
Kiln	Dapoer pembakaran kapoer.
Kin	Kambrat ; sanak soedara.
Kind	Baek hati ; matjem atawa roepa.
Kindle	Pasang api.
Kindliness	Kabaean atawa kamoerahan hati.
Kindly	Dengen baek hati.
Kindness	Kabaean ; boedi.
Kindred	Sanak-soedara ; kaoem kaloewarga.
Kine	Sampi-sampi.
King	Radja-lelaki.
Kingdom	Keradjaän.
Kingly	Sebagi radja.
Kink	Boentelan tali ; bisa bikin orang tertawa atawa batok.
Kinsfolk	Sanak-soedara ; kaoem kaloewarga ; familie.
Kinsman	Satoe sanak-soedara, kaoem kaloewarga atawa familie.
Kiss	Tjioem ; djalanken peradatan dengen bibir.
Kit	Pakean soldadoe atawa matros.
Kitchen	Dapoer.
Kitten	Anak koetjing.
Knack	Barang permaenan.
Knag	Mata kajoe ; boekoe kajoe.
Knag	Barang jang menondjol kaloear ; kantjing.
Knap	Gigit ; tempiling.
Knapsack	Kantong soldadoe.
Knal	Mata atawa boekoe kajoe.
Knarled	Mempoenjai mata atawa boekoe kajoe.
Knave	Bangsat ; orang boesoek ; kartoe maen.
Knavery	Perboeatan bangsat atawa boesoek.
Knavish	Sebagi bangsat ; boesoek ; tiada djoedjoer.
Knead	Kerdjaken dengen tangan.
Knee	Loetoet ; dengkoel.
Kneel	Berloetoet ; berkoewi.
Kneepan	Toelang loetoet.

Knell	Soeara lotjeng ; gojang ; boenjiken.
Knew	Soeda taoe.
Knife	Piso.
Knight	Orang berpangkat.
Knighterrant	Orang berpangkat jang mengglandangan atawa djalan sana-sini dengen tiada mempoenjai toedjoehan jang betoel.
Knightghood	Pangkat atawa deradjatnja saorang berpangkat ; koempoelan orang berpangkat.
Knit	Hoehoengken dengen benang dan djaroem ; djait.
Knob	Boentelan ; barang jang menondjol kaloear.
Knobby	Penoe boentelan.
Knock	Ketok.
Knocker	Knob pintoe.
Knoll	Boekit ketjil.
Knop	Knob ; kantjing ; tangkee atawa rentjengan kembang jang boender.
Knot	Boentelan ; persariketan.
Knotty	Penoe boentelan.
Knout	Pekakas hoekoeman bangsa Rus.
Know	Taoe.
Knowingly	Dengen mempoenjai pengatahoean atawa kepinteran.
Knowledge	Pengatahoean ; kapinteran.
Knuckle	Boekoe tangan.
Koran	Boekoe sembajang kaoem Mohamad.
Kraal	Pondok atawa kampoeng bangsa Hottentot.
Kyanize	Simpen kajoe dengen ditaroin obat soepaja tiada gampang boesoek.

L.

Label	Soerat ketrangan ; kertas nama ; taroin soerat ketrangan atawa kertas nama.
Laboratory	Bengkel pakerdjahan ; tempat pranti jakinken ilmoe pisa, preksa orang poenja dara dan sebaginja.
Labour	Kerdja berat ; pakerdjahan berat.
Labourer	Orang jang bekerdja berat ; toekang bekerdja berat.
Laborious	Bisa bekerdja berat ; perloe pakerdjahan barat.
Lace	Rinda ; soelaman ; rindain ; soelam.
Lack	Kakoerangan ; perloe tambahan.
Lackey	Boedjang ; jongos ; rawatin ; toenggoein.
Laconic	Pendek ; ringkes.
Lacquer	Vernish tjat.
Lad	Djedjaka.
Ladder	Tangga.
Lade	Moewatin.
Lading	Moewatin.
Ladle	Gajoeng ; sendokan.
Lady	Njonja bangsawan.
Lag	Djato ka blakang.
Lagoon	Empang jang tjetek.
Lair	Sarang binatang galak.
Lake	Tasik ; empang besar.
Lamb	Anak kambing.
Lame	Pintjang ; bikin pintjang.
Lament	Berdoeka ; bersoesa hati.
Lamentation	Doekaän ; soeara tangisan atawa ratapan.
Lamp	Lampoe ; penerangan.
Lance	Toembak.
Lancet	Piso ketjil pranti belek orang.

Land	Tana ; negri ; naek ka darat.
Landau	Kreta jang beroda ampat.
Landlady	Pengoeroes prempoean dari satoe roema menginep.
Landlord	Toean-tana ; pengoeroes lelaki dari satoe roema menginep atawa logement.
Landmark	Wates negri ; barang jang keliatan dari djaoe.
Landscape	Landschap ; pemandangan dari tempat ; gambar dari pemandangan tempat-tempat.
Lane	Gang ; djalanan ketjil.
Language	Bahasa.
Languid	Lema tawa lemes ; kenji.
Languish	llang tenaga.
Languor	Kepajahan tenaga.
Lank	Koeroes ; langsing.
Lantern	Lentera.
Lap	Sabagian dari tana lapang adoe koeda ; loetoet atawa dengkoel ; pankoean ; reba ; djilat.
Lapse	Liwatin ; terpelesetin
Larceny	Katjoerian jang ketjil.
Larch	Samatjem poehoen tjemara atawa siong.
Lard	Minjak atawa gemoek babi.
Larder	Tempat simpen barang makanan ; goedang ramsoem.
Large	Besar.
Lark	Boeroeng lark ; saroepa boeroeng jang pande menjanji ; loetjoe ; soeka berbanjol.
Larynx	Bagian sebla atas dari pipa angin dalem toeboe menoesia.
Lascar	Boedak-laskar ; matros boemipoetra di Oost Hindia.
Lash	Tjamboek, .
Lass	Anak prawan ; gadis.
Lassitude	Kalelahan ; katjapean.

Last	Tjitakan sepatoe ; paling blakang ; teroes; tahan ; pengabisan ; achir-achir.
Latch	Glender pintoe.
Late	Laat ; sasoedanja liwat tempo.
Latent	Tersemoeni ; tiada keliatan.
Later	Lebi laat ; let i blakang.
Lath	Sakeping kajoe.
Lathe	Masin boeat memoeter.
Lather	Boesa saboen.
Latitude	Djaoenja dari djalanan mata-hari ; lebarnja ; kamerdikaän.
Latter	Jang blakangan ; jang kedoea.
Lattice	Palangan ; lankan besi ; palangin ; taroin lankan besi.
Laud	Poedjian ; poedji.
Laudable	Boleh dipoedji ; haroes dipoedji.
Laugh	Tertawa atawa ketawa ; tertawahan atawa ketawahan.
Laughter	Soeara tertawahan ; soeara bekakakan.
Launch	Kasi djalan di atas aer ; lepas ka aer.
Laudress	Toekang-tjoetji prempoean.
Laundry	Bengkel binatoe ; tempat tjoetji pakenn kotor
Laurel	Samatjem poehoen kembang.
Lavatory	Tempat pranti menjoetji.
Lavish	Boros ; borosken.
Law	Wet ; oendang-oendang ; atoeran.
Lawyer	Advocaat ; procureur.
Lax	Longgar ; kendor.
Lay	Lagoe ; soeda taro ; bertarohan ; bertelor.
Layer	Tatakan ; fondament.
Layman	Orang jang bekerdja menjemben.
Lazar	Orang jang dapet sakit pest.
Lazy	Males.
Lead	Tima.
Lead	Toentoen ; pimpin.
Leaf	Daon ; lembaran.

League	Persariketan ; oekoeran dari 3 paal.
Leak	Botjornja ; botjorin.
Leaky	Botjor.
Lean	Koeroes ; isi jang zonder minjak atawa gemoek.
Leap	Lompat atawa lontjat.
Learn	Beladjar ; dapet denger
Lease	Sewaken.
Leasehold	Harta banda jang disewaken.
Leash	Koempoelan ; kawanan.
Least	Paling sedikit ; paling ketjil.
Leather	Koelit mateng.
Leave	Kamerdikaän ; idjin ; verlof ; brenti ; tinggalken.
Leaven	Dek pranti bikin koewe ; taroin dek.
Lectern	Medja pranti batja boekoe.
Lecture	Lezing ; yan-swat ; pembitjaraän di hadepan orang banjak.
Ledge	Karang tergantoeng.
Ledger	Boekoe accounts ; boekoe peritoengan.
Lee	Melawan angin ; tempat melawan angin.
Leech	Linta.
Leek	Daon bawang.
Left	Kiri ; soeda tinggalin.
Leg	Kaki.
Legacy	Pengasihan dengen soeka sendiri ; boedel.
Legal	Menoeroet atoeran ; menoeroet wet ; sah.
Legate	Oetoesan ; wakil keradjaän.
Legend	Tjerita romance ; tjerita doeloe.
Legging	Iketan kaki.
Legible	Boleh dibatjah.
Legion	Koempoelan besar ; koempoelan soldadoe.
Legislate	Bikin wet.
Legislature	Kekwasaän besar dalem oeroesan pamerentahan.
Legitimate	Sah ; terlahir oleh istri kawin.

Leisure	Tempo sempet atawa menganggoer.
Lend	Kasi pindjem.
Length	Pandjangnja.
Lengthen	Bikin pandjang.
Lenient	Sabar; tiada bengis.
Lens	Katja api.
Leonine	Mempoenjai prilakoe sebagi singa.
Leper	Orang jang dapet sakit tay-ko.
Leprosy	Penjakit tay-ko.
Less	Koerang.
Lessee	Orang jang disewaken.
Lessen	Bikin koerang.
Lesson	Peladjaran.
Lest	Slempang; kwatir.
Let	Halangan; kasi; mari; sewaken; halangin.
Lethargy	Mengantoek; njenjak.
Letter	Soerat; letter; hoeroef.
Lettuce	Selada.
Level	Rata; bikin rata.
Lever	Palangan; angkat.
Levity	Kaentengannja.
Levy	Geraken; siapken.
Lewd	Kotor; berhati serong.
Liable	Teritoeng; terbilang.
Liar	Pendjoesta; pembohong.
Libel	Soerat jang menghinaken orang; hinaken.
Liberal	Rojaal; boros.
Liberality	Karojaalan; kaborosan; kabaean-hati.
Liberate	Lepas; kasi kamerdikaän.
Liberty	Kamerdikaän.
Library	Bibliotheek; gedong dalem mana ada disimpen boekoe-boekoe dan soerat-soerat kabar pranti dibatja oleh orang banjak.
License	Idjin; tanggoengan; akoe sah.
Licentious	Kotor; berhati serong.

Lick	Djilat.
Lie	Djoesta ; mendjoesta.
Lie	Reba.
Liege	Toean ; pembesar ; boleb dipertjaja.
Lien	Pemintaän jang sah.
Lieu	Tempat
Lieutenant	Luitenant ; satoe pangkat di bawa Kapitein.
Life	Djiwa ; pengidoepan.
Lifeless	Tiada berdjiwa atawa bernjawa ; mati.
Lift	Angkat.
Ligament	Band jang mengiket toelang.
Ligature	Pengiket ; barang jang mengiket.
Light	Trang ; enteng ; pasang.
Lighten	Bikin trang ; bikin enteng.
Lightly	Dengen enteng ; dengen trang ; dengen gesit.
Lightness	Sinar jang trang ; kaentengan.
Lightning	Kilap atawa kilat.
Like	Soeka ; sama ; seperti atawa sebagi ; brangkali.
Likelihood	Doegahan jang brangkali.
Likely	Brangkali ; roepa-roepanja.
Liken	Padoe.
Likeness	Portret ; gambar ; miripnja.
Likeness	Begitoepoen ; demikian djoega.
Liking	Soekahan.
Limb	Anggota toeboe ; tjabang ; pinggiran.
Limber	Lemes ; gampang dibikin bengkok.
Lime	Kapoer aloes ; djeroek tipis ; getain ; lengketin.
Limit	Wates ; watesin.
Limitation	Watesnja.
Limp	Djalan pintjang-pintjang.
Limpid	Bening ; trang.
Line	Benang ; garisan ; derekan ; lapisin ; derekin.
Lineage	Lombahan ; toeroenan.

Lineal	Lineal ; kajoe pranti menggeret garisan sama garisannja ; sama pandjangnja.
Lineament	Roman ; aer moerka.
Linen	Kaen linen ; terbikin dari linen.
Linger	Seleder ; berlambat.
Link	Kantjing manchet ; samboengan ; samboeng.
Lion	Singa.
Lip	Bibir.
Liquefy	Bikin djadi aer.
Liquid	Barang beraer.
Liquidate	Bikin slese ; bikin bersi.
Liquor	Minoeman.
Lisp	Bitjara tiada terang atawa teges ; bitjara dengen pelo ; kapeloan.
List	Lijst ; tjatetan ; tjatet.
Listen	Denger.
Listless	Tiada bisa diam ; tiada perhatiken.
Literil	Menoeroet soerat ; berhoeboeng dengen soerat.
Literature	Peladjaran soerat ; boen-hak.
Lithe	Lemes ; gampang dieloek atawa dibengkokin.
Lithograph	Cliche ; tjitakan gambar dari zink atawa batoe.
Lithography	Ilmoe membikin cliche atawa tjitakan dari zink atawa batoe,
Litigation	Perbantahan dalem wet ; dakwaän.
Litigious	Soeka berbantah ; soeka mendakwa ; soeka tjari perkara.
Litter	Barang jang gampang di goeloeng ; peranakan babi ; barang boewangan ; sebar.
Little	Ketjil ; sedikit.
Littoral	Termasoek dalem bilangan daratan.
Live	Hidoep ; tinggal.
Lively	Gesit ; sebat.
Liver	Djatoeng hati.
Livery	Pakean jongos.

Livid	Bewarna seperti tima ; bewarna poetjet.
Living	Pengidoepan ; jang hidoep.
Lizard	Tjetjek ; kadal.
Lo	Tengok ! liatlah !
Load	Moewatan ; tanggoengan.
Loadstone	Besi-brani.
Loaf	Potongan roti.
Loam	Tana lempoeng.
Loan	Pindjeman.
Loath	Tiada ingin ; tiada soedi.
Loathe	Bentji dengen sanget.
Loathsome	Membentji-in ; bikin orang djadi bentji atawa gedek.
Lobby	Gang dari pertengahan roema.
Lobe	Bagian dari peparoe atawa koeping.
Lobster	Oedang besar ; oedang pantjet.
Local	Termasoek dalem bilangan tempat.
Locality	Tempat ; letaknja.
Loch	Tasik ; tangan laoet.
Lock	Koentji ; koentji-in ; gompiokan ramboet ; moeloet soengei.
Locket	Peti atawa dos pranti simpen ramboet.
Locomotion	Keadaän bergerak.
Locomotive	Kepala kreta api, stoöm-tram dan sebaginja,
Lodge	Roema menginep , menginep.
Lodging	Tempat tinggal boeat samentara waktoe.
Loft	Kamar pranti simpen barang.
Lofty	Tinggi ; sombong.
Log	Balok ; daja boeat oekoer djalanan kapal.
Logic	Ilmoe meroending ; loen-li-hak.
Loin	Bebokong.
Loiter	Seleder ; berlambat.
Lonely	Sepi ; soenji.
Long	Pandjang ; lama ; kepingin.
Longing	Kapinginan atawa kainginan jang heibat.
Longitude	Djaoenja antara Timoer dan Barat.

Look	Roman ; pengliatan ; liat ; tengok.
Looking-glass	Katja-moeka ; tjermin.
Loom	Perkakas menenoen.
Loop	Koeping ; mata ; lobang.
Loose	Longgar ; tiada teriket.
Lop	Potong ; tabas.
Loquacious	Dikasi omong teroes.
Lord	Toean ; orang bangsawan agoeng ; Toehan Allah.
Lordly	Agoeng.
Lordship	Gelaran dari satoe **Lord.**
Lorn	Soenji ; ditinggalken saorang diri.
Lose	Ilang ; kala.
Loss	Kailangan ; karoegian ; kakalahan.
Lot	Bagian ; bagi ; banjak ; peroentoengan.
Lotion	Aer wangi ; aer ramboet.
Lottery	Lotery ; pengadoean oentoeng.
Loud	Kentjeng ; bersoeara keras.
Loudness	Soeara jang kentjeng atawa keras.
Lough	Tasik.
Lounge	Tempat jang enak ; ilangken tempo dengen menganggoer.
Lout	Orang kate jang djelek.
Love	Katjintahan ; tjinta.
Lovely	Bagoes ; tjakap ; tjantik.
Lover	Orang jang menjinta ; katjintahan.
Loving	Jang tertjinta ; jang terkasehi.
Low	Renda ; tiada tinggi ; pendek ; kate ; ber-boenji sebagi sampi.
Lower	Kasi toeroen ; toeroenin.
Lower	Mendjadi gelap ; menakoetin.
Lowermost	Paling renda ; paling dalem.
Lowliness	Tabiat jang tiada soeka mengagoengken diri.
Lowly	Renda ; hina.
Loyal	Setia ; tiong.
Loyalty	Kasetiaän ; tiong-sin.

Lozenge	Daging manis ; kembang-goela.
Lubricate	Minjakin ; taroin minjak.
Lucid	Terang ; tegas.
Luck	Peroentoengan ; nasib.
Lucky	Beroentoeng ; bernasib bagoes.
Lucrative	Boleh djadi oentoeng ; mengoentoengin.
Lncre	Kaoentoengan.
Ludicrous	Tertawa dengen maksoed menghinaken.
Luff	Balikin ka hadepan angin.
Luggage	Bagage ; barang bawahan atawa bekelan.
Lugger	Kapal dengen 3 tiang.
Lukewarm	Anget.
Lull	Diam ; pendiam.
Lumbago	Sakit pingang.
Lumbar	Dari bebokong.
Lumber	Kajoe ; barang jang tiada bergoena.
Luminary	Barang atawa pekakas jang mengasi penerangan.
Luminious	Terang ; gilang-goemilang.
Lump	Potongan ketjil.
Lunacy	Koerang ingetan.
Lunar	Berhoeboeng dengen remboelan.
Lunatic	Orang gila ; gila.
Lunch	Makanan jang tiada mengenjangin.
Lung	Peparoe.
Lunge	Toesoek dengen pedang.
Lurch	Gojangnja kapal ; keadaän atawa tempat jang soetji ; gojang atawa glindingin.
Lure	Oempan ; oempanin ; boedjoek.
Lurid	Gelap ; petang.
Lurk	Reba tersemboeni.
Luscious	Manis rasanja.
Lust	Napsoe birahi ; bernapsoe.
Lustre	Warna jang mengkilap.
Lustrous	Mengkilap atawa berkilat ; mengkredep.
Lusty	Gemoek ; sehat.

Luxuriance	Toemboehan jang sarat ; banjak dan senang.
Luxuriate	Toemboe dengen sarat ; liwatin hari dengen memboros ; katjelep.
Luxury	Karojaalan ; penghidoepan jang boros.
Lying	Berdjoesta ; djoesta.
Lymph	Geta dalem toeboe machloek.
Lyre	Terengteng ; perabot muziek jang pake tali.
Lyric	Lagoe jang dinjanji'in menoeroet soearanja terengteng ; termasoek dalem pembilangan terengteng atawa perabot muziek jang pake tali.

M.

Ma'am	Njonja ; hoedjin ; ringkesnja dari perkataän *Madam*.
Mab	Radja dari dewi.
Mac	Anak lelaki.
Macaroni	Macaroni ; so-oen besar ; orang bodo ; barang tjampoeran.
Macaroon	Koewe ketjil ; orang jang lantjang.
Mace	Roejoeng ; bendera ; kabesaran ; leng-ki ; boenoe.
Macerate	Bikin kisoet ; tjelep.
Machine	Masin ; pekakas.
Mad	Gila ; edan,
Madam	Njonja ; hoedjin ; pribahasa boeat orang prempoean.
Madden	Bikin gila.
Madly	Dengen tjara gila.
Madness	Kagilaän ; kaedanan,
Magazine	Goedang obat ; soerat kabar jang didjilid djadi boekoe.
Maggot	Belatoeng,
Magic	Soenglap ; ilmoe setan,

Magician	Toekang soenglap.
Magistrate	Hakim.
Magnanimous	Besar pikiran.
Magnet	Besi-brani.
Magniricence	Kabagoesan ; katjakapan.
Magnificent	Bagoes ; tjakap.
Magnify	Bikin besar.
Magnifying-glass	Keker pranti bikin besar barang ; microscoop.
Magnitude	Besarnja, lebarnja, dan pandjangnja.
Mahogany	Samatjem kajoe jang koewat dari tana Centraal Amerika.
Maid	Gadis ; anak prawan ; boedjang prempoean atawa baboe.
Maiden	Gadis ; anak prawan ; seger ; belon dipake.
Mail	Pakean prang ; pembawahan post.
Main	Laoetan besar ; oetama.
Mainland	Binoewa.
Mainly	Teroetama.
Maintain	Toendjang ; djaga.
Maintainance	Daja boeat menoendjang.
Maize	Djagoeng.
Majestic	Angker ; agoeng.
Majesty	Kaängkeran ; kaägoengan.
Major	Majoor ; officier di sebla atas dari Kapitein; lebi besar.
Majority	Sabagian besar ; sampe oemoer.
Make	Pembikinan ; roman ; bikin ; paksa ; soeroe.
Malady	Penjakit.
Malaria	Demem malaria.
Male	Lelaki.
Malediction	Koetoekan.
Malefactor	Pemboenoe ; penghianat.
Malice	Kabentjian atawa kedengkian di dalem hati.
Malicous	Dengki ; djoedes.
Malign	Djahat ; tiada baek ; dengki ; bikin tjilaka.

Malignant	Soeka bikin tjilaka orang ; djoedes.
Mallet	Martil ketjil.
Malt	Tape.
Maltreat	Berboewat djahat ; maki.
Mammal	Binatang jang soesoein anaknja.
Mammon	Kekajahan.
Man	Orang ; manoesia : lengkepin dengen orang.
Manage	Atoer ; berdaja ; gantiken.
Management	Atoeran ; daja ; gantihan.
Manager	Agent ; peminpin.
Mandate	Mahloemat ; firman.
Mandolin	Mandoline ; pekakas muziek sebagi kton-tjong.
Mane	Soeri koeda atawa singa.
Manful	Brani ; berhati besar.
Mange	Penjakit bisoel dari heiwan.
Manger	Bak pranti taro makanan heiwan.
Mangle	Masin boeat bikin litjin kaen lenen ; potong robek ; bikin litjin kaen linen.
Manhood	Dewasa ; keadaän soeda djadi orang.
Mania	Kagenitan,
Maniac	Orang edan atawa gila.
Manifest	Teges ; terann ; njata ; hoendjoek ; bikin terang.
Manisfesto	Ketrangan ; pemberitaän.
Manifold	Banjak.
Maniple	Sagengeman tangan ; koempoelan soldadoe.
Mankind	Bangsa menoesia.
Manly	Djadi orang ; brani.
Manner	Atoeran ; djalanan.
Manners	Aadat-istiadat; atoeran.
Manoeuvre	Gerakan ; tipoe-daja ; permaenan perang-prangan.
Mansion	Gedong ; roemah besar-
Manslaughter	Pemboenoehan orang.
Mantel	Kous gas.

Mantle	Mantel ; badjoe orang prempoean.
Manual	Boekoe ketjil ; dikerdjaken dengen tangan,
Manufactory	Fabriek ; tempat bikin barang-barang.
Manufacture	Pembikinan barang-barang; bikin barang-barang.
Manure	Boemboe boeat bikin gemoek tana; bikin gemoek tana.
Manuscript	Toelisan.
Many	Banjak.
Map	Peta boemi.
Marauder	Penghianat.
Marble	Batoe Marmer; goendoe; 'terbikin dari marmer.
March	Djalannja soldadoe; boelan katiga dari taon kalender atawa Yang-lek Sha-gwe; djalan berbaris.
Mare	Koeda prempoean.
Margin	Pinggiran ; wates.
Marine	Marine ; matros kapal ; pasoekan laoet termasoek dalem bilangan laoet.
Mariner	Matros.
Maritime	Berhoeboeng dengen laoet.
Mark	Tanda ; tjap ; boelan-boelan ; tandain ; tjap.
Market	Pasar.
Marksman	Toekang tembak jang gapé.
Marmalade	Manisan.
Marriage	Nikahan ; kawinan.
Marriageable	Boleh dikawinin ; sampe oemoer koeat dikasi kawin.
Marrow	Soemsoem.
Marry	Nika ; kawin.
Marsh	Tempat bèlok ; tempat loempoer.
Marshal	Maarschalk ; atoer.
Marshy	Basa ; bèlok ; penoe loempoer.
Martial	Sebagi soldadoe ; militair.
Martyr	Orang jang brani korbanken djiwanja boeat perkara jang baek.

Martyrdom	Kematiannja satoe orang jang brani korbanken djiwanja boeat perkara jang baek.
Marvel	Heran ; kaheranan.
Marvellous	Heran ; adjaib.
Masculine	Lelaki ; termasoek dalem fihak lelaki
Mash	Makanan jang panas.
Mask	Kedok ; topeng; pake kedok ; pake topeng
Mason	Toekang batoe.
Mass	Goemploekan ; potongan besar.
Massacre	Pemboenoehan.
Massive	Besar ; belongkotan·
Mast	Tiang kapal ; boea dari poehoen *beech* atawa *oak*.
Master	Toean ; madjikan ; tauw-kee; goeroe ; prenta.; oeroesin.
Masterpiece	Pakerdjahan jang paling baek.
Masticate	Koenja atawa mama ; njanjal ; papak.
Mat	Tiker ; oelat sebagi tiker.
Matador	Toekang adoe banteng.
Match	Pertandingan; nikahan; geretan atawa kajoe api ; pasangin ; bikin sembabat ; adoe.
Matchless	Tiada ada saingannja.
Mate	Temen ; officier di atas kapal.
Material	Boemboe ; perloe.
Maternal	Berhoeboeng dengen iboe atawa mah.
Maternity	Sanak-soedara dari iboe.
Mathemetics	Ilmoe itoeng.
Matrimony	Nikahan ; perkawinan.
Matron	Iboe dari satoe familie atawa kaoem kaloe-warga ; baboe.
Matter	Barang ; nana ; sebab ; kenapa ; bikin terang.
Mattress	Bulzak ; djok.
Mature	Dewasa ; sampe besar ; mateng ; tamatken. bikin mateng.
Maturity	Kamatengan ; katjoekoepan.

Maxim	Mitsal pepata ; peribahasa.
Maximum	Djoembla jang paling besar atawa tinggi.
May	Boelan ka lima ; Yang-Iek Go-gwee ; boleh ; di-idjinken.
Mayor	Hakim besar dari satoe kota.
Me	Saja ; akoe (dipake di boentoet omongan).
Meadow	Lapangan ; padang.
Meagre	Koeroes ; miskin.
Meal	Makanan.
Mean	Itoengan poeeoel rata ; pelit ; djahat ; hina ; maksoedken ; trangin.
Meaning	Maksoed ; ketrangan.
Meanness	Kedjahatan ; kehinaän;
Means	Djalan ; oewang penghidoepan.
Measure	Oekoeran ; oekoer.
Measurement	Oekoeran, oepama, lebar, tinggi, dan besarnja satoe barang.
Meat	Daging,
Mechanic	Toekang bekerdja.
Mechanical	Berhoeboeng dengan masin atawa pekakas.
Mechanics	Ilmoe peladjaran masin.
Medal	Medaille; bintang kahormatan.
Meddle	Ganggoe ; oesil.
Mediaeval	Dari abad pertengahan.
Mediate	Jang tiada berfihak ka sana-sini ; bikin dami.
Mediation	Keadaän tiada berfihak ka sana-sini ; pembikinan dami.
Mediator	Orang jang tiada berfihak ka sana-sini ; toekang bikin dami.
Medical	Berhoeboeng dengen obat--obatan.
Medicine	Obat.
Meditate	Pikir.
Medium	Peranteran ; djalan ; sedeng (tiada besar tiada ketjil).
Meek	Lema-lemboet ; baek.
Meekness	Tabeat jang lema-lemboet.

Meet	Pertandingan; pertemoehan; satoedjoe; bertemoe.
Meeting	Pertemoehan; perhimpoenan; vergadering.
Melancholy	Kadoekaän; kakeselan; doeka; kesel.
Mellow	Mateng; bikin mateng.
Melodrama	Pertoendjoekan di atas panggoeng.
Melody	Lagoe; bagian soeara tinggi dalem njanjian.
Melt	Loemer.
Member	Anggota; kaki-tangan; tjabang poehoen.
Membrane	Koelit tipis.
Memoir	Tjatetan dari penghidoepan.
Memorable	Haroes dibikin peringetan.
Memorandum	Tjatetan; peringetan.
Memorial	Tjatetan; peringetan; jang haroes ditjatet atawa dibikin peringetan,
Memory	Ingetan; pikiran.
Menace	Autjeman; antjem.
Menagerie	Koempoelan binatang boewas.
Mend	Betoelin; bikin betoel.
Mendacity	Kapalsoean; kadjoestaän.
Mendicant	Pengemis; toekang minta-minta.
Menial	Boedjang; termasoek dalem bilangan boedjang.
Mensuration	Ilmoe mengoekoer.
Mental	Pikiran poenja.
Mention	Seboetan; seboet; kata.
Mercantile	Berhoeboeng dengen dagangan.
Mercenary	Orang atawa soldadoe jang bekerdja dengen gadji; temaha; sekaker.
Mercer	Toekang djoewal barang-barang dari soetra.
Merchandise	Barang-barang klontong.
Merchant	Soedagar.
Merchantman	Kapal dagang.
Merciful	Mempoenjai hati kesian.
Mercury	Aer perak.
Mercy	Pengrasaän kesian; maäf; kaämpoenan.

Mere	Empang ketjil ; tjoema ; sadja.
Merge	Tenggelem ; ilang dalem aer.
Meridian	Tengahari ; boenderan jang di liwatin oleh mata-hari pada waktoe tengahari.
Mernio	**Kambing** Blanda.
Merit	Kahargaän ; kaharoesan ; haroes.
Meritious	Haroesnja begitoe.
Merriment	Kasenangan ; kagoembirahan.
Merry	Girang ; goembira.
Mess	Makanan ; temen-makan ; makan sama-sama.
Message	Perhoeboengan ; kabaran ; soeroehan.
Messenger	Orang soeroehan ; pembawa kabar.
Metal	Logam seperti emas, perak, besi, tembaga dan sebagainja.
Metallic	Termasoek dalem bilangan logam.
Mete	Oekoer.
Meter, metre	Oekoeran dari satoe meter atawa 100 centi-meter.
Method	Atoeran ; djalanan.
Metropolis	Iboe-kota ; kota besar.
Mettle	Kabranihan ; kagagahan.
Mew	Soeara koetjing ; berboenji sebagi koetjing ; ditoetoep dalem koeroengan.
Mews	Tempat berentinja kreta dan koeda.
Microscope	Microscoop ; katja api.
Mid	Di tenga-tenganja ; antaranja.
Middle	Tenga-tenganja ; antaranja.
Midst	Tengattenganja ; antaranja.
Midwife	Doekoen beranak.
Mien	Roman di loear.
Might	Kakoewatan ; tenaga ; boleh.
Mighty	Koewat ; bertenaga.
Mifrate	Pinda dari satoe ka laen negri.
Mikado	Keizer Japan.
Milch	Bisa mengeloearken soesoe.
Mild	Baek ; lema lemboet.

Mildew	Sekohan ; boeloekan.
Mildness	Kabaean ; kalema-lemboetan.
Mile	Paal ; li ; 1760 ijards.
Militant	Berada dalem oeroesan prang.
Military	Soldadoe ; militair ; seperti soldadoe atawa orang peprangan.
Militia	Soldadoe jang terdiri dari anak-rahajat
Milk	Soesoe ; peres soesoe.
Mill	pengilingan.
Miller	Toekang pengilingan.
Millet	Gandoem ; trigoe.
Milliner	Toekang bikin topi orang prempoean.
Million	Millioen ; 1000000.
Milt	Telor ikan ; troeboek.
Mimic	Toekang adjok-adjokin orang ; adjok-adjok-kin.
Mince	Potong ketjil-ketjil.
Mind	Pikiran ; kamaoehan ; perdoeli ; perhatiken.
Minded	Berpikiran ; beringin.
Mindful	Berati-ati.
Mine	Parit ; gali ; saja poenja.
Miner	Toekang gali parit.
Mineral	Barang atawa logam jang terdapet di parit ; berhoeboeng dengan parit.
Mineralogy	Ilmoe peladjaran parit.
Mingle	Tjampoer.
Minium	Nomor jang paling sedikit.
Minister	Boedjang ; Minister dari negri ; wesio atawa padri ; kasi.
Ministry	Kantoor ; departement ; pakerdjahan padri ; koempoelan minister-minister.
Minor	Orang di bawa oemoer 21 taon ; koerang ; lebi ketjil.
Minority	Tempo dari hari kelahiran hingga beroe-moer 21 taon ; djoembla jang lebi ketjil atawa koerang.

Minstrel	Toekang musiek ; toekang njanji.
Mint	Fabriek oewang ; tempat tjitak · oewang ; tjitak oewang.
Minuet	Dansa ; tandakan.
Minute	Minuut atawa menit ; tjatetan ; tjatet ; ketjil.
Miracle	Kaädjaiban ; kaheranan.
Miraculous	Jang tiada bisa diperboeat oleh menoesia.
Mirage	Bajangan.
Mire	Loempoer.
Mirror	Katja-moeka ; tjermin.
Mirth	Kagirangan ; kaentengan hati.
Misapply	Pake ; sala.
Misapprehend	Sala. artiken.
Misapprehension	Artian jang sala ; kesalaän.
Misbehaviour	Pri lakoe jang djelek.
Miscarriage	Kasialan ; perdjalanan jang tiada baek.
Miscarry	Bikin sial atawa sala.
Miscellaneous	Tjampoer-tjampoer.
Miscellany	Tjampoeran ; boekoe dari roepa-roepa karangan.
Mischance	Kasialan.
Mischief	Kadjinakaän ; loeka ; berbahaja.
Mischievous	Djinaka ; berbahaja.
Misconduct	Prilakoe jang djelek atawa tiada senoenoe.
Miscreant	Orang jang tiada haroes dikesiani orang
Misdeed	Perboewatan jang tiada baek atawa tiada halal.
Misdemeanour	Dosa enteng.
Miser	Orang pelit ; orang tai idoeng-asin.
Miserable	Bersengsara.
Misery	Kasengsaraän.
Misfortune	Kasialan.
Misgiving	Katjoerigaän ; kasangsian.
Mishap	Kasialan.
Misinform	Kasi kabar sala.

Mislead	Toentoen ka djalan sala; bikin djadi kliroe.
Misogyny	Kabentjian pada orang prampoean.
Miss	Nona; gelaran bagi orang prampoean jang belon menika; sala; bilang.
Missing	Kailangan; kasalaän,
Mission	Soëroehan; kiriman koempoelan zendeling.
Missionary	Zendeling; orang jang dikirim boeat siarken agama.
Misstatement	Pembritaän jang sala.
Mist	Halimoen; pedoet.
Mistake	Kesalaän; bikin sala.
Misletoe	Pasilan poehoen.
Mistress	Nona; njonja-roema.
Mistrust	Sangkahan; katjoerigaän
Mistrustful	Bertjoeriga; mempoenjai hati jang tjoeriga.
Misty	Penoe halimoen atawa pedoet.
Misunderstand	Sala mengarti.
Misuse	Sala pake; rawat tiada baek.
Mite	Koetoe ketjil; oewang.
Mitre	Topi atawa kopianja bisschop atawa padri kepala.
Mitigate	Toeroenin; bikin rata.
Mitton	Saroeng tangan.
Mix	Tjampoer.
Mixture	Tjampoeran.
Moan	Menggroetoe; bersoesa hati.
Moat	Solokan.
Mob	Koempoelan orang jang riboet; kroeboetin.
Mock	Palsoe; lewein atawa djengekin.
Mockery	Lewean atawa djengekan.
Mode	Atoeran; roman; Kwan-sit atawa model.
Model	Model; tjonto; bikin model atawa kwan-sit.
Moderate	Sedeng; toe-ho bikin dingin; bikin koerang.
Moderation	Kasedengan; katoe-ho-an.
Modern	Matjem baroe.
Modest	Taöe adat; hormat,

Modesty	Prilakoe jang taoe adat atawa hormat.
Modify	Trangin maksoednja ; toekar.
Mohair	Kaen mohair.
Moiety	Satenganja.
Moist	Semek atawa demek ; basa.
Moisten	Bikin semek atawa demek ; bikin basa.
Moisture	Kasemekan atawa kademekan; aer
Mole	Tai-lajar ; toetoel.
Molest	Ganggoe ; tjah-nauw ; oesil.
Molestation	Ganggoean ; oesilan.
Mollity	Bikin lembek ; bikin diging ; bikin akoer.
Moment	Tempo ; kedjadian.
Momentous	Perloe ada sangkoetan.
Monarch	Radja.
Monarchy	Keradjaän.
Monastery	Klenteng paranti tempat tinggal weshio atawa padri.
Monetary	Berhoeboeng dengen oewang.
Money	Oewang ; doewit.
Monitor	Moerid jang bisa bri bantoean pada goeroenja ; kapal meriam.
Monk	Wesio atawa padri.
Monkey	Monjet.
Monopoly	Monodolie ; hak boeat djoewal atawa berniaga sendiri.
Monosyllable	Perkataän dari satoe seboetan atawa soeara batjaän.
Monotony	Kasamaän ; kamiripan.
Monster	Binatang besar ; orang kedjem.
Monstrous	Adjaib ; gaib ; boekan terdjadi dengen maoenja Allah.
Month	Boelan dari almanak.
Monument	Batoe peringetan.
Mood	Adat ; tabiat.
Moody	Bawel ; bo-sioh.
Moon	Boelan di langit ; remboelan

Moor	Tana jang tiada dipake ; bangsa Moor dari Afrika Oetara ; bikin brenti praoe jang berdjalan.
Moot	Boleh dibantah ; berbantahan.
Mop	Rakbol ; bikin bersi dengen rakbol,
Mope	Tiada mempoenjai kegesitan ; gelap ; kesel
Moral	Pri-boedi kebedjikan ; to-tek ; betoel.
Morality	Pri-boedi kebedjikan ; to-tek.
Morals	Jakinan tentang kewadjiban menoesia.
Morass	Tempat loempoer.
Morbid	Tiada sehat ; tiada seger.
More	Lebi banjak ; lebi.
Moreover	Lebi djaoe.
Morning	Pagi.
Morphia	Morphine ; tai madat.
Morrow	Esok harinja ; kabesokannja.
Morsel	Keping-keping ketjil.
Mortal	Machloek jang moesti mati ; moesti mati ; bakal mati ; membikin kematian.
Mortality	Keadaän jang moesti atawa bakal mati.
Mortar	Mortier ; loempang ; meriam pendek.
Mortgage	Tanggoengan.
Mortuary	Roema orang mati ; tempat koeboeran.
Mosquito	Njamoek.
Most	Paling banjak ; paling.
Mostly	Kabanjakan ; sebagian besar.
Mote	Antjoeran ; boeboek.
Moth	Samatjem koepoe-koepoe.
Mother	Mah ; iboe ; tana aer.
Motion	Bergerakan ; voorstelan.
Motive	Boedjoekan ; bikin bergerak.
Motor	Motor ; kreta motor.
Motorist	Orang jang menoenggang motor
Motto	Pribahasa ; mitsal ; omongan pendek.
Mould	Tana lempoeng ; tjitakan.
Mound	Gili-gili.

Mount	Boekit ; bangoen ; naek koeda.
Mountain	Goenoeng.
Mountainous	Banjak goenoeng ; penoe goenoeng.
Mourn	Berdoeka ; bersoesa hati.
Mournful	Penoe doeka.
Mourning	Kadoekahan ; kasoesaän hati ; berkaboeng atawa twaha.
Mouse	Tikoes.
Moustache	Koemis.
Mouth	Moeloet.
Movable	Boleh digerakin ; voorstel.
Movement	Gerakan ; pindahan tempat.
Mow	Potong roempoet.
Much	Banjak.
Mucus	Ingoes.
Mud	Loempoer.
Muff	Saroeng tangan ; orang jang djelek.
Muffin	Koewe-boeloe.
Muffle	Boengkoes.
Mug	Tjangkir ; thee-auw.
Mulatto	Peranakan dari bangsa item dan poeti.
Mule	Kalde ; peranakan dari kalde dan koeda.
Mulish	Bandel ; berkepala batoe ; sebagi kalde.
Multiplication	Itoengan kali atawa poekoel.
Multiply	Kali ; poekoel, (itoengan).
Multitude	Koempoelan orang.
Mumble	Koenja ; papak ; mama.
Mummer	Anak komedi.
Mummery	Pertoendjoekan komedi ; wajang wong.
Mummy	Mait jang soeda ditaroin obat.
Munch	Mama ; papak ; koenja.
Mundane	Dari ini doenia.
Municipal	Berhoeboeng dengen kota.
Munificence	Karojaalan.
Munificent	Rojaal.
Munition	Pendjagaän.

Murder	Pemboenoehan ; boenoeh.
Murderer	Pemboenoe ; orang jang memboenoe
Murky	Gelap petang.
Murmur	Soeara menggroetoe atawa menjomel ; meng-groetoe atawa menjomel ; menggrendeng.
Murrain	Penjakit heiwan.
Muscle	Oerat daging.
Muscular	Beroerat daging ; koewat.
Museum	Gedong artja ; gedong tempat simpen ba-rang-barang koenoe, adjaib dan sebaginja.
Mushroom	Djamoer.
Music	Musiek ; tetaboean.
Musk	Binatang ; wadas ; tetaneman.
Musket	Senapan ; sendjata api.
Muslin	Kaen muslin atawa mousseline.
Mussel	Kiong ; kerang.
Must	Pati atawa aer boea anggoer jang baroe diperes atawa ditoemboek ; moesti.
Muster	Permaenan baris dari soldadoe ; berkoempoel.
Musty	Sekohan ; basi.
Mutation	Toekaran.
Mute	Orang bisoe atawa gagoe ; diam ; tiada bersoeara.
Mutilate	Beset ; antjoerken.
Mutinous	Membikin hoeroe-hara.
Mutiny	Hoeroe hara.
Mutter	Omong dengen swara pelahan.
Mutton	Daging kambing.
Mutual	Satjara persobatan ; rapet.
Muzzle	Moeloet jang bertjotjot.
My	Saja poenja
Myriad	Koempoelan ; kawanan.
Mysterious	Tersemoeni ; terpegang resia.
Mystery	Resia ; barang jang tersemoeni.
Mythology	Kadjoesta'an tjerita kadongengan.
Mythoplasm	Dongeng ; tjerita djoesta atawa karangan.

N.

Nadir	Sorga jang letaknja di bawa boemi.
Nail	Koekoe ; pakoe ; 2¼ duim ; pakoein.
Nag	Koeda ketjil ; teroes memaki.
Naked	Telandjang ; zonder pakean.
Name	Nama ; gelaran ; namaken.
Namely	Jaitoe ; jalah.
Nap	Tidoer sabentaran ; wool jang pendek di atas kaen.
Nape	Tengkok leher.
Napkin	Serbeta.
Narrate	Tjeritaken ; bilang.
Narrative .	Tjerita pendek,
Narrow	Sempit ; tiada lebar.
Nasty	Mesoem ; djorok.
Nation	Bangsa ; rahajat negri.
National	Termasoek dalem bilangan bangsa atawa rahajat negri ; bangsa atawa rahajat negri poenja.
Native	Boemipoetra ; anak peranakan.
Natural	Dikaloearken atawa didjadiken oleh alam ; thian-djian.
Naturalise	Mendapet hak sama rata seperti rahajat dari negri dimana kita menoempang,
Nature	Alam ; adat.
Naught	Tiada apa-apa ; djelek.
Naughty	Nakal ; djahat.
Nausea	Enak ; penjakit maoe moenta.
Nautical	Berhoeboeng dengen kapal atawa laoet.
Naval	Termasoek dalem bilangan kapal.
Nave	Tenganja roda ; badannja gredja,
Navel	Poeser.
Navigate	Kemoedi-in kapal atawa praoe ; belajar,

Navigation	Ilmoe boeat kemoedi-in atawa kasi djalan kapal.
Navvy	Orang jang bekerdja di nataran
Navy	Pasoekan kapal prang.
Nay	Tiada ; boekan.
Near	Deket.
Nearly	Mendeketin ; ampir,
Neat	Netjis ; bersi.
Neatness	Kanetjisan ; kabersian.
Necessary	Perloe
Necessity	Kaperloean.
Neck	Leher.
Need	Kaperloean ; kamaoehan ; kasoesaän ; perloe ; maoe.
Needful	Perloe.
Needle	Djaroem.
Needy	Miskin ; sengsara.
Negative	Perkataän jang menjataken kamoengkiran.
Neglect	Kateledoran ; teledorin ; tiada perhatiken.
Negligence	Adat jang bisa teledor atawa tiada soeka perhatiken.
Negligent	Teledor ; tiada soeka perhatiken,
Negotiate	Oeroes ; bitjarain.
Negotiation	Oeroesan ; pembitjaraän.
Negro	Orang bangsa Niger ; orang item.
Neigh	Soeara atawa boenjinja koeda.
Neighbour	Tetangga.
Neither	Tiada satoe atawa laen dari doea.
Nephew	Neef; tjoe-tjoe dari soedara.
Nerve	Oerat ; zeniuw.
Nervous	Ketakoetan ; sakit zeniuwachtig.
Ness	Idoeng ; tandjoeng.
Nest	Sarang boeroeng.
Nestling	Anak boeroeng.
Net	Djala.
Nether	Reba di bawa.

Nettle	Saroepa tetaneman jang bidoeri.
Neuralgia	Sakit di oerat ; sakit kepala thauw-hong.
Neuter	Boekan ini atawa itoe ; tiada berdjiwa.
Neutral	Neutraal ; tiong-lip ; tiada berfihak ka sana sini.
Never	Tiada perna ; belon sakali.
Nevertheless	Begimana djoega.
New	Baroe ; seger.
Newness	Kabaroean ; kasegeran.
News	Kabar.
Next	Laen ; di sebla.
Nibble	Gigitan ketjil ; gigit sedikit-sedikit.
Nice	Enak ; bagoes.
Niche	Lobang di tembok.
Nick	Lobang ; oekiran ; setan aer.
Nickel	Nikkel ; tembaga poeti.
Niece	Tit-li tjoetjoe prempoean dari soedara ; nicht.
Niggard	Orang jang pelit ; pelit.
Nigger	Orang Niger ; boedak item.
Nigh	Deket ; ampir.
Night	Malem.
Nightly	Dengen itoeng malem ; pada waktoe malem.
Nightmare	Ngigo ; mengimpi jang heibat.
Nihilist	Orang kaoem Kekbeng atawa revolutie bangsa Rus.
Nimble	Sebat ; gesit.
Nip	Tjoebit ; tjingkong ; roesakin.
Nippers	Kakatoea ; pekakas pranti tjaboet pakoe.
Nipple	Pentil tete.
Nit	Telor koetoe,
No	Tiada ; boekan.
Nobility	Pembesar ; atceran memerenta.
Noble	Orang berpangkat ; pembesar ; gaga ; keren.
Nobleman	Orang berpangkat atawa mempoenjai gelaran ; pembesar ; orang bangsawan.

Nobleness	Kabesaran atawa kakerenannja pangkat,
Nobody	Tiada ada orang.
Nocturnal	Malem poenja ; pada waktoe malem.
Nocuous	Berbahaja,
Nod	Manggoet ; manggoetan.
Noise	Soeara riboet ; tersiar.
Noisome	Berbahaja.
Noisy	Riboet.
Nomad	Pelantjong ; toekang djalan.
Nominal	Nama sadja.
Nominate	Namaken ; voorstel
Nominative	Perkataän jang trangin orang atawa binatang jang melakoeken perboeatan.
Non	Perkataän tambahan jang bermaksoed *tida*.
None	Tiada ada.
Nonplus	Bingoeng.
Nonsense	Djoesta ; bohong.
Nook	Peloksok atawa pepodjok.
Noon	Tengahari ; djam 12 tengahari.
Nor	Perkataän jang menjataken kamoengkiran.
North	Oetara ; kaler , Lor.
Nothern	Mengadep djoeroesan Oetara ; djoeroesan Oetara poenja.
Nose	Idoeng.
Nosegay	Rentjengan kembang
Nostril	Lobang idoeng.
Not	Tiada ; boekan.
Notable	Termashoer ; ternama ; kaseboet.
Notch	Lobang ; potongan.
Note	Noot ; ketrangan ; noot musiek ; tjatet ; liat.
Noted	Kaseboet ; termashoer.
Nothing	Tiada ada barang ; tiada apa-apa.
Notice	Pembrian taoe ; liat.
Notify	Bri taoe ; wartaken.
Notion	Pikiran.
Notorious	Termashoer ; terkenal.

Noun	Nama dari satoe orang, binatang atawa barang.
Nourish ·	Kasi makan ; oempanin.
Nourishment	Barang makanan.
Novel	Tjerita ; baroe.
Novelty	Kabaroean.
Novice	Orang jang baroe moelai beladjar.
Now	Sekarang ; pada ini waktoe.
Nude	Terlandjang boelet ; zonder berpakean.
Nudity	Ketelandjangan.
Nugget	Potongan dari mas.
Nuisance	Barang jang mengganggoe atawa sala.
Null	Tiada berhasil ; nul ; kosong.
Numb	Tiada mempoenjai pengrasaän ; bikin mati.
Number	Nummer atawa angka ; djoembla; reken atawa itoeng.
Numeral	Terbilang dalem nummer ; nummer poenja
Numeration	Bikin atawa kasi nummer.
Numerator	Nummer jang ada di atas garisan dalem itoengan *fraction*.
Numerous	Banjak.
Nun	Padri atawa wesio prempoean.
Nunnery	Tempat tinggalnja padri atawa wesio prempoean.
Nuptial	Kawinan ; nikahan ; termasoek dalem oeroesan kawin.
Nurse	Bahoe ; baboein.
Nursery	Kamar anak ketjil ; tana pranti tanem poehoen jang moeda.
Nurture	Pengadjaran jang baek ; kasi makan ; kasi peladjaran.
Nut	Boea kenari ; poeteran glenderan.
Nutriment	Jang bisa piara atawa bikin hidoep orang.
Nutrition	Barang makanan.
Nutritious	Bisa piara atawa bikin hidoep orang.
Nymph	Djin prempoean ; blatoeng koepoe-koepoe.

O.

Oaf	Orang bodo; orang goblok.
Oak	Poehoen *oak* sebagi disini poenja poehoen djadi.
Oasis	Tempat toemboe roempoet di tenga padang pasir.
Oar	Penggajoe.
Oat	Gandoem; beras Blanda.
Oath	Soempa.
Obedience	Hati jang menoeroet; adat jang maoe denger kata.
Obedient	Berhati menoeroet; beradat denger kata.
Obey	Menoeroet; denger kata.
Obituary	Tjatetan dari orang-orang jang meninggal doenia.
Object	Haloean; kamaoehan; barang jang keliatan.
Object	Bantah; protest.
Objection	Bantahan; protest
Obligation	Obligatie; kewadjiban; persariketan; bond.
Oblige	Paksa; trima kasi.
Obliging	Taoe adat; baek-boedi.
Oblong	Londjong; barang londjong.
Obscene	Kotor; tiada sopan.
Obscure	Gelap petang; semoeni.
Obscurity	Kagelapan; keadaän renda.
Observant	Hati-hati; soenggoe-soenggoe hati.
Observation	Perhatian; pengliatan; pemandangan.
Observe	Liat; pandang.
Obsolete	Liwat tanggal; tiada dipake lagi.
Obstacle	Tjegatan; tjegahan; barang atawa hal jang mengandangin.
Obstinate	Bandel; berkepala batoe.
Obstruct	Tjegat: tjega; ngandangin.
Obstruction	Tjegatan; tjegahan; barang atawa hal jang mengandangin.

Obtain	Dapet ; beroleh.
Obtuse	Poentoel ; tiada tadjem.
Obtuseness	Kapoentoelan.
Obverse	Moeka doewit.
Obvious	Terang ; gampang diliat,
Occasion	Sebab; alesan ; tempo ; kaperloean.
Ockasional	Tempo-tempo ; kadang-kadang.
Occupant	Orang jang menempatin.
Occupation	Pakerdjahan ; kapoenjaän
Occupy	Tempatin ; pake.
Occur	Terdjadi ; dateng dalem pikiran,
Occurence	Kedjadian.
Ocean	Laoetan besar.
Ocular	Berhoeboeng dengen mata.
Odd	Heran ; adjaib ; loear biasa.
Oddly	Dengen heran ; dengen adjaib ; dengen loewar biasa.
Ode-	Sairan jang pendek.
Odour	Baoe ; baoe jang wangi.
Of	Dari ; tentang hal.
Off	Pergi ; terpisa dari.
Offence	Kesalaän ; kedosahan.
Offend	Kasi sala.
Offensive	Bikin sala.
Offer	Voorstelen ; tawaran ; voorstel; kasi persen,
Offering	Sembajang ; sedekaän.
Office	Kewadjiban ; pakerdjaän ; kantoor.
Officer	Officier ; orang jang pegang pekerdjahan.
Official	Officier ; orang jang pegang djabatan ; dengen officiel atawa dengen sah.
Officiate	Djalanken kewadjiban.
Offset	Moentjoek.
Offspring	Anak tjoetjoe ; toeroenan.
Oft	Sring-sring ; sringkali.
Oil	Minjak ; gemoek ; minjakin.
Oily	Meminjak ; penoe gemoek.

Ointment	Zalf ; kojo.
Old	Toea ; lama.
Olden	Didjeman doeloe.
Olive	Kana.
Omen	Tanda ; alamat.
Omission	Kateledoran ; barang atawa soerat jang ka-tinggalan.
Omit	Tinggalken ; terledorin.
Omnipotent	Semoea berpengaroe.
Omniscient	Semoea taoe.
On	Di atas ; teroes.
Once	Satoe kali ; didjeman doeloe.
One	Satoe : satoe orang atawa barang.
Onion	Bawang.
Only	Tjoema ; sadja ; melaenken ; sakedar.
Onset	Labrakan.
Onward	Madjoe.
Opal	Saroepa batoe permata jang mempoenjai warna boenglon.
Open	Boeka ; troes-trang ; orang banjak.
Opening	Lobang ; permoelaän.
Openly	Dengen troes-trang ; dinjataken dihadepan orang banjak.
Operate	Lakoeken ; bikin berdjalan.
Operation	Pakerdjahan jang moesti dilakoeken ; operatie
Operative	Orang pakerdjahan ; bekerdja.
Opinion	Pikiran ; timbangan.
Opium	Tjandoe ; madat.
Opponent	Moesoe.
Opportune	Dikasi tempo jang baek.
Opportunity	Tempo jang baek.
Oppose	Bantah ; protest ; lawanan.
Opposite	Di sebrang ; contra.
Oppisition	Bantahan ; lawanan.
Oppress	Tindi ; tindes ; pidjit.
Oppression	Tindian ; tindesan ; pidjitan ; kedjagoan.

Oppressor	Djago ; orang jang menindi, menindes atawa memidjit.
Optics	Ilmoe peladjaran dari penerangan...
Option	Hak boeat memili.
Opulence	Harta banda ; kekajahan.
Or	Atawa ; kaloe tiada.
Orange	Djeroek ; warna koening djeroek.
Oration	Pembitjaraän atawa batjaän di hadepan orang banjak.
Orator	Orang jang pande bitjara.
Oratory	Ilmoe bitjara atawa omong.
Orb	Barang boender.
Orbit	Djalanan doenia atawa bintang.
Orchard	Kebon boeah-boeahan,
Ordain	Angkat ; benoemd.
Order	Prentahan ; ataoeran ; prenta.
Ordinance	Reglement ; atoeran.
Ordinary	Biasa.
Ordure	Kotoran ; nadjis.
Ore	Logam dari parit.
Organ	Orgel ; piano ; anggota.
Organic	Mempoenjai anggota.
Organize	Gerakan ; dapetken.
Oriental	Terbilangan sebla Timoer.
Orifice	Moeloet.
Origin	Permoelaän ; poko.
Original	Bermoela ; berpoko ; pertama kali ; mata aer.
Originate	Pertama kali dapetken.
Ornament	Periasan ; mas inten.
Orphan	Anak piatoe.
Orthography	Spellan atawa toelisan jang betoel.
Oscillate	Bergeter atawa bergoemeter,
Ostensible	Terang ; tegas.
Ostentation	Pertoendjoekan di loewar.
Osteology	Peladjaran prihal toelang.

Ostrich	Boeroeng kasoewari.
Other	Laen ; jang laen.
Otherwise	Sebaliknja ; kaloe tiada.
Ought	Patoet ; soeatoe barang.
Ounce	Satoe per doea-blas dari satoe pond ; ons.
Our	Kita orang poenja.
Out	Kaloear ; di loear.
Outcast	Pemboewangan.
Outer	Lebi loear
Outermost	Paling loear.
Outfit	Pakean.
Outlast	Tahan lebi lama dari.
Outlaw	Orang jang melanggar oendang-oendang. negri ; penghianat negri.
Outlay	Ongkos.
Outline	Geret ; garisan.
Outpost	Post di tempat djaoe.
Outrage	Mara ; goesar.
Outright	Dengen tjoekoep.
Outset	Permoelaän.
Outside	Loearnja ; di loear.
Outskirt	Wates negri.
Outstanding	Belon terbajar loenas.
Outward	Di loear.
Oval	Londjong ; beroman sebagi telor.
Oven	Dapoer besar.
Over	Di atas ; lebi ; liwat.
Overbearing	Sebagi djago.
Overcast	Pentjarin ; mendoeng.
Overcome	Kalaken ; poenaken.
Overflow	Lebi dari tjoekoep.
Overhaul	Preksa.
Overhead	Di atas kepala.
Overlay	Toetoep atasnja.
Overlook	Preksa ; maäfken.
Overseer	Mandoor ; kwasa.

Oversight	Kasalaän ; kateledoran.
Overt	Toendjoekan di hadepan orang banjak.
Overtake	Soesoel.
Overthrow	Djatonja ; kebinasaännja.
Overture	Voostelan ; musiek jang maen paling doeloe.
Overturn	Terbalik ; keleboe.
Overwhelm	Berkwasa besar ; terkoeroeng.
Owe	Oetang.
Owing	Sebab ; oleh kerna ; lantaran.
Own	Sendiri poenja ; akoe.
Owner	Jang poenja.
Ox	Sampi lelaki ; banteng.
Oxygen	Samatjem hawa gas jang bikin orang djadi hidoep.
Oyster	Tiram.
Ozone	Bagian ; petjahan dari hawa oedara jang mengoeroeng boemi.

P.

Pace	Tindakan ; itoeng dengen tindakan.
Pacific	Diam ; dami ; tedoe.
Pacify	Bikin dami.
Pack	Boengkoesan ; iket ; pak.
Package	Boengkoesan ; pakket.
Packet	Boengkoesan ketjil ; kapal.
Pact	Perdjandjian ; kontract.
Pad	Bantal jang rata.
Padding	Barang djedjelan.
Paddle	Pengajoe ; pedal sepeda ; dajoeng.
Paddock	Lapangan atawa padang ketjil ; kodok atawa anak kodok.
Padlock	Koentji slot.
Pagan	Orang jang memoedja-laen agama dari Kristen.

Page	Boedak; pengikoet; lembaran atawa katja boekoe; pagina.
Pageant	Pertoendjoekan jang inda.
Pagoda	Mertjoe.
Pail	Ember.
Pain	Sakit; kesoesaän.
Paint	Tjat.
Painting	Gambar jang di bikin dengen tjat.
Pair	Pasang; pasangin.
Palace	Astana.
Palatable	Enak rasanja.
Palate	Laklakan; rasa
Palaver	Omongan iseng-iseng.
Pale	Kajoe beroedjoeng; koeroengan; district; poetjet; goerem.
Palfrey	Koeda toenggang.
Paling	Pager kajoe.
Palisade	Pager kajoe.
Pall	Toetoepan peti mati; ilang rasanja.
Pallet	Pembaringan dari roempoet-kering; kasoer ketjil.
Palliate	Koerangin.
Pallid	Poetjet.
Palm	Telapakan tangan; tipoe.
Palmistry	Ilmoe membilang peroentoengan orang dengen meliat oerat-oerat tangan.
Palmy	Bersemi; madjoe.
Palpable	Jang boleh di rasaken.
Palpitate	Bergontjang.
Palay	Kegilaän; kaedanan.
Palter	Tipoe; akalin.
Paltry	Hina; tiada beharga
Pamphlet	Boekoe ketjil jang terdjait.
Pan	Kwali besi.
Pancreas	Njali.
Pander	Ba-tauw; toekang kasi djalan; ba-tauwin; kasi djalan.

Pane	Katja djendela.
Panegyric	Omong-omongan poedjian.
Pang	Rasa sakit jang heibat.
Panic	Kagoegoepan.
Pannier	Bakoel jang dislendangin di atas koeda.
Panoply	Pakean prang besi jang lengkep.
Pansy	Samatjem kembang oengoe.
Pant	Sengal-sengal ; dengen sanget.
Pantechnicon	Grobak. pranti angkoet barang-perabotan ; tempat orang berniaga.
Pantry	Kamar tempat simpen barang makanan.
Pap	Pentil tete ; barang makanan jang lembek.
Papa	Bahasanja anak ketjil boeat ajah.
Papal	Berhoeboeng dengen kepala padri (pope).
Paper	Kertas ; soerat-kabar ; terbikin dari kertas toetoepin dengen kertas.
Papist	Orang jang beragama Romaan Katholiek.
Parable	Dongeng jang berhoeboeng dengen pri-boedi kebedjikan.
Parachute	Pajoeng dipake boeat toeroen dari ballon.
Parade	Parade ; pengadjaran baris dari soldadoe ; pertoendjoekan ; pertoendjoekin ; koempoelin.
Paradox	Kabeneran jang beroepa sebagi katjoerigaän ; omongan jang koerang masoek akal.
Paradise	Sorga.
Paraffin	Minjak tana.
Paragon	Toeladan atawa tjonto jang sedjati.
Paragraph	Ajat.
Parallel	Sama rebanja ; rata.
Paralysis	Penjakit beroete ; pian-soei.
Paralyze	Tjega djalanannja.
Paramount	Jang tiada mempoenjai bandingan ; nummer satoe.
Paramour	Orang jang bisa poera-poera tjinta laen orang ; soendel ; gladak.

Parapet	Langkan tembok.
Paraphrase	Ketrangan jang tjoekoep ; kasi ketrangan dengen tjoekoep.
Parasite	Orang jang bisa bermoeka-moeka ; pasilan.
Parasol	Pajoeng ketjil.
Parboil	Reboes stenga mateng.
Parcel	Boengkoesan ; pakket.
Parch	Keringin ; bikin mengkedoes.
Parchment	Koelit kambing pranti toelis soerat.
Pardon	Maäf ; ampoen ; maäfin ; ampoenin.
Pare	Koepas ; boewang koelitnja.
Parent	Orang toea ; ajah atawa iboe.
Parents	Iboe bapa.
Parentage	Kelahiran ; tarikan.
Parental	Sebagi satoe ajah atawa iboe.
Parish	District jang terprenta oleh satoe bisschop atawa kepala padri.
Parity	Kesamaän ; deradjat jang sama rata.
Park	Park ; lapangan roempoet jang terkoeroeng.
Parlance	Omongan sehari-hari.
Parley	Conferentie ; perhimpoenan besar ; berhimpoen.
Parliament	Parlement ; madjelis dari oeroesan negri ; kok-hwee.
Parlour	Pertengahan ; thia.
Parole	Perdjandjian atas kahormatan diri.
Parricide	Pemboenoehan atas orang-toea dan kadosahannja.
Parry	Singkirken ; laloeken.
Parsimony	Ilmoe himat ; kabisahan aken ati-ati pake oewang.
Parson	Padri ; wesio.
Pasonage	Roema padri ; tempat tinggalnja padri.
Part	Bagian ; bagi pisaken.
Partake	Mempoenjai bagian ; bagian.
Partial	Berhati serong ; tida adil,
Participate	Membagi.

Participle	Perkataän jang mempoenjai tabiat dari *noun* dan *verb*.
Particular	Loear-biasa ; tjerewet.
Parting	Berpisahan.
Partisan	Orang sakambrat
Partition	Bagian.
Partly	Sabagian.
Partner	Persero ; orang jang mempoenjai bagian.
Partnership	Perserohan ; maatschappij ; kong-sì.
Parly	Koempoèlan orang ; partij atawa kaoem politiek.
Pass	Djalanan ; tempat berbahaja ; liwatin.
Passage	Perdjalanan ; djalanan masoek; onkost kapal.
Passenger	Passigier ; penoempang.
Passing	Pengliwatan ; nummer satoe.
Passion	Kehilapan ; pengrasaän ; kainginan.
Passionate	Gampang hilap atawa mera ; bo-sioh.
Passive	Jang menerima ; jang terkena pada diri.
Past	Tempo jang soeda liwat ; soeda liwat ; soeda abis.
Paste	Gom ; kouw ; tempel.
Pasteboard	Kertas karton.
Pastel	Potlood bewarna.
Pastime	Permaenan sport.
Pastor	Padri.
Pastoral	Sairan jang merantjaken penghidoepan di desa ; padri poenja ; desa poenja.
Pastry	Koewe taartjes,
Pasture	Padang roempoet : makan roempoet.
Pasty	Sematjem koewe ; sebagi gom atawa kouw.
Pat	Tepokan ; tedok.
Patch	Tambelan ; tambel.
Patent	Patent ; perkenannja hak ; terboeka ; dilindoengi dengen hak kamerdikaän.
Patentee	Orang jang memegang hak patent,
Paternal	Berhoeboeng dengen ajah atawa bapa.

15.

Path	Djalanan ketjil.
Pathetic	Menggeraken hati.
Pathos	Keangetan ; pengrasaän.
Patience	Kesabaran.
Patient	Orang sakit ; orang jang berobat ; sabar.
Patriarch	Kepala dari satoe familie atawa kaocm koelawarga.
Patrimony	Harta-banda dari leloehoer.
Patriot	Penjinta negrinja.
Patriotism	Ketjintahan pada negri.
Patrol	Pendjagaän ; ronda.
Patron	Pendjaga ; ahliwaris.
Patronage	Toendjangan ; langganan ; aer moeka.
Patronize	Langganin.
Patter	Berboenji sebagi djato ketelan aer.
Pattern	Tjonto ; monster.
Patty	Sematjem koewe ketjil ; bah-pauw.
Paunch	Peroet.
Pauper	Orang miskin.
Pause	Pauze ; pembrentian boeat samentara waktoe ; brenti.
Pave	Plester dengen cement.
Pavement	Djalanan jang terplester dengen cement.
Paw	Telapakan kaki binatang ; garoek.
Pawn	Barang gadehan ; gade.
Pawnbroker	Toekang penggadean.
Pay	Gadji ; pembajara ; bajar.
Payable	Boleh di bajar.
Payment	Pembajaran.
Peace	Kadiaman ; perdamian.
Peaceful	Diam ; dami.
Peak	Poentjak boekit atawa goenoeng
Peal	Soeara klenengan.
Peasant	Orang oedik ; orang tani.
Pebble	Batoe koral.
Peck	$1/_4$ bushel ; patok.

Paculiar	Terpoenja dada; tjoema satoe-satoenja; loear biasa,
Pecuniary	Berhoeboeng dengen oewang.
Peddler	Toekang klontong.
Peddle	Djoeal barang dengen djalan koeliling.
Pedestrian	Orang jang berdjalan kaki; berdjalan kaki.
Peel	Koelit kajoe; koepas.
Peep	Intipan; intip.
Peer	Deradjat sama rata; orang bangsawan; tengok deket-deket.
Peerage	Koempoelan orang bangsawan; atawa berpangkat.
Peerless	Tiada mempoenjai bandingan.
Peevish	Gampang mara; bo-sioh.
Peg	Kajoe gantoengan; gantoeng.
Pelf	Oewang; doewit.
Pellet	Bola ketjil.
Pellmell	Dalem keadaän kalang-kaboet.
Pellucid	Bening; terang.
Pelt	Lempar; koelitin.
Peltry	Koelit bersama boeloe.
Pen	Pena; koeroengan.
Penal	Jang menerima hoekoeman.
Penalty	Hoekoeman.
Penance	Kesoekahan aken trima hoekoeman.
Pencil	Potlood; griffel
Pendant	Giwang; barang permata; bendera tjabang-gas.
Pendent	Tergantoeng.
Pending	Pada waktoe; dalem tempo toendahan.
Pendulum	Batoe lotjeng.
Penetrate	Toesoek; masoeken.
Penetration	Toesoekan; masoeknja; kepinteran.
Peninsula	Tana separo poelo; djazirat.
Penis	Kemaloean orang lelaki.
Penitence	Seselan boeat kedosahan,

Penitent	Jang menjesel dari kedosahan.
Penitentiary	Tempat pranti bikin bersi hati orang.
Penmanship	Toelisan.
Pennant	Bendera ketjil.
Pennate	Berboeloe.
Penny	Oewang Inggris jang beharga disini kira-kira 5 cent; 1/12 dari satoe *shilling*.
Penniless	Tiada mempoenjai sakeping boeta; sengsara.
Pension	Pension; kasi pension
Pensive	Mempoenjai banjak pikiran dan doeka.
Penurious	Pelit.
Penury	Kemiskinan
People	Orang-orang; bangsa; ditempatin oleh orang.
Pepper	Lada.
Peradventure	Brangkali
Perambulate	Djalan teroes atawa meliwatin.
Perambulator	Kreta anak ketjil.
Perceive	Liat; mengatahoei.
Percentage	Commissie dan laen-laen atas 100.
Perception	Kepinteran; kasedaran.
Perch	Samatjem ikan; koeroengan ajam; satoe rod atawa 5½ ijard; mentjlok.
Perchance	Brangkali; kabetoelan.
Percolate	Menetes sebagi aer; saring.
Percussion	Gelagat saling poekoel; poekoelan.
Perdition	Keroesakan; karoegian
Perfect	Tjoekoep; betoel; rapi.
Perfection	Keadaän jang paling tjoekoep atawa memoewasken.
Perfectly	Dengen tjoekoep; antero.
Perform	Bikin; kerdjaken; maen.
Performance	Pakerdjahan; permaenan.
Performer	Orang jang bekerdja; anak komedi.
Perfume	Baoe.
Perhaps	Brangkali; bole djadi.

Peril	Ketjilakaän ; behaja.
Perilous	Berbahaja ; penoe ketjilakaän.
Period	Djeman ; tempo ; oedjoeng ; tanda.brenti.
Periodical	Soerat-kabar jang diterbitken pada tempo jang ditentoeken ; ada waktoenja.
Perish	Boesoek ; mati.
Perishable	Bakalan boesoek atawa mati.
Perjure	Soëmpa palsoe.
Perjury	Soempahan palsoe.
Permanent	Awet ; bisa tahan lama.
Permeate	Djalan teroes di lobang keringet.
Permission	Permisi ; idjin.
Permissive	Boleh dipermisi-in atawa di-idjinken.
Permit	Permisi-in ; idjinken ; soerat permisi atawa idjin.
Permutation	Penoekaran.
Pernincious	Berbahaja ; bisa menjilakain orang.
Perpendicular	Lempeng ; dongak ka atas.
Perpetrate	Bikin ; berboeat.
Perpetual	Awet ; tahan selama-lamanja.
Perpetuate	Bikin tahan selama-lamanja.
Perplex	Bingoéng ; goegoep.
Perplexing	Membingoengin ; menggoegoepin.
Perplexity	Kabingoengan ; kagoegoepan.
Perry	Aer ·boewa peer jang soeda dibikin arak.
Perquisite	Kaoentoengan jang tiada dikira.
Persecute	Bikin soesa ; kasi sakit.
Perseverance	Hati jang tiada merasa bosen ; hati jang tetep
Persevere	Bekerdja dengen tiada marasa bosen ; bekerdja dengen hati tetep.
Persist	Berkeras.
Person	Orang.
Personal	Terbilangannja orang lelaki atawa prempoean.
Personate	Wakilken orang.

Perspective	Ilmoe meneeken gambar sebagimana diliat dengen mata.
Perspicuous	Njata , teges ; trang.
Perspiration	Keringetan ; keringet.
Perspire	Berkringet.
Persuade	Boedjoek ; pikat.
Pert	Gesit ; binal.
Pertain	Terbilang ; termasoek bilangan.
Pertinacity	Hati jang tiada merasa bosen ; hati tetep.
Pertinent	Ka haloean ; dengen maksoed.
Perturbation	Keadaän tiada bisa diam.
Peruse	Batja dengen ati-ati.
Pervade	Siarken ; temboesken.
Perverse	Bandel ; bengal.
Perversion	Perobahan djadi lebi djelek.
Pervert	Bikin roesak.
Pessimist	Orang jang selaloe menjomel atas segala barang atawa oeroesan.
Pest	Penjakit pest.
Pester	Ganggoe ; bikin soesa.
Pestilence	Pest ; penjakit jang menoelarin.
Pestilent	Menoelarin ; mendjelekin.
Pestle	Aloe ; toemboekan.
Pet	Piarahan ; piara.
Petal	Takepan kembang.
Petition	Rekest ; permoehoenan ; bermoehoen.
Petrify	Djadi batoe.
Petroleum	Minjak tana.
Petticoat	Pakean bagian sebla bawa dari orang prempoean ; koen atawa rok ; kaen saroeng.
Pettish	Tjerewet ; bo-sioh.
Petty	Ketjil ; koerang harga.
Petulant	Gampang mara ; bo-sioh.
Phantom	Setan ; iblis.
Phase	Roman ; roepa.
Pheasant	Sabangsa boeroeng jang mempoenjai boeloe bagoes.

Phenomenon	Barang jang loear-biasa.
Phial	Botol ketjil.
Philanthropy	Ketjintahan pada sesama manoesia,
Phlegm	Rejak ; tham.
Phonetic	Menoeroet lagoenja soeara.
Phonograph	Tanda soeara ; masin bitjara.
Phosphorus	Phosphorus ; saroepa dzat jang gampang, menjala.
Photograph	Portret ; gambar.
Phrase	Omongan pendek.
Phraseology	Atoeran mengomong ; model mengomong.
Physic	Obat ; ilmoe thabib ; makan obat.
Physical	Menoeroet tabiat ; berhoeboeng dengen toeboe,
Physician	Doktor ; thabib.
Physics	Ilmoe peladjaran barang-barang jang ada di ini doenia ; boet-li-hak.
Physiology	Ilmoe peladjaran dari machloek jang hidoep.
Physique	Pembikinan atawa keadaän toeboe ; sikap.
Piano	Piano.
Piazza	Djalanan jang tertoetoep.
Pick	Poengoet ; petik ; koempoelin.
Picked	Jang terpoengoet, terpili, atawa terkoempoel.
Picket	Pendjaga ; djaga dengen pager.
Pickle	Tjoeka pranti asinin atjar ; atjar ; asinin bikin atjar.
Picnic	Plesiran ; pasiaran.
Pictorial	Terhias dengen gambar.
Picture	Gambar ; pikir.
Picturesque	Bagoes dalem pemandangan.
Pie	Samatjem koewe dalem mana ada terboengkoes daging ; bah-pauw.
Piebald	Dari matjem-matjem warna.
Piece	Keping ; tambel.
Piece-meal	Sakeping-keping.

Pier	Djagaän pintoe melengkoeng ; boom ; pelaboean ketjil.
Pierce	Toesoek.
Piercing	Menoesoek ; tadjem.
Piety	Kealiman ; kesoetjian,
Pig	Babi.
Pigeon	Boeroeng dara jang bisa bawa soerat.
Pike	Toembak ; samatjem ikan.
Pile	Toemploekan ; gedong ; kajoe fondament atawa tee-ki.
Pilfer	Tjoeri ; tjolong ;
Pilgrim	Palantjongan ka tempat jang soetji.
Pilgrimage	Pelantjongan dengen maksoed soetji.
Pill	Pill ; obat sebagi katjang ; yoh-wan.
Pillage	Rampasan ; rampas.
Pillar	Pilar tiang ; derekan.
Pillow	Bantal kepala ; reba.
Pilot	Djoeroe moedi ; toentoen kapal.
Pimple	Djerawat.
Pin	Djaroem pentol ; kentjengin.
Pinch	Tjoebit.
Pine	Samatjem poehoen ; iindoein.
Pinion	Boeloe ; roda bergigi jang ketjil ; iket lengan.
Pink	Boenga atawa kembang ; warna dadoe.
Pinnace	Samatjem praoe.
Pint	1/8 dari satoe gallon ; pentji.
Pioneer	Orang jang pergi paling doeloe ; pemboeka negri.
Pious	Alim ; soetji.
Pip	Bidji boea appel dan laen-laen boea ; penjakit ajam.
Pipe	Pipa ; tong atawa tahang ; soeling.
Piper	Orang jang maenken soeling.
Pipkin	Teko tana.
Piquancy	Ketadjeman ; kagetiran.
Piquant	Getir ; bengis,

Piracy	Pembadjakan di laoet.
Pirate	Badjak laoet.
Pistol	Pistol ; sendjata api.
Piston	Samatjem trompet; pekakas dalem pompa dan sebaginja.
Pit.	Lobang dalem ; tandain dengen lobang; djebak.
Pitch	Pek atawa dedekan ter ; wates; plester dengen pek ; bangoen dan djato ; djorokin.
Pitcher	Kendi ; boejoeng.
Piteous	Membikin orang djadi kesian ; berdoeka.
Pith	Ati kajoe ; kembangnja banjak barang.
Pithy	Dengen kekoewatan ; berkeras, ati kajoə poenja.
Pitiful	Kesian ; bikin orang djadi kesian.
Pity	Pengrasaän kesian.
Pivot	As, sakoeliling mana barang terpoeter.
Placable	Boleh diampoenin atawa dimaäfin.
Placard	Pembrian taoe.
Place	Tempat ; pangkat ; taro.
Placid	Diam ; lema-lemboet
Plague	Penjakit pest ; kesoesaän ; bikin mara.
Plaid	Tja'a pandjang terbikin dari wool ; diploei.
Plain	Lapang ; padang ; rata ; saderhana ; poetsit ; sebagi diroema sendiri.
Plainness	Kenjataän ; kasederhanaän ; kanetjisan.
Plaint	Menggroetoean ; menggrendengan.
Plaintiff	Orang jang mendakwa.
Plaintive	Mengggeraken hati orang.
Plait	Kepangan ; kepang.
Plan	Haloean ; model ; peta ; membikin model atawa peta ; berdaja.
Plane	Seroet ; rata ; bikin rata ; seroetin.
Panet	Bintang jang bergerak.
Plank	Papan.
Plant	Tetaneman ; tanem.

Plantation	Tetaneman ; poehoen-poehoen jang ditanem.
Plaster	Plesteran tembok ; plester.
Plastic	Boleh ditjitak.
Plat	Sakeping tana.
Plate	Piring ; sepoe ; lapisin.
Platinum	Platina ; saroepa logam jang berat.
Platter	Piring jang tjetek.
Plaudit	Poedjihan.
Plausible	Jang boleh dipoedji ; jang boleh diambil.
Play	Permaenan ; pertoendjoekan komedi ; bermaen.
Playful	Gesit ; loetjoe.
Plaything	Barang permaenan.
Plea	Dakwaän di hadepan pengadilan ; alesan.
Plead	Minta dengen sanget.
Pleasant	Enak.
Please	Soeka ; soedi ; bersoekoer.
Pleasure	Kesoekahan hati ; plesir.
Pledge	Gadean ; tanggoengan ; perdjandjian ; kasi sebagi tangoengan.
Plenteous	Tjoekoep banjak.
Plentiful	Banjak.
Plenty	Keadaän sanget banjak.
Pliable	Gampang dibengkokin ; lemes.
Pliant	Gampang dibengkokin ; djinek.
Pliers	Kakatoea ketjil.
Plight	Tanggoengan ; keadaän ; kasi tanggoengan.
Plod	Madjoe dengen pelahan tapi tetep
Plot	Tipoe resia ; sakeping tana ; berdaja ; merampas.
Plough	Loekoe.
Pluck	Kebranihan ; petik ; koempoelin ; gentak.
Plug	Soempelan ; soempel.
Plum	Boea bidji ; kismis.
Plumage	Boeloe boeroeng.
Plumb	Batoe atas tali ; batoe datjin ; dongak ka atas.

Plumber	Toekang tima.
Plume	Boeloe ; periasan.
Plummet	Tima pranti mengimbangin timbangan ; batoe datjin.
Plump	Denok ; montok.
Plumpness	Kadenokan ; kamontokan.
Plunder	Meroesakin ; rampas ; rampok.
Plunge	Seloeloepan ; lemparken ka dalem aer.
Plural	Lebi dari satoe.
Play	Lipetan ; goeloengan ; bekerdja.
Pneumatic	Termasoek dalem bilangan hawa oedara berisi hawa.
Pneumonia	Sakit paroe.
Poach	Masak atawa reboes sedikit ; mentjoeri binatang.
Poacher	Toekang tjoeri binatang ; maling ajam,
Pocket	Kantong ; kantongin.
Pod	Koelit katjang.
Poem	Sairan ; pantoenan.
Poesy	Sairan ; pantoenan.
Poet	Pengarang sair atawa pantoen.
Poetical	Berhoeboeng dengen sairan atawa pantoenan.
Poetry	Sairan ; pantoenan.
Poignant	Amat sakit.
Point	Oedjoeng ; punt atawa kalimat pertanjaän djoedjoe ; hoendjoek ; bikin trang dengen taro tanda brenti ; bikin tadjem.
Pointed	Beroedjoeng ; tadjem.
Poise	Beratnja ; timbangan ; timbang.
Poison	Ratjoen ; ratjoenin.
Poisonous	Beratjoen.
Poke	Toelak ; soeroeng.
Poker	Tapelan besi ; permaenan kartoe.
Polar	Dari atawa deket *poles* atawa oedjoeng as doenia.
Pole	Djoran ; bamboe ; $5\frac{1}{2}$ ijards ; oedjoeng dari as doenia.

Police	Politie ; pembesar negri,
Policeman	Oppas ; agent politie.
Policy	Atoeran memerenta; djoeroesan perboeatan; polis atawa perdjandjian assurantie.
Polish	Polesan ; poles ; politoer.
Polite	Tane adat ; berprilakoe hormat.
Politic	Pinter ; pande.
Political	Berhoeboeng dengen polit.ek atawa negri.
Pilitics	Politiek ; atoeran memberesin negri
Polka	Dansa bangsa Hungarie.
Poll	Kepala ; pemilihan ; pili.
Pollute	Bikin mesoem ; bikin kotor.
Poltroon	Pengetjoet.
Polygamy	Kedosahan lantaran mempoenjai banjak istri atawa soeami.
Polypus	Saroepa koetoe laoet.
Polysyllable	Perkataän jang lebi dari tiga soeara batjanja.
Pomatum	Pomade ; zalf ramboet.
Pomp	Parade ; pengadjaran baris.
Pompous	Sombong ; angkoe.
Fond	Empang.
Fonder	Pikir ; timbang.
Ponderous	Berat ; bebel.
Pony	Koeda ketjil.
Pool	Empang ketjil.
Poop	Boentoet kapal.
Poor	Miskin ; kesian.
Pop	Soeara njaring ; nondjolin.
Pope	Kepala padri Katholiek jang berdiam di kota Rome ; paus atawa radja-agama.
Poplin	Barang jang terbikin dari soetra dan benang wool.
Populace	Rahajat negri.
Popular	Disoekai oleh orang banjak ; berhoeboeng dengen orang banjak.
Population	Pendoedoek negri ; anak rahajat,

Populous	Mempoenjai banjak pendoedoek negri atawa anak rahajat.
Porcelain	Porcelein ; tana lempoeng jang aloes ·dan bagoes.
Porch	Djalanan masoek jang tertoetoep
Pore	Lobang keringet ; tengok dengen tetep.
Pork	Daging babi.
Porous	Mempoenjai lobang kringet.
Porridge	Boeboer.
Port	Pelaboean ; anggoer mera.
Portable	Boleh di bawa atawa diangkat.
Portend	Soeda larang.
Portent	Firasat jang tiada baek.
Porter	Pengawal atawa pendjaga pintoe ; koeli· pranti mengangkat barang-barang ; sama tjem bier.
Portfolio	Peti pranti taro kertas jang terlepas.
Portion	Portie ; bagian.
Portly	Besar keren.
Portmanteau	Koffer ; tasch.
Portrait	Portret ; gambar.
Portray	Teeken portret atawa gambar.
Pose	Tempat ; gelagat ; roman ; bikin goegoep dengen pertanjaän : membingoengin hati.
Position	Tempat ; tingkatan.
Positive	Pasti tentoe.
Possess	Poenjaken
Possession	Barang kapoenjaän ; milik.
Possible	Boleh djadi.
Post	Pakerdjahan ; djabatan ; tiang ; post ; paker- djaken ; tempatin ; masoeken dalem boe- koe besar.
Postage	Franco ; onkost pembawahan soerat.
Postal	Berhoeboeng dengen post.
Post-office	Kantoor post.
Postpone	Toenda ; bikin lambat.

Postscript	Nota Benne ; omongan jang ditambahken di boentoet soerat.
Posture	Roman ; matjem ; taro dalem keadaän loearbiasa.
Pot	Pot; paso atawa kwali; simpen; taro dalem pot.
Potash	Samatjem *alkali* (aer keras).
Potato	Kentang ; obi-landa.
Potent	Berpengaroe ; koewat.
Potentate	Orang jang berpengaroe ; radja.
Potter	Toekang bikin barang-barang dari tana.
Pottery	Barang-barang jang terbikin dari tana ; tempat dimana barang-barang dari tana ada dibikin ; lio.
Pouch	Kantong.
Poultice	Zalf ; koh-yoh
Poultry	Ajam, bebek dan sebaginja.
Pounce	Boeboek ; toebroek ; terkam.
Pound	Pond ; timbangan dari 16 atawa 12 ons ; oewang emas dari 20 *shillings* (=oewang disini ƒ 12. −), toemboek.
Pour	Toewang.
Pout	Djebian bibir ; djebi-in bibir.
Poverty	Kamiskinan ; kasengsaraän.
Powder	Poeier ; boeboek ; obat-senapan ; bikin aloes ; berarakin.
Power	Pengaroe ; kakoewatan ; kepandean.
Powerful	Berpengaroe ; koewat.
Practicable	Boleh dikerdjaken.
Practical	Terdapet dari kabiasahan.
Practice	Kabiasahan ; kaoeloengan ; tabiat.
Practise	Biasain ; oeloeng ; bikin djadi tabiat.
Prairie	Padang malem mana ada sedikit sekali papoehoenan.
Praise	Poedjian ; poedji.
Prance	Lompat atawa lontjat.
Prank	Loetjoe berbanjol:

Prate	Omong banjak dan mengalantoer.
Prattle	Omong mengalantoer ; bitjara seperti anak ketjil.
Pray	Sembajang ; bermoehoen.
Prayer	Sembajangan ; permoehoenan
Preach	Siarken omongan ; berpridato atas oeroesan agama.
Preamble	Peranteran; penoetoer kata ; pendahoeloean.
Precarious	Tiada tentoe.
Precaution	Hati jang teliti ; perhatian.
Precede	Djalan doeloean.
Precedence	Perdjalanan lebi doeloe ; kamoedahan.
Precedent	Tjonto ; toeladan.
Precept	Mitsal-pepata ; atoeran ; pengadjaran.
Preceptor	Goeroe.
Precinct	Wates.
Precious	Beharga ; mahal.
Precipicel	Karang djoerang.
Precipitate	Kaboeroe napsoe ; jang djadi endek atawa ampas ; lemparken.
Precipitous	Sanget djoerang.
Precise	Betoel ; tjotjok.
Precisely	Dengen betoel ; dengen tjotjok.
Precision	Kabetoelannja ; katjotjokannja.
Preclude	Alangin ; ngandangin.
Precocious	Jang siang-siang soeda djadi mateng atawa dewasa
Precursor	Pemboeka djalan ; djoeroe kabar.
Predatory	Terampas ; terampok.
Predecessor	Orang jang bekerdja paling doeloe.
Predict	Ramalken ; bilang lebi doeloe ; tenoeng.
Prediction	Ramalan; pembilangan lebi doeloe; tenoengan.
Predominant	Jang berdjalan ; jang digoenaken.
Pre-eminence	Keadaän jang paling termashoer.
Pre-exist	Berada lebi doeloe ; hidoep lebi doeloe.
Preface	Permoelaän-kata ; pendahoeloean.
Prefer	Lebi soeka.

Preference	Pemilihan.
Preferment	Kemadjoean.
Pre-figure	Hoendjoeken lebi doeloe dengen tjitakan.
Pregnant	Hamil; boenting.
Prejudice	Pertimbangan jang berat sebla; behaja; timbangan dengen berat sebla.
Preliminary	Tindakan jang pertama kali; penoentoen.
Prelude	Peranteran; penoetoer-kata.
Pre-mature	Sablon waktoenja.
Pre-meditated	Soeda pikir lebi doeloe.
Pre-mediation	Pikiran jang soeda ditetepken lebi doeloe.
Premier	Prime Minister; tjaij-siang; pertama; oetama.
Premises	Roema-roema atawa tana-tana.
Premium	Premie; sadjoembla oewang jang dibajar boeat polis assurantie; madjoe atas harga pertama.
Premonitory	Mengengem nasehat.
Preparation	Persediaän.
Prepare	Bikin sedia; sadji.
Prepay	Bajar di moeka.
Preposition	Perkataän jang menjataken perhoeboengan antara *verbs, nouns* dan *pronouns.*
Pre-possessing	Kasi pikiran baek.
Pre-posterous	Bertentangan dengen atoeran sedjati.
Pre-rogative	Hak loear-biasa.
Presage	Pendahoeloean; ramalan; ramalin.
Presbyter	Orang jang lebi toea; padri.
Prescribe	Merentjanaken; toentoen; prenta.
Prescription	Recept; soerat obat.
Presense	Beradaän; hadirnja.
Present	Barang bingkisan atawa persenan; tempo pada sekarang ini; sekarang; ada; hadlir.
Present	Kasi; persembahken,
Presently	Dengen sigra; lantas.
Preservation	Keslamatan; persimpenan jang slamat.
Preserve	Jam; gelei atawa manisan; simpen,

Preside	Djaga ; pimpin.
President	President ; kepala dari satoe negri republiek atawa pakoempoelan.
Press	Pers ; tindian soerat ; kaperloean ; koempoelan. orang ; tindi ; boedjoek ; berdesek
Pressing	Perloe ; penting.
Pressure	Tindian ; tindesan.
Prestige	Deradjat jang tinggi ; kakerenan.
Presume	Kira ; doega.
Presumption	Kiraän ; doegahan.
Pretence	Poera-poerahan ; belagaän ; alesan.
Pretend	Poera-poera ; belaga ; kasi alesan.
Preternatural	Bertentangan dengen natuur atawa maoenja. Allah.
Pretext	Poera-poerahan ; berlagaän ; alesan.
Pretty	Tjakap ; tjantik ; sedeng.
Prevail	Menangken ; kalaken ; berdjalan.
Prevaling	Jang menang ; jang mengalaken ; jang berdjalan.
Prevalent	Paling loemrah atawa biasa.
Prevent	Tjega ; tahan.
Prevention	Penjegaän ; tahanan.
Previous	Jang berdjalan lebi doeloe ; terlaloe lekas.
Prey	Barang rampasan ; restant ; rampas dan makan dengen rakoes.
Price	Harga.
Priceless	Tiada beharga ; bertentangan dengen harga.
Prick	Toesoekan ; antoekan ; toesoek ; antoek.
Prickle	Doeri..
Pride	Kasombongan ; kaägoengan diri ; menjombongin ; mengagoengin diri.
Priest	Padri ; wesio.
Pristhood	Kewadjibannja padri atawa wesio.
Prig	Orang jang berkepala besar atawa angkoe.
Prim	Kliwat bagoes.
Primary	Tingkatan bermoela

Prime	Terang-tana; pertama; oetama; paling bagoes.
Primer	Boekoe tingkatan ka satoe boeat orang-orang jang baroe moelai beladjar.
Primeval	Pertama; toelen; origineel.
Priming	Obat-senapan; sapoehan tjat jang pertama kali.
Primitive	Pertama; ka satoe kali.
Prince	Anak-radja; prins.
Princely	Djadi sebagi anak-radja.
Princess	Poetri dari satoe radja; istri dari anak-radja; prinses.
Principal	Pemimpin; goeroe kepala; poko oewang; oetama.
Principality	Tana djadjahan dari satoe anak-radja.
Principally	Teroetama; sebagian besar; kebanjakan.
Principle	Kabeneran jang tiada bisa disangkal lagi.
Print	Tjitak.
Printing	Kepala padri; tjitakan.
Prior	Lebi moeda; lebi siang.
Priority	Kamoedahannja; kasiangannja.
Prison	Pendjara; pemboewihan.
Prisoner	Orang prantean; orang jang terpendjara.
Privacy	Keadaän saorang diri.
Private	Saorang diri; prive.
Privateer	Kapal prang jang boekan djadi kapoenjaän-nja negri.
Privation	Kesoesaän; keroegian.
Privilege	Kamerdikaän; kalonggaran.
Privily	Dengen resia; dengen prive.
Privy	Mengatahoei; bertaoe.
Prize	Persenan; oepahan; barang rampasan; hargaken.
Probability	Keadaän jang brangkali.
Probable	Brangkali; boleh djadi.
Probate	Ketrangan.

Probation	Pamereksaän boeat dapet ketrangan.
Probationer	Orang jang ditilik atawa dipreksa; orang jang bekerdja zonder gadji.
Probe	Djaroem pranti preksa loeka; tjari ketrangan.
Probity	Kadjoedjoeran hati; kasetiaän hati.
Problem	Pertanjaän jang dihadepken; namanja saroepa itoengan.
Proceed	Madjoe.
Proceeding	Permoelaän dalem pakerdjahan,
Proceeds	Djoembla jang terdapet.
Process	Haloean; atoeran.
Proclaim	Kaloearken firman atawa soerat mahloemat.
Proclamation	Firman atawa soerat mahloemat; seng-tji.
Proclivity	Kainginan; kapinginan.
Procrastination	Toendahan; pembikinan lambat.
Procreation	Kelahirannja anak.
Proctor	Procureur; Pekelor bamboe; pengrawat roema sekola.
Procure	Dapetken,
Prodigal	Boros; rojaal
Prodigious	Heran; loear-biasa.
Prodigy	Kaheranan; keadaän loear-biasa.
Produce	Kaloearan; kaloearin.
Product	Pendapetan; barang kaloearan; hasil-boemi.
Production	Barang kaloearan; hasil boemi atawa touwsan.
Productive	Gemoek; mengaloearken banjak hasil,
Profess	Akoe sah; siarken omongan betoel.
Profession	Penghidoepan; Pakerdjahan; peroesahan.
Proffer	Tawarken; kasi.
Proficient	Orang jang pande dalem soeatoe ilmoe; pande.
Profile	Sampingnja; roman diloear.
Profit	Kaoentoengan; kagoenaän.
Profitable	Jang boleh mengoentoengin; bergoena.
Profound	Dalem; terpeladjar
Profuse	Rojaal; boros.

Profusion	Karojaalan ; kaborosan.
Progeny	Toeroenan ; anak-tjoetjoe.
Prognosticate	Hoendjoek lebi deeloe ; menjataken lebi doeloe ; ramalin.
Programme	Programma ; tjatetan.
Progress	Madjoenja ; kemadjoean.
Progressive	Madjoe.
Prohibit	Larang.
Prohibition	Larangan.
Project	Tipoe-daja ; haloean.
Project	Nondjol kaloear ; berdaja.
Projectile	Barang jang diondjolin.
Prolific	Gemoek ; berhasil.
Prologue	Peranteran ; penoentoen.
Prolong	Bikin pandjang.
Prominent	Termashoer ; djantoek.
Promiscuous	Tertjampoer ; kalang-kaboet.
Promise	Perdjandjian ; berdjandji.
Promising	Ada membri pengharepan besar.
Promontory	Tandjoeng ; kepala tana.
Promote	Naeken ; madjoeken.
Promotion	Naeknja ; kemadjoean.
Prompt	Sebat ; tjepet ; gara-garain.
Promulgate	Bri taoe dengen firman atawa soerat mahloemat.
Promulgation	Pembrian taoe dengen firman atawa soerat mahloemat.
Prone	Ka bawa ; toendoek.
Prong	Garpoe ; tjagak.
Pronoun	Peganti *noun* atawa nama machloek atawa barang.
Pronounce	Seboet ; batja.
Pronunciation	Soeara batjanja.
Proof	Ketrangan.
Prop	Toendjangan ; toendjang.
Propagate	Tambahken ; siarken.

Propel	Paksa madjoe.
Proper	Bener ; satoedjoe.
Property	Harta banda ; matjem ; qualiteit.
Prophecy	Ramalan ; pembilangan tentang peroentoengan orang.
Prophesy	Ramalin ; meliatin peroentoengan.
Prophet	Orang jang bisa trangken hal-hal jang belon dateng ; nabi.
Propitiate	Akoer kombali ; ganti ; teboes.
Proportion	Hoeboengan ; bandingan ; namanja saroepa itoengan.
Proposal	Voorstel ; tawaran ; pikiran jang dikasi.
Propose	Voorstel ; tawarin kasi pikiran.
Proposition	Hal jang dimadjoeken.
Propound	Kasi aken ditimbang.
Proprietary	Terpoenja pada jang poenja.
Proprietor	Jang poenja ; eigenaar.
Propriety	Kasatoedjoean adat-lembaga.
Prorogue	Berlambat ; toenda perdjalanan.
Prosaic	Geblek ; tiada menjoekain hati.
Proscribe	Hoekoem boewang hoekoeman jang dibri satjara militair.
Proscription	Hoekoeman jang meliwatin wet ; hoekoeman militair.
Prose	Karangan pendek ; karangan dengen pake omongan sahari-hari.
Prosecute	Iringin ; klacht ; dakwa di pengadilan.
Prospect	Pemandangan ; pengharepan.
Prospective	Liat ka depan.
Prospestus	Peta dari pakerdjahan jang hendak dilakoeken ; rentjana.
Prosper	Djadi madjoe ; djadi beroentoeng.
Prosperity	Kabroentoengan ; kemadjoean.
Prosperous	Madjoe , beroentoeng.
Prostitute	Orang prempoean jang latjoerken diri ; prempoean hina ; latjoerken ; bikin djadi hina.
Protect	Djaga ; lindoengin.

Protection	Djagaän ; lindoengan.
Protector	Pendjaga ; orang jang bri perlindoengan.
Protest	Pembrian taoe satjara officieel ; verklaring.
Protest	Protest ; bantah.
Protestant	Kaoem protestant, jaitoe kaoem jang soeda bikin perobahan dalem agama Kristen.
Protract	Bikin pandjang.
Protrude	Soeroeng ; nondjolin.
Protuberance	Penjakit bengkak.
Proud	Sombong ; berkepala besar.
Prove	Tjoba ; tjari ketrangan.
Provender	Barang makanan boeat binatang.
Proverb	Tjekoe ; mistal-pepata.
Provide	Lengkepin ; sediaken.
Providence	Perlindoengan dari Toehan Allah.
Provident	Ati-ati ; dilindoengin.
Province	Provincie ; bagian dari satoe negri ; she.
Provincial	Termasoek dalem bilangan provincie ; terbilangan itoe tempat djoega.
Provision	Barang makanan ; ramsoem.
Provocation	Djengekan atawa lewean.
Provoke	Djengekin atawa lewein ; bikin mara.
Prowess	Kebranihan.
Prow	Memboeaja ; djalan mengglandangan.
Proximity	Deketnja.
Proxy	Gantinja ; wakil.
Prude	Prempoean jang bisa memegang kahormatan dirinja ; tjiat-hoe.
Prudence	Kepinteran kepandéan ; katelitian.
Prudent	Teliti ; pinter ; pande.
Prune	Boea pruim ; oh-tjouw.
Pry	Intip.
Psalm	Njanjian soetji.
Psalter	Boekoe njanjian soetji.
Puberty	Matengnja ; dewasanja.
Public	Orang banjak ; loemrah ; biasa.

Publican	Toekang roema makan ; pendjaga logement.
Publicly	Dengen teroes-trang.
Publish	Terbitken ; kaloearken.
Pucker	Mengkeroetan ; djadi mengkeroet.
Pudding	Koewe podding.
Puddle	Empang ketjil.
Puerile	Sebagi anak ketjil.
Puff	Tioepan ; sengal-sengal.
Fugilist	Orang jang berklai sama kepelan.
Fugnacious	Sedia boeat berklai atawa bertanding.
Pugnacity	Persediaän boeat berklai atawa bertanding.
Fuke	Moenta ; toempa.
Pull	Tarikan ; sentakan ; tarik ; sentak.
Pullet	Ajam dadara.
Pulley	Roda ketjil ; kerekan.
Pulp	Barang jang lembek ; daging jang empoek.
Pulpit	Medja tinggi ; medja pranti berpridato atawa yan-swat.
Pulpy	Lembek ; berdaging.
Pulse	Meh atawa nadi ; katjang.
Pulverise	Toemboek djadi tepoeng.
Pump	Pompa atawa kompa.
Pun	Tebakan atawa badean dalem omongan.
Punch	Poesoet ; minoeman ; poekoelan ; bikin lobang ; poekoel.
Punctual	Tjotjok dengen tempo.
Punctuate	Kasi tanda tempat brentinja.
Puncture	Loeka ketjil ; toesoek.
Pungent	Getir ; pait.
Punish	Hoekoem ; seksa.
Punishment	Hoekoeman ; seksahan.
Punt	Praoe jang bawanja rata.
Puny	Ketjil dan kenji.
Pupil	Moerid ; anak-sekola ; anak-anakan mata.
Puppet	Boneka ketjil.
Puppy	Anak andjing.

Purchase	Pemblian ; bli.
Purchaser	Pembli.
Pure	Bening ; bersi.
Purgetive	Obat boewang aer.
Purge	Boewang aer ; berak ; bersiken peroet.
Purify	Bikin bersi.
Puritan	Orang jang pegang betoel agamanja.
Purity	Kabeningan ; kabersihan,
Purl	Anjoet ; pelahan-pelahan.
Purloin	Tjoeri ; tjalong.
Purple	Warna oengoe.
Purport	Maksoednja;
Purpose	Kemaoehan ; kainginan.
Purr	Mengeong sebagi koetjing.
Purse	Dompet.
Purser	Orang jang pegang oewang atawa ramsoem di atas kapal.
Pursue	Ikoet ; oedek.
Pursuit	Pengikoetan ; pengoedekan.
Purvey	Bli barang makanan atawa ramsoem.
Purveyor	Pembli barang makanan atawa ramsoem ; toekang blandja; pengoeroes makanan.
Pus	Nana.
Push	Toelakan ; toelak.
Pustule	Djerawat ketjil.
Put	Taro ; rebaken.
Putrefy	Djadi boesoek.
Putrid	Boesoek ; dangkalan.
Puzzle	Kabingoengan ; kagoegoepan ; bingoeng ; goegoep.
Pygmy	Orang kate ; orang jang melaenken dikira ada.
Pyramid	Mertjoe jang beroedjoeng, didiriken atas fondament jang lebar; goenoeng-goenoenan.
Pyrotechnics	Ilmoe membikin kembang api atawa yan-hwee.

Python	Oeler santja jang besar.
Pyx	Doos ; peti.

Q

Quack	Orang bodo jang soeka belaga pinter ; soeara bebek ; bersoeara atawa berboenji seperti bebek.
Quadrant	Bagian ka ampat ; 90 karat ; saroepa pakekas pranti oekoer boenderan.
Quadruped	Binatang kaki ampat.
Quadruple	Ampat kali ganda.
Quaggy	Lembek lemes.
Quagmire	Tempat belek ; tempat penoe loempoer.
Quail	Goemeter dengen ketakoetan.
Quaint	Heran ; adjaib.
Quake	Goemiter atawa gojang lantaran ketakoetan.
Quaker	Orang jang bergoemeter atawa bergojang lantaran ketakoetan.
Qualification	Kepandean ; pendapetan ; prilakoe.
Qualify	Trangken maksoednja ; bikin djadi bergoena.
Qualm	Ennek ; penjakit moenta-moenta.
Quantity	Goempoelan ; oekoeran.
Quarrel	Berklai moeloet ; riboet moeloet.
Quarry	Tempat dimana batoe ada digali ; barang pemboeroean jang didapet ; gali batoe.
Quart	Saprapat gallon.
Quarter	Saprapat ; takeran dari 8 bushel ; bagi djadi ampat ; menginep.
Quarters	Tempat tinggal ; wijk.
Quarterly	Saban 3 boelan ; tiap-tiap 3 boelan.
Quartemaster	Pembesar di atas kapal.
Quartern	Bagian ka ampat ;
Quartz	Samatjem batoe permata.
Quay	Pelaboean ; boom atawa tempat bagi kapal atawa praoe barlaboe.

Queen	Radja prempoean ; permisoeri.
Queer	Heran ; adjaib.
Quench	Ilangken aoes.
Query.	Pertanjaän.
Quest	Tanja ; tjari.
Question	Pertanjaän ; sangkahan ; tanja ; sangka.
Queue	Thauwtjang atawa tjatjing ; ramboet terkepang.
Quick	Tjepet ; sebat ; lekas.
Quicken	Bikin tjepet ; bikin sebat ; sedarin.
Quicksilver	Aer pérak.
Quiet	Diam ; bikin diam.
Quill	Boeloe gangsa jang dibikin pena.
Quilt	Toetoepan randjang ; toetoesin.
Quince	Boea-boeahan.
Quintal	Berat dari 100 atawa 112 pond.
Quip	Bikin maloe ; hinaken.
Quire	Doea poeloe ampat lembar ; koor.
Quit	Brenti ; lepas.
Quite	Amat ; sama-sekali.
Quittance	Kalepasan ; pembrentian.
Quiver	Peti atawa doos pranti anak pana.
Quiz	Tebakan ; orang jang loear-biasa ; bikin maen.
Quoin	Pepodjok ; oedjoeng.
Quoit	Samatjem tjintjin jang berat.
Quorum	Sakoempoelan orang boeat oeroesan pakerdjahan.
Quota	Pembagian.
Quotation	Omongan boeat mempikat ; harga jang ditetepin.
Quote	Pikat ; namain ; taro atawa tetepin harga.
Quoth	Kata ; berkata.
Quotient	Pendapetan dari itoengan bagi (—)

R.

Rabbet	Pinggir takepan; bikin pinggir takepan.
Rabbi	Gelaran bangsa Jood.
Rabbit	Klentji.
Rabble	Koempoelan orang.
Rabid	Kalap; gila.
Race	Lombahan; bangsa; berlomba.
Rack	Pekakas pranti menjeksa orang; garoekan roempoet; awan jang tipis; seksa.
Racket	Soeara riboet jang kaloet; tamparan bola tennis.
Racy	Getir; menggeraken hari.
Radiant	Mentjorong.
Radiate	Mentjorongin sinar.
Radical	Akar; orang oetama jang bikin perobahan; sampe ka akar.
Radish	Lobak.
Radius	Palangan roda, satenga boenderan.
Raffle	Permaenan top; pemboekahan loterij; maen top; boeka loterij.
Raft	Getek.
Rag	Sowekan atawa rombengan kaen.
Rage	Kegoesaran; kemarahan; goesar; mara.
Ragged	Berpakean rombeng.
Raging	Hilap; goesar; mara.
Rail	Besi djalanan kreta api; koeroeng dengen besi djalanan kreta api.
Railing	Lan-kan; kajoe pengoeroengan.
Raillery	Djengeka; tertawaän,
Railroad, Rail-way	Djalanan kreta api.
Raiment	Pakean.
Rain	Oedjan; toeroen oedjan.
Rainbow	Bianglala.

Raise	Angkat; tambahken; koempoelin; geraken.
Raisin	Kismis.
Rajah	Radja; sultan.
Rake	Garoekan roempoet; garoek.
Rally	Bersiap kombali; dapetken kombali kekoewatan.
Ram	Kambing Olanda; oesir; giring.
Ramble	Pasiaran; perdjalanan; djalan-djalan.
Rampant	Sarat.
Rampart	Tembok pendjaän.
Rancid	Asem; boesoek.
Rancour	Kagedekan atawa kabentjian jang paling heibat.
Random	Sembarangan; toengkoelan.
Range	Derekan; anglo pranti masak; atoer; derekin.
Rank	Barisan; pangkat; koewat; perlente; masoeken dalem barisan.
Ransom	Oewang teboesan; teboes.
Rant	Omongan lantjang; omong dengen lantjang.
Rap	Poekoelan jang heibat; poekoel.
Rapacious	Rakoes; sekaker.
Rapacity	Kerakoesan; kasekakeran.
Rape	Perkosahan; saroepa tetaneman.
Rapid	Lekas; tjepet.
Rapidity	Lekasnja; katjepetannja.
Rapier	Pedang ketjil.
Rapine	Rampokan dengen perkosa.
Rapt	Jang menggeraken hati.
Rapture	Kagirangan jang boekan terhingga.
Rare	Djarang.
Rarety	Kadjarangan.
Rarely	Dengen djarang; tiada sering.
Rarity	Kadjarangannja.
Rascal	Bangsat; orang jang tiada boleh dipertjaja.
Rase, Raze	Ratain dengen tana; roesakin sama sekali.
Rash	Kabinalan; kasembarangan; katjompongan; binal; sembarangan; tjompong.

Rasher	Keping-keping ketjil dari babi ham.
Rashness	Katjompongan ; kasembarangan.
Rasp	Kikir jang kasar ; kikirin
Rate	Harga ; tingkatan ; hargain.
Rather	Rada-rada; sada-sada.
Ratify	Akoe sah dan perkenanken.
Ratio	Timpalan ; bandingan.
Ration	Makanan sahari-hari.
Rational	Patoet ; mempoenjai pengatahoean.
Rattle	Soeara klentengan ; permaenan ; bikin soeara klentengan.
Raucous	Serak ; kasar.
Ravage	Rampas ; binasaken.
Rave	Omong dengan garang.
Ravel	Lilit atawa boeka.
Raven	Gowak atawa gaok ; makan dengen rakoes.
Ravenous	Kelaparan ; rakoes.
Ravine	Lobang goenoeng ; gowa.
Ravish	Bawa dengen perkosa ; angkoet ; perkosa.
Raw	Menta atawa belon didjadiken karang ; dingin ; zonder mempoenjai koelit.
Ray	Sorot ; sinar.
Razor	Piso tjoekoer.
Reach	Sampe ; sampein.
Reaction	Perboeatan jang berbalik.
Read	Batja ; membatja.
Reading	Pembatjaän ; pridato ; lezing atawa yan-swat.
Ready	Sedia ; klaar.
Real	Betoel ; toelen.
Reality	Kabetoelannja ; katoelenanja.
Realize	Mengarti ; anggep bener ; djadiken doewit.
Really	Betoel-betoel dengen sasoenggoenja,
Realm	Keradjaän.
Ream	20 *quires*, djoembla 480 lembar.
Reap	Potong padi ; kaoentoengan sebagi oepahan,

Rear	Bagian blakang ; angkat ; piara ; berdiri atas kaki blakang.
Reason	Pikiran aken menimbang ; gerakan ; sebabnja atawa lantaran ; pertengkaran.
Reasonable	Pantes.
Reasoning	Pertimbangan pikiran.
Reassure	Berhati besar kombali.
Rebate	Potong ; pembikinan koerang.
Rebel	Pembrontak ; brontak ; geraken hoeroe-hara.
Rebellion	Pembrontakan ; hoeroe-hara.
Rebuff	Tjegahan ; tahanan ; tjega ; tahan.
Rebuke	Tjomelan ; tjomelin.
Rebus	Samatjem badehan
Rebut	Bantah dengen peroendingan.
Recall	Panggilan aken balik ; panggil balik.
Recede	Moendoer.
Receipt	Penerimaän ; rekening ; ketrangan ; kasi ketrangan dengen soerat.
Receive	Trima.
Recent	Baroe-baroe ini ; seger.
Reception	Receptie ; perdjamoean.
Recess	Lobang dalem tembok ; pengasohan boeat sabentaran.
Recipe	Recept ; soerat obat.
Recipient	Orang jang menerima.
Reciprocal	Satjara sobat.
Recital	Pembatjaän dengen tiada liat boekoe.
Recitation	Pembatjaän dengen tiada liat boekoe.
Recite	Batja dengen tiada liat boekoe.
Reckless	Teledor ; koerang ati-ati.
Reckon	Reken ; itoeng ; hargaken ; menggandelin.
Reckoner	Table atawa takwim itoengan.
Reckoning	Rekening ; peritoengan.
Reclaim	Roba ; bikin lebi baek.
Recline	Bersender ka belakang.
Recognition	Perkenalan kombali ; akoean sah.

Recognize	Kenalin ; akoe sah.
Recoil	Lari poelang.
Recollect	Inget kombali.
Recollection	Ingetan jang dateng kombali.
Recommend	Poedjiken.
Recommenda-tion.	Poedjian.
Recompense	Pembalesan ; bales.
Reconcile	Djadi baek kombali ; dami kombali.
Reconcilation	Perdamian kombali.
Reconsider	Pikir lagi.
Record	Tjatetan dari barang jang soeda kedjadian ; plaat gramophone.
Record	Tjatet hal-hal jang bener soeda kedjadian.
Recount	Rentjanaken ; tjeritaken.
Recourse	Permintaän toeloeng.
Recover	Dapet kombali ; djadi baek atawa semboe.
Recovery	Pendapetan kombali ; pendjadian baek atawa semboe.
Recreant	Pengetjoet ; penakoet.
Recreate	Bikin seger badan.
Recreation	Pembikinan seger badan ; permaenan sport.
Recruit	Soldadoe baroe ; dapetken kombali.
Rectify	Bikin bener atawa betoel ; bikin bersi dengen saringan.
Rectitude	Kadjoedjoeran ; kabeneran.
Rector	Padri ; kepala roema sekola.
Rectory	Tempat tinggalnja padri ; tempat-tinggalnja kepala roema sekola.
Recumbent	Mereba.
Recuperate	Dapetken kombali ; bikin seger kombali.
Recur	Terdjadi ; terkenang dalem pikiran.
Recurrence	Baliknja ; dengen adanja lagi.
Red	Warna mera.
Redeem	Tbeoes.
Redeemeor	Nabi.

Redemption	Teboesan.
Redouble	Besarken ; bikin berlipet ganda.
Redoubtable	Menakoetin.
Redress	Pembikinan betoel ; betoelin,
Reduce	Toeroenin.
Reduction	Pembikinan toeroen.
Redundance	Keadaän terlaloe banjak.
Redundant	Terlaloe banjak.
Reed	Alang-alang.
Reef	Goeloengan lajar ; tingkatan karang ; goe-loeng lajar.
Reek	Hawa ; asep ; bernapas kaloear.
Reel	Pekakas menenoen ; djalan seperti orang. maоok ; sempojongan.
Refection	Pembikin seger badan.
Refer	Tjari ketrangan ; tjari perhoeboengan.
Reference	Pentjarian taoe ; perhoeboengan ; adres.
Refine	Bikin teges atawa terang.
Refined	Soeda dibersiken.
Refinement	Prilakoe atawa adat jang baek.
Reflect	Bersorot berbalik ; pikir ; pikir kombali.
Reflection	Sorot jang dateng kombali ; pikiran.
Reflector	Moeka jang soeda di poles atawa di bikin mengkilap.
Reflex	Boewang balik.
Reform	Roda ; bikin lebi baek ; memperbaiki ; kek-beng.
Reformation	Perobahan ; pembikinan lebi baek.
Reformer	Orang jang membikin perobahan.
Reformation	Pembikinan lebi baek ; kek-beng.
Refrain	Singkirken ; djaoeken.
Refresh	Bikin seger.
Refreshing	Pembikinan seger ; djadi seger.
Refreshment	Pembikinan seger ; barang makanan.
Refrigerator	Peti pranti rendem minoeman aken dibikin dingin.

Refuge	Perlindoengan
Refund	Bajar kombali.
Refusal	Kamoengkiran.
Refuse	Barang tetek-bengek ; barang jang tida bergoena.
Refuse	Moengkir.
Regain	Sampeken ; dapetken kombali.
Regal	Sebagi radja poenja.
Regale	Rawatin.
Regard	Perhatian ; kahargaän ; perhatiken ; hargaken.
Regatta	Perlombahan praoe.
Regenerate	Hidoep kombali ; bikin baroe
Regeneration	Kelahiran jang baroe.
Regent	Regent ; wakil radja.
Regicide	Pemboenoenja radja.
Regime	Atoeran penghidoepan ; atoeran pamerentahan.
Regiment	Barisan soldadoe.
Region	District ; bagian tana.
Register	Tjatetan ; lijst.
Registrar	Penjimpen dari tjatet-tjatetan orang banjak.
Regret	Seselan ; menjesel.
Regular	Menoeroet atoeran ; tentoe.
Regularity.	Atoeran ; perdjalanan jang tentoe.
Regulate	Atoer ; bikin rapi.
Regulation	Reglement ; atoeran.
Rehearse	Batja loear kepala.
Reign	Djeman bertachtanja ; bertachta.
Reigning	Lagi bertachta.
Rein	Tahan ; tjega.
Reinforce	Tamba soldadoe.
Reinforcement	Tambahan soldadoe.
Reins	Les koeda ; klemboengan.
Reinstate	Memperbaiki kombali ; bikin baek kombali.
Reiterate	Oelangken ; kerdjaken lagi.

Reject	Toelak ; tiada soedi trima.
Rejection	Toelakan ; kamoengkiran.
Rejoice	Bergirang ; senang-senang.
Rejoin	Samboeng ; djawabin.
Rejoinder	Djawaban ; pembalesan.
Rejuvenate	Bikin moeda lagi.
Relapse	Balik kombali.
Relate	Rentjanaken ; tjeritaken.
Relation	Rentjana ; tjerita ; hoeboengan sanak-soedara.
Relative	Sanak-soedara ; kaoem koelawarga ; familie.
Relax	Bikin longgar ; bikin kendor.
Release	Kalepasan ; lepas.
Relegate	Oesir boewang.
Relent	Djadi lebi baek ; djadi lebi djinek.
Reliable	Boleh dipertjaja.
Reliance	Kapertjajaän.
Relic	Peninggalan ; sisa.
Relict	Prempoean djanda.
Relief	Penoeloengan.
Religion.	Agama ; kapertjajaän pada Toehan Allah.
Religious	Soetji ; beragama ; alim.
Relinquish	Hapoesken ; boewang.
Relish	Bikin senang ; hiboerin.
Reluctance, Reluctancy	Kabentahanan ; hati jang tiada ingin.
Reluctant	Bentahan ; berkepala batoe.
Rely	Pertjaia.
Remain	Tinggal ; katinggalan.
Remainder	Katinggalannja.
Remains	Katinggalannja ; sisa.
Remand	Kirim atawa panggil balik.
Remark	Pemandangan ; pandang.
Remarkable	Loear-biasa ; heran ; termashoer.
Remedy	Obat ; obatin.
Remember	Inget ; simpen dalem pikiran.
Remembrance	Peringetan.

Remind	Ingetin.
Reminiscence	Peringetan kombali.
Remiss	Teledor ; koerang ati-ati.
Remission	Keampoenan ; maäf.
Remit	Kirim oewang ; ampoenin.
Remittance	Pengiriman oewang.
Remnant	Peninggalan ; sisa.
Remonstrance	Pertengkaran omong ; peroendingan.
Remonstrate	Boedjoek ; bertengkar.
Remorse	Seselan ; hati kesian.
Remote	Djaoe
Removal	Pindahan.
Remove	Pinda ; pindaken.
Remunerate	Bales ; oepaken.
Remuneration	Pembalesan ; oepahan.
Rend	Robek ; keset.
Render	Kasi ; bri.
Renew	Bikin baroe ; betoelin.
Renewal	Pembikinan baroe.
Renounce	Tiada akoe boewang.
Renovate	Bikin baroe ; betoelin.
Renown	Nama jang termashoer.
Rent	Petja-bling ; oewang sewa roema ; sewa.
Repair	Pembikin betoel ; bikin betoel,
Reparation	Pembikinan betoel ; reparatie.
Repast	Makanan.
Repay	Bajar kombali ; bales.
Repeat	Oelangken ; kerdjaken atawa kata lagi.
Repeatedly	Sringkali.
Repel	Tangkis ; tjega.
Repent	Menjesel ; bertobat.
Repentance	Seselan ; hati jang ingin bertobat.
Repetition	Repetitie ; perboeatan oelangken kombali apa jang soeda dikerdjaken lebi doeloe.
Reply	Djawaban ; djawab.
Report	Raport ; kabar ; soeara ; kasi rapport atawa kabar.

Repose	Reba ; berbaring.
Repository	Goedang ; depot.
Reprehend	Kasi sala.
Reprehensible	Boleh dikasi sala.
Represent	Menoendjoeken ; wakilken.
Representation	Pertoendjoekan ; wakilannja.
Representative	Wakil ; peganti.
Repress	Pademken.
Reproach	Dakwaän ; hinaän ; dakwa ; hinaken.
Reproachful	Hina ; jang haroes dikasi sala.
Reproduce	Bikin djari baroe.
Reproductive	Mengeloearken hasil.
Reproof	Dakwaän.
Reprove	Dakwa.
Reptile	Binatang merajap.
Republic	Repuliek ; negri dalem mana orang jang memerenta ada diangkat oleh anak rahajat ; kiong-hokok.
Republican	Kaoem Republiekein ; berhoeboeng dengen republiek.
Repngnant	Boleh dibantah.
Repulse	Tangkisan ; tangkis.
Repulsive	Melarang.
Reputable	Boleh dihargaken ; boleh ditaksir.
Reputation	Kahargaän ; keagoengan.
Repute	Prilakoe ; keagoengan ; hargaken.
Reputed	Soeda direken atawa di-itoeng.
Request	Permintaän ; permoehoenan.
Require	Perloe pake.
Requirement	Kaperloean.
Requisite	Barang jang perloe ; perloe.
Requite	Bales.
Rescind	Singkirken ; boewang.
Rescue	Penoeloeng ; toeloeng.
Research	Pertanjaän jang melit ; tanja dengen melit.
Resemblance	Gambar ; miripnja.

Resemble	Mirip ; bersamaän.
Resent	Menoendjoeken mara.
Reserve	Pendjaga,
Reserved	Teliti ; pendiam.
Reservoir	Tempat menjimpen ; goedang.
Reside	Tinggal ; berdiam.
Residence	Roema ; tempat-tinggal.
Resident	Orang jang tinggal ; pendoedoek negri ; pangkat resident.
Residue, Resiuum	Sisa ; kotorannja endekannja.
Resin	Lepas ; meletaken.
Resignation	Kalepasan ; letakan ; penjeraän pada kemaoehannja Allah.
Resin.	Minjak kajoe ; siongka.
Resist	Tahan ; bantah.
Resistance	Tahanan ; bantahan.
Resolute	Tetep pikiran.
Resolution	Katetepan pikiran.
Resolve	Tetepken pikiran.
Resort	Tempat jang sring dipergi-in ; koendjoengin ; pergi-in.
Resound	Berboenji.
Resource	Haloean ; daja ; bantoean.
Respect	Hormatken ; hargaken
Respectable	Boleh dihormatken.
Respectful	Berprilakoe hormat.
Respiration	Napas.
Respire	Bernapas.
Respite	Kelambatan ; lambatin.
Resplendent	Terang ; gilang-goemilang.
Respond	Djawab ; bales dengen soerat.
Response	Djawaban.
Responsibility	Tanggoengan.
Responsible	Djadi tanggoengan.
Rest	Ngasohan ; ngaso ; tidoer ; taro.

Restaurant	Restauratie ; roema makan.
Restive	Bentahan tiada sabar.
Restless	Tiada bisa diam.
Restoration	Pengasihan poelang.
Restore	Bawa poelang.'
Restrain	Tjega ; tahan.
Restraint	Tjegahan ; tahanan.
Restrict	Watesin.
Restriction	Wates.
Result	Kedjadiannja ; boeanja ; achirnja.
Resume	Ambil lagi.
Resurrection	Bangoennja kombali.
Retail	Djoeal ketengan.
Retain	Tahan ; pake
Retainer	Orang jang berlengket ; onkost advocaat.
Retard	Lambat ; pelahan.
Retinue	Pengikoet ; pengiring.
Retire	Moendoer ; brenti dari pakerdjahan.
Retirement	Moendoernja dari pakerdjahan ; brentinja dari pakerdjahan.
Retort	Djawaban jang tadjem ; paso pranti taro obat ; djawabin.
Retrace	Balik dengen sama djalanan.
Retract	Panggil balik.
Retreat	Moendoernja ; tempat sendirian ; moendoer.
Retrench	Koerangin ; potong.
Retribition	Pembajaran kombali pegantian.
Retrieve	Dapet atawa baek kombali.
Retrograde	Moendoer ka blakang.
Retrospect	Balesan ; oelangan ; perboeatan jang kadoea kalinja.
Return	Baliknja ; balik bales.
Reunion	Samboengan atawa hoeboengan kombali.
Reunite	Djadiken satoe.
Reveal	Bikin djadi orang taoe ; boeka.
Revel	Pesta dengen disertain soeara riboet.

Revelation	Pemboekaän ; firman A'llah pada manoesia.
Revenge	Bales kedjahatan.
Revenue	Hasil pendapetan.
Reverberate	Soeara berbalik.
Revere	Hormatken dengen tinggi.
Reverence	Kahormatan ; kaägoengan.
Reverend	Jang agoeng ; gelaran dikasi pada padri.
Reverie	Ngingoan. .
Reverse	Terbalikan ; terbalik.
Revert	Balik.
Review	Pamereksaän ; oelangan ; pikir lagi ; preksa.
Revise	Preksa dan bikin betoel.
Revival	Baliknja penghidoepan ; semboenja.
Revive	Semboe kombali.
Revocation	Penghapoesan ; boewangan.
Revoke	Panggil balik ; hapoesken ; boewangan.
Revolt	Bangoennja kombali ; geraken hoeroe-hara.
Revolution	Revolutie ; hoeroe-hara jang berhasil.
Revolve	Terpoeter ; pikir pergi pikir dateng.
Revolver	Revolver ; saroepa sendjata api jang terpoeter.
Reward	Oepa ; pembalesan ; oepahin ; bales.
Rhetoric	Ilmoe boeat omong di hadepan orang banjak.
Rheumatism	Penjakit entjok.
Rhyme	Akoernja soeara perkataän ; sairan atawa pantoen.
Rhythm	Tjotjoknja oekoeran dan tempo.
Rib	Toelang iga ; kajoe di samping kapal.
Ribaldry	Omongan jang kotor.
Ribbon	Pita.
Rich	Kaja ; hartawan ; goeri.
Riches	Kekajahan.
Richly	Dengen tjoekoep ; dengen rébo.
Rickety	Kenji ; lemes.
Rid	Bebasken ; terbebas ; terlepas.
Ride	Penoenggangan ; toenggang ; berlaboe.
Ridge	Bagian blakang atawa atas ; poentjak.

Ridicule	Djengekan ; lewean ; tertawaän.
Ridiculous	Boleh didjengekin ; boleh dilewein atawa ditertawain.
Rife	Banjak ; jang loemrah atawa biasa.
Rifle	Sendjata api ; senapan ; rampas.
Rift	Lobang.
Rigging	Tambang kapal.
Right	Keadilan ; hak ; kanan ; betoel ; lempeng ; berboeat keadilan,
Righteous	Adil ; alim.
Righteousness	Pri-boedi kesoetjian.
Rightful	Betoel ; menoeroet keadilan.
Rigid	Kakoe ; keren ; ketoes.
Rigour	Kekakoean ; kakerenan ; kaketoesan.
Rigourous	Keren kedjem.
Rill	Kali atawa soengei ketjil.
Rim	Pinggiran.
Rime	Emboen jang djadi aer batoe.
Rind	Koelit ; badjoe sebla loear.
Ring	Tjintjin ; boenderan ; soeara klenengan ; gojang.
Ringleader	Toekang gara-gara ; kepala dari satoe per-sakoetoean.
Ringlet	Kritingnja ramboet.
Ringworm	Koerap.
Rinse	Bersiken dalem aer.
Riot	Hoeroe hara ; ganggoean ; geraken hoeroe-hara ; djadi terlaloe banjak.
Riotous	Kaloet ; kalang-kaboet.
Rip	Potongan ; robekan ; potong ; robek.
Ripe	Mateng ; sedia.
Ripen	Bikin mateng ; djadi mateng.
Ripple	Berombak.
Rise	Bangoennja ; permoelaännja ; tambahannja ; bangoen ; tambah.
Rising	Bangoennja ; gerakan hoeroe-hara.

Risk	Katjilakaän ; bikin tjilaka.
Rite	Adat-istiadat.
Rival	Saingan ; bersaingan.
River	Kali ; soengei.
Rivet	Djaroem ; tjantoem.
Rivulet	Kali atawa soengei ketjil.
Road	Djalanan ; tempat kapal berlaboe.
Roam	Djalan-djalan.
Roar	Soeara mengaoeng ; mengaoeng.
Roast	Panggang.
Ro	Tjoeri ; tjolong.
Robber	Perampok ; ketjoe.
Robbery	Perampokan.
Robe	Pakean pandjang ; thung-sa.
Robust	Koewat ; gaga.
Rock	Karang ; ajoen.
Rocket	Kembang api ; yan-hwee.
Rocky	Penoe karang.
Rod	Toengket ; $5^{1}/_{2}$ yards.
Rodent	Binatang jang menjalnjal.
Rogue	Orang jang tiada boleh dipertjaja; bangsat.
Roll	Gelindingan ; lijst nama ; gelindingin.
Romance	Tjerita ; kedjoestaän.
Romantic	Garang ; boros.
Roof	Woewoengan ; atasnja genteng roema.
Room	Kamar ; tempat.
Roomy	Mempoenjai banjak kamar atawa tempat.
Roost	Mentjlokan boeroeng ; mentjlok.
Root	Akar ; berakar ; gali.
Rope	Tambang.
Rosy	Mera sebagi kembang roos.
Rot	Djadi boesoek.
Rotation	Terpoeternja
Rote	Oelangan ; repetitie.
Rotten	Boesoek ; boeroek.
Rotund	Boénder.

Rouge	Tjat mera pranti moeka ; gin-tjoe.
Rough	Kasar ; berombak.
Roughness	Kekasaran.
Round	Boenderan ; boender ; koelilingin.
Rouse	Bangoen ; bergerak.
Rout	Kekalahan.
Reute	Djalanan.
Rove	Djalan-djalan ; menggelandangan.
Row	Riboet ; ganggoean.
Royal	Seperti radja ; radja poenja.
Royälty	Keradjaän.
Rub	Gosok.
Rubbish	Tektek-bengek ; barang jang sisa boewangan.
Ruby	Batoe permata jang mera.
Rudder	Kemoedi.
Rude	Koerang adjar ; kasar.
Ruffian	Orang kedjem ; bangsat ; badjingan,
Ruffle	Bikin mara ; ganggoe.
Rug	Sikatan kaki.
Rugged	Kasar ; bergoempiok.
Ruin	Keroesakan ; roeboean roema ; bikin roesak.
Ruinous	Jang keroesakan ; membehajaken.
Rule	Wet ; atoeran ; prentahan ; oekoeran ; prenta ; garisan.
Ruler	Orang jang memerentah ; radja.
Rumble	Bikin berisik.
Rumour	Kabar angin ; rapport.
Run	Lari ; anjoet.
Rupee	Oewang Hindu beharga kira-kira ƒ 1.20.
Rupture	Petjahan ; bikin petja.
Rural	Termasoek dalem bilangan oedik ; oedik poenja.
Rush	Toebroekan ; saroepa tetaneman ; toebroek.
Russet	Mera sawo.
Rust	See-sian ; tai-an.
Rustic	Orang oedik; termasoek dalem bilangan oedik.

Rustle	Bikin soeara klentengan.
Rut	Lobang bekas roda.
Ruthless	Kedjem ; tiada mempoenjai hati kesian.
Rye	Samatjem padi.
Ryot	Orang tani bangsa Hindu.

S.

Sabbath	Hari ngaso ; hari minggoe.
Sable	Tenggiling
Sabre	Pedang lebar
Sack	Karoeng ; rampasan kota ; ramsoem.
Sackcloth	Kaen karoeng.
Sacred	Soetji ; alim.
Sacrifice	Sembajangan ; soedjoetan ; keroegian ; korban ; bersoedjoet pada Toehan Allah ; dapet keroegian ; korbanken.
Sad	Kesel ; doeka.
Saddle	Zadel atawa sela, tempat doedoek dari koelit boeat koeda, soeda dan laen-laen ; selain ; moewatin.
Safe	Lemari besi ; lemari makanan ; slamat.
Safeguard	Pendjagaän ; perlindoengan
Safety	Keslamatan.
Sagacious	Pinter ; mengarti.
Sagacity	Kapinteran ; pengartian.
Sage	Nabi ; achli ; pande.
Sail	Kaen lajar ; belajar.
Sailer	Kapal lajar.
Sailor	Matroos ; anak kapal ; orang belajaran.
Saint	Nabi ; orang soetji
Sake	Kebaean ; kaperloean.
Salad	Roedjak selada.
Salary	Gadji.
Sale	Pendjoealan.

Salesman	Toekang djoeal.
Saliva	Loeda.
Sallow	Bewarna poetjet.
Salmon	Ikan zalm.
Saloon	Salon ; kamar jang terhias.
Salver	Piring ; nenampan ; lojang.
Salt	Garem ; asinin.
Saltish	Asin.
Salutary	Sehat ; seger.
Salute	Saluut ; tanda hormat dengen kasi naek tangan di djidat ; kasi tanda hormat dengen kasi naek tangan di djidat.
Salvage	Pembajaran boeat barang jang ditoeloeng simpenin.
Salvation	Pertoeloengan ; teboesan dosa ; keslamatan.
Salve	Zalf ; kojo.
Same	Sama ; mirip.
Sameness	Kesamaän ; kamiripan.
Sample	Tjonto ; monster.
Sanctify	Bikin soetji.
Sanctuary	Tempat bikin soetji badan ; tempat perlindoengan.
Sand	Pasir.
Sandal	Sepatoe sandaal.
Sandwich	Daging jang ditaro antara doea keping roti.
Sane	Berhati terang atawa gaga.
Sauguinary	Kedjem ; soeka memboenoe orang.
Sanguine	Ada pengharepan ; bergiat.
Sanitary	Berhoeboeng sama pri kasehatan badan.
Sanity	Hati jang terang atawa gaga.
Sap	Geta ; gali.
Sapient	Pinter ; mengarti.
Sapling	Poehoen jang masi moeda.
Sapphire	Batoe permata jang berwarna biroe.
Sash	Angkin ; band ; kajoe djendela.
Satan	Setan ; iblis.

Satanish	Sebagi setan ; terlaloe djahat.
Satchel	Kantong ketjil.
Satiate	Isi hingga loeber.
Satin	Kaen satijn atawa pangsi.
Satisfaction	Kapoewasan hati.
Satisfy	Bikin poewas ; poewasin.
Sauce	Saus ; ketjap Inggris.
Saucer	Piring ketjil.
Saucy	Gesit ; nakal.
Saucage	Saucijs atawa soesis ; daging terboengkoes.
Savage	Bangsa biadab ; biadab.
Savannah	Padang roempoet jang besar.
Save	Simpen ; slamatin atawa toeloeng ; malaen-ken.
Saving	Berhimat ; bisa pelit.
Saviour	Nabi.
Savour	Rasa ; baoe.
Savoury	Enak rasanja atawa baoenja.
Saw	Gergadji ; mitsal-pepata ; soeda liat.
Sawyer	Toekang gergadji.
Say	Kata ; bilang ; begitoelah kira-kira.
Saying	Mitsal pepata.
Scabbard	Saroeng pedang.
Scaffold	Kajoe pergantoengan.
Scald	Loeka lantaran kasedoe.
Scale	Timbangan ; sisik ; tingkatan ; timbang ; sisikin ; tingkatin.
Scalp	Koelit kepala ; batok kepala.
Scamp	Bangsat ; penipoe.
Scamper	Lari terboeroe-boeroe.
Scan	Preksa dengen teliti.
Scandal	Kehinaän ; kadjelekan ; rasa maloe.
Scandalous	Hina ; djelek ; menerbitken rasa maloe.
Scanty	Sedikit ; ampir koerang.
Scar	Tanda bekas bisoel ; botak.
Scarce	Sedikit ; djarang.

Scarcely	Dengen soesa ; ampir tiada biasa.
Scarcity	Kesoesaän ; kamelaratan.
Scare	Bikin takoet.
Scarf	Tjala jang pandjang ; tjoekin ; samboeng.
Scarlatina	Demem mera atawa panas.
Scarlet	Mera toea.
Scatter	Sebar ; siarken,
Scavenger	Toekang bikin bersi djalanan.
Scene	Pengliatan ; scherm atawa keree komedie.
Scenery	Pemandangan ; landschap.
Scent	Baoe ; baoein ; endoes.
Sceptre	Toengket radja,
Schedule	Tarief ; tjatetan.
Scheme	Tjonto ; peta.
Scholar	Moerid ; anak sekola.
School	Sekólahan ; tempat-pergoeroean.
Schoolmaster	Goeroe sekola.
Schooner	Kapal bertiang doea.
Science	Ilmoe peladjarant pengatahoean.
Scientific	Berhoeboeng sama ilmoe peladjaran atawa pengatahoean.
Scissors	Goenting ketjil
Scold	Tjomelin ; maki-in.
Scoop	Gajoeng ; lobangin ; keroek.
Scope	Derekan ; kamaoehan.
Scorch	Angoes ; geseng.
Score	Kodi atawa doea-poeloe; lobang potongan; garisan ; peritoengan; tandain dengen lobang.
Scorn	Hati jang mendongkol.
Scornful	Berhati mendongkol.
Scorpion	Kaledjengking.
Scoundrel	Bangsat ; boekan orang baek-baek.
Scour	Bersiken dengen digosok.
Scourge	Tjamboek ; tjamboekin.
Scout	Mata-mata ; intip ; mandjet.
Scowl	Roman jang mara ; beroman mara.

Scramble	Terkem ; mandjet.
Scrap	Keping-keping ketjil.
Scrape	Kerik.
Scratch	Tjakaran ; tjakar ; garoek.
Scrawl	Toelisan jang djelek ; toelis dengen djelek.
Scream	Treakan jang njaring ; bertreak dengen njaring
Screech	Treakan jang kolok ; bertreak dengen kolok.
Screen	Schutsel ; pedengan.
Screw	Schroef ; kekoewatan machine ; taro schroef ; pelintir.
Scribble	Toelis dengen tjompong atawa sembarangan.
Scribe	Penoelis ; krani.
Scrip	Kantong ; soerat ketrangan.
Scripture	Kitab soetji ; bijbel.
Scrub	Orang bangsa renda ; gosok.
Scrubby	Renda ; hina ; tiada berharga.
Scrutiny	Pamereksaän jang teliti.
Scuffle	Pergoeletan jang heibat.
Scull	Penggajoe pendek.
Scullery	Dapoer blakang.
Scullion	Boedjang dapoer.
Sculptor	Toekang oekir kajoe atawa batoe.
Sculpture	Oekiran di atas kajoe atawa batoe.
Scum	Boesa koelit.
Scurf	Kotoran kepala ; ketoembe.
Scurvy	Penjakit koelit ; hina ; renda.
Scuttle	Kapal areng batoe ; bikin lobang di pantat kapal.
Scythe	Arit.
Sea	Laoet.
Seafaring	Bekerdja sebagi matroos.
Seal	Andjing laoet ; tjap ; kentjengin.
Seam	Samboengan djaitan ; tandain.
Seaman	Orang pelajaran ; matroos.

Seamanship	Ilmoe belajar.
Seamstress	Toekang djait prempoean.
Sear	Moeka jang terbakar ; kering ; lajoe.
Search	Tjarian ; selidikan ; tjari ; selidik.
Season	Moesin ; waktoe jang satoedjoe ; satoedjoe ; bisa ; kasi rasa.
Seasonable	Dalem waktoe jang baek.
Seasoning.	Tjampoeran rasa ; boemboe.
Seaworthy	Boleh dipake di laoet ; boleh digoenaken boeat belajar.
Seat	Tempat doedoek ; kadoedoekan ; doedoekin.
Secede	Oendoerken diri dari orang banjak.
Seclusion	Oendoeran diri dari orang banjak.
Second	Seconde ; kadoea.
Secrecy	Keadaän resia atawa prive.
Secret	Resia ; geheim.
Secretary	Secretaris ; soe-kie.
Secrete	Semoeniken.
Sect	Kaoem jang memoedja soeatoe agama.
Section	Bagian ; sectie.
Secular	Loemrah ; biasa; tersiar; di sakoeliling doenia.
Secure	Slamat ; bikin slamat ; dapet.
Security	Tanggoengan ; borgtocht.
Sedate	Pendiam ; keren.
Sedentary	Pendiam ; tiada gesit.
Sediment	Endekan ; ampasnja
Sedition	Gerakan hoeroe-hara ; pembrontakan.
Seduce	Bikin tersesat ; bersatoeboe.
See.	Provincie dari satoe bisschop ; liat.
Seed	Bidji ; bibit.
Seek	Tjari ; minta.
Seem	Roepa-roepanja,
Seeming	Roepanja ; keliatannja ; romannja.
Seemly	Mendjadi , menoeroen.
Seer	Nabi ; orang jang meliat
See-saw	Endjot-endjotan ; ajoenan.

Seethe	Reboes ; tjwee.
Segment	Bagian jang terpotong.
Segregate	Pisaken dari jang laen.
Seismograph	Pekakas jang bisa bri ketrangan tentang tana-gojang.
Seize	Tangkep ; terkam.
Seldom	Djarang.
Select	Pili ; terpili.
Selection	Pilihan.
Self	Sendirian , sama ; tjoema satoe-satoenja.
Selfevident	Teges ; njata ; terang.
Selfish	Temaha ; sekaker ; sirik.
Selfishness	Katemahaän ; kasekakeran ; hati jang sirik.
Selfisame	Sama ; mirip.
Self-will	Kabentahanan ; kepala batoe ; menoeroet kemaoehan sendiri.
Sell	Djoeal.
Selvage	Pinggiran kaen.
Semblance	Kesamaän ; kamiripan.
Semicircle	Stenga boenderan ; boelan sebla.
Semi-colon	Tanda (;).
Seminary	Sekolahan ; temgat-pergoeroean.
Senate	Senaat ; kaoem jang mendjalanken wet.
Senator	Lid senaat.
Send	Kirim.
Senile	Toea ; koeno.
Senior	Lebi toea ; lebi tinggi.
Sensation	Pengrasaän.
Sense	Kabisahan aken merasa ; maksoed.
Senseless	Tiada mempoenjai pengrasaän ; kelenger atawa pangsan ; bodo ; tiada berotak.
Sensibility	Katadjeman pengrasaän.
Sensible	Liat dengen pengrasaän ; berotak.
Sentence	Poetoesan hakim ; zie atawa omongan ; hoekoem.
Sentiment	Pengrasaän ; pikiran.

Sentinel	Pendjaga ; orang djaga ; pengawal.
Sentry	Soldadoe djaga ; schilwacht.
Separate	Pisaken ; teges.
Separation	Pisahan.
September	Boelan ka sembilan ; Jang-lek Kauwgwee.
Sepulchre	Koeboeran.
Sepuel	Bagian jang mengikoet.
Sepuence	Bandingan ; timpalan.
Seraph	Bidadari dari tingkatan jang paling atas.
Sere	Lajoe ; kering.
Serene	Diam ; dami.
Serenity	Kadiaman ; kadamian.
Serf	Boedak.
Serge	Barang wool jang tipis.
Sergeant	Sergeant atawa sersan.
Serenade	Pesta barisan pada waktoe malem.
Series	Stel atawa prangkat ; tingkatan.
Serious	Pendiam ; keren.
Sermon	Pembitjaraän jang soetji.
Serpent	Oeler santja.
Serum	Bagian jang beraer dari dara atawa soesoe.
Servant	Jongos atawa boedjang ; baboe atawa boe-djang prempoean.
Serve	Bekerdja.
Service	Pakerdjahan ; dienst.
Serviceable	Bergoena ; boleh dipake.
Servile	Djahat ; kedjem.
Servitude	Hoeboengan ; pakerdjahan djadi boedak.
Session	Kadoedoekan dalem pengadilan ; vergade-ring ; waktoenja boeka vergadering.
Set	Stellan atawa prangkat ; taro.
Settle	Bangkoe dengen senderan ; tetepken pikiran ; bajar ; tinggal tetep ; bikin slese.
Settlement	Tana djadjahan.
Several	Banjak ; bebrapa.
Severally	Dengen pisa.

Severe	Bengis ; kedjem.
Severity	Kabengisan ; kakedjeman.
Sew	Djait.
Sewer	Pakerdjahan mendjait ; solokan.
Sex	Fihak, lelaki atawa prempoean.
Shabby	Bedjat ; djelek.
Shackle	Iket ; rante kaki tangan.
Shade	Tempat tedoe.
Shadow	Bajangan ; schaduw.
Shaft	Kajoe ; as roda ; anak-pana ; sabagian ko-lom ; djalanan ka bawa parit.
Shaggy	Gompiok ; kasar.
Shah	Radja dari negri Persie.
Shake	Gojangnja ; gojang ; bergoemeteran.
Shallow	Tjetek ; tiada dalem.
Sham	Poera-poerahan ; poera-poera ; tiroean.
Shambles	Roema djagal.
Shame	Pengrasaän maloe.
Shameful	Penoe dari rasa maloe.
Shampoo	Tjoetji kepala , kramas.
Shank	Bagian kaki dari loetoet ka mata-kaki.
Shape	Roman ; pantesin.
Share	Andeel ; bagian ; besi-meloekoe ; bagi.
Shark	Ikan tjoetjoet.
Sharp	Tadjem ; njaring ; tiada adil.
Sharpen	Bikin tadjem.
Sharper	Penipoe ; bangsat.
Shatter	Keset ; robek.
Shave	Tjoekoer.
Shaving	Tatal.
Shawl	Tjala.
She	Dia (prempoean).
Sheaf	Gaboengan padi.
Shear	Potong.
Shears	Goenting besar.
Sheath	Saroeng pedang.

Sheathe	Saroengin ; masoeken dalem saroeng.
Sheave	Roda kerekan.
Shed	Goeboek ; lempar ; djatoken.
Sheen	Ketrangan ; kabagoesan.
Sheepish	Pemaloean.
Sheer	Djoengdjang ; lempeng ; balik dari keadaän jang betoel.
Sheers	Machine pranti angkat barang berat.
Sheet	Spree ; lembaran.
Shelf	Rak ; lemari,
Shell	Kerang ; koelit ; peti mait jang enteng, tjopotin dari koelitnja.
Shelter	Perlindoengan ; lindoengin.
Shelve	Miringin ; taro ka samping.
Shepherd	Toekang angon ; gombala.
Sheriff	Officier dalem afdeeling jang djalanken wet ; schout.
Sherry	Anggoer Spanjol jang paling enak.
Shield	Tameng ; tamengin.
Shift	Pemindahan ; pindain.
Shiling	Oewang Inggris dari doeablas *pence*, djadi oewang disini kira-kira 60 cent.
Shimmer	Mengkilap ; bertjahia.
Shin	Moeka kaki ; moeka betis.
Shine	Bertjahia ; mentjorong.
Shining	Bertjahia ; mentjorong ; terang.
Ship	Kapal ; naekin di kapal.
Shipwreck	Kapal petja.
Shipwright	Toekang bikin kapal.
Shire	District.
Shirt	Kemedja.
Shiver	Goemeter ; antjoer.
Shoal	Kawanan ikan.
Shock	Poekoelan ; bentoeran ; bikin kaget ; kasi sala.
Shoe	Sepatoe ; taro sepatoe atawa besi koeda.

Shoot	Moentjoek ; reboeng ; tembak ; bermoentjoek.
Shop	Toko ; waroeng atawa kedei ; belandja.
Shore	Pinggir laoet ; darat.
Short	Pendek ; kate.
Shortly	Tiada lama ; lekas djoega.
Shot	Tembakan ; peloeroe atawa pelor ; soeda tembak.
Shoulder	Poendak.
Shout	Bertereak ; berseroe.
Shove	Toelak ; soeroeng.
Shovel	Sendokan bara.
Show	Pertoendjoekan ; hoendjoek.
Shower	Oedjan besar.
Showy	Perlente ; rébo.
Shred	Keping jang pandjang ; potong ketjil-ketjil.
Shrew	Orang prempoean jang bawel.
Shrewd	Pinter ; mengarti.
Shriek	Soeara treakan ; bertreak.
Shrill	Njaring serta membikin pengeng koeping.
Shrink	Kisoet : mengkeroet.
Shround	Pakean orang-mati ; sie-ie.
Shrub	Oetan ketjil ; raroempoetan.
Shrug	Angkatan poendak ; angkat poendak.
Shudder	Goemeter.
Shun	Singkirken ; djaoeken.
Shut	Toetoep.
Shutter	Kajoe djendela.
Shuttle	Pekakas toekang-tenoen ; sekotji machine mendjait.
Shy	Pemaloean.
Sick	Sakit.
Sicken	Djato sakit.
Sickly	Sakitan.
Sickle	Arit ; ani-ani.
Sickness	Penjakit.
Side	Pinggir atawa tepi ; sebla atawa fihak ; menjebla

Sideways	Njamping ; njerong.
Siege	Pengoeroengan ; labrakan atas benteng.
Sieve	Saringan.
Sift	Saring.
Sigh	Tarikan napas ; tarik napas.
Sight	Pengliatan ; pemandangan.
Sign	Tanda ; tandain.
Signal	Tanda ; heran.
Signature	Teekenan nama.
Significant	Beharga ; diboeat seboetan.
Signification	Maksoed ; ketrangan.
Signify	Trangin ; kasi maksoednja.
Silence	Pendiaman.
Silent	Diam.
Silk	Soetra.
Sill	Bagian sebla bawa dari pintoe atawa djendela.
Silly	Bodo ; goblok.
Silver	Perak.
Similar	Sama roepanja.
Similarity	Kesamaän roepa.
Simmer	Reboes dengen api pelahan.
Simper	Tertawa jang ada maksoednja.
Simple	Gampang ; saderhana.
Simplicity	Kagampangan ; kasaderhanaän.
Simplify	Bikin gampang ; bikin terang.
Simply	Melaenken ; asal sadja.
Simulate	Tiroe ; tipoe.
Sin	Dosa ; berboeat dosa.
Since	Sasoedahnja dari itoə tempo ; dari itoe sebab.
Sincere	Berhati betoel ; setia.
Sincerity	Kesetiaän hati.
Sinew	Zinuw ; oerat-daging.
Sinewy	Berboeat ; koewat.
Sinful	Berdosa.

Sing	Njanji
Single	Satoe ; belon menika ; pili.
Singular	Tjoema satoe.
Oink	Solokan ; tenggelem.
Sinner	Orang jang berdosa.
Sinuous	Berlengkak-lengkok ; legat-legot.
Sip	Isep.
Sir .	Toean ; goeroe ; gelaran *Sir*.
Sire	Ajah ; bahasa boeat radja.
Sister	Soedara prempoean; djoeroe rawat prempoean
Sit	Doedoek.
Site	Tempat ; tana.
Sitting	Koempoelan ; tempat doedoek dalem gredja.
Situation	Pakerdjahan ; tempat ; keadaän
Size	Besarnja.
Skate	Ikan pari ; sepatoe ijs ; djalan dengen se-patoe ijs.
Skeleton	Toelang machloek atawa binatang; tengkorak.
Sketch	Tjonto ; peta ; tjontoin ; petain.
Skilful	Pande ; berakal.
Skill	Kapandean ; akal.
Skilled	Mempoenjain kapandean.
Skim	Boewang boesa atawa koelitnja ; kenalin.
Skin	Koelit ; tjopotin koelitnja.
Skip	Lompatan ; lompatin.
Skirmish	Prang ketjil.
Skirt	Pinggiran ; rok.
Skittish	Pemaloean ; gesit.
Skulk	Seloemoetin ; semoeni-in.
Skull	Tengkorak kepala.
Sky	Langit.
Slab	Keping jang litjin.
Slack	Kendor.
Slacken	Bikin kendor.
Slake	Ilangin aoes.
Slam	Kamenangan atas semoea akal ; banting.

Slander	Tjelahan ; tjela.
Slang	Oetjapan jang renda dan biasa ; omongan pasar.
Slant	Miring ; dojong.
Slash	Loeka jang pandjang ; loekain ; potong.
Slate	Papan lei.
Slattern	Prempoean jang mesoem.
Slaughter	Pemboenoehan ; potong heiwan.
Slave	Boedak.
Slavery	Pakerdjahan memboedak.
Slavish	Kedjem ; djahat.
Slay	Boenoe ; basmi.
Sleek	Litjin mengkilap.
Sleep	Tidoeran ; tidoer.
Sleet	Oedjan bertjampoer dengen saldjoe.
Sleeve	Tangan badjoe.
Sleigh	Kreta saldjoe.
Slender	Koeroes ; langsing.
Slice	Potongan ketjil.
Slide	Djalanan jang litjin ; mengglinding.
Slight	Enteng ; tipis.
Slim	Tipis dan koeroes.
Slime	Tana lempoeng.
Sling	Gesper ; selitan ; gesperin ; selitin.
Slip	Terpelesetan ; kesalaän ; keping ; terpeleset ; berboeat kesalaän.
Slipper	Kasoet slof.
Slippery	Litjin ; tiada tentoe.
Slit	Petjahan.
Sloop	Kapal satoe tiang.
Slop	Aer jang ditoempaken ; makanan jang beraer; pakean jang soeda sedia djadi ; toempaken.
Slope	Dojongnja ; djoerangnja ; dojong ; djoerang.
Sloth	Kemalesan jang soeda djadi toeman.
Slothful	Males.

Slough	Tempat jang berloempoer.
Slough	Koelit boeaja dan laen-laen binatang merajap jang soeda dikeset; keset; pisaken.
Sloven	Orang jang mesoem.
Slow	Pelahan; lambat.
Slug	Linta darat.
Sluggard	Pemales; oreng jang males bekerdja.
Sluggish	Geremet; males.
Slumber	Tidoeran lajap-lajap; tidoer lajap-lajap.
Slut	Prempoean jang mesoem
Sly	Berakal; tjerdik,
Smack	Poekoelan; bikin soeara dengen bibir.
Small	Ketjil; tiada beharga.
Smart	Tjepat; pinter; peri.
Smash	Antjoerken; terdjang.
Smattering	Pengatahoean jang tiada tjoekoep.
Smear	Olesin.
Smell	Baoe; baoeien endoes
Smelt	Logam jang soeda dibikin loemer.
Smile	Mesem; bermesem.
Smite	Poekoel; boenoe.
Smith	Toekang kerdja dalem logam, oepama toekang mas besi dan sebaginja.
Smithy	Bengkel dari satoe toekang mas, besi dan sebaginja.
Smoke	Asep; roko; isep roko.
Smooth	Litjin; bikin litjin.
Smother	Bikin pangpet atawa rapet.
Smoulder	Bakar; ganggang.
Smuggle	Seloemoetin; bawa masoek barang gelap.
Smut	Noda dari sawang api.
Snake	Oeler.
Snap	Tjerokotan; tjerokot; patain pendek-pendek;
Snappish	Gampang menggigit; gampang mara.
Snare	Djebakan; djebak.
Snarl	Mengaoeng.

Snatch	Terdjang ; reboet,
Sneak	Tjolong ; tjoeri ; seloemoetin.
Sneer	Roman jang asem; hoendjoeken roman jang asem ; djengekin.
Sneeze	Soeara bangkesan ; berbangkes.
Snip	Potong.
Snore	Menggeros.
Snout	Tjongtjot.
Snow	Saldjoe.
Snub	Tahan ; tjega.
Snuff	Boeboek tembako ; soemboe lilin jang soeda dipotong ; potong soemboe lilin.
Snug	Anget ; enak.
So	Begitoe ; demikian.
Soak	Tjelep dalem aer.
Soap	Saboen.
Soar	Moemboel ; melajang.
Sob	Tangisan jang sedi ; menangis dengen sedi.
Sober	Pendiaman ; tiada soeka minoem-minoeman keras.
Sociable	Soeka bertemen ; soeka bergaoel.
Socialism	Pergaoelan menoesia ; sia-hwee.
Socialist	Kaoem socialist atawa jang niat bikin baek pergaoelan menoesia.
Society	Pakoempoelan.
Sock	Kous kaki.
Socket	Lobang ; tempat tjeglok.
Sod	Tana roempoet.
Sofa	Sofa atawa divan.
Soft	Lembek ; lema-lemboet.
Soil	Tana ; bikin noda.
Sojourn	Kadiaman boeat samentara waktoe ; berdiam boeat samentara waktoe.
Solace	Hiboeran ; hiboerin.
Solar	Berhoeboeng dengen matahari.
Solder	Solderan ; solder (kaleng.)

Soldier	Soldadoe.
Sole	Saroepa ikan; zool-sepatoe; tjoema satoe-satoenja; sendiri; pasang zool sepatoe.
Solely	Dengen sendirian.
Solemn	Pendiam; keren.
Solemnity	Adat-istiadat jang soetji.
Solemnize	Lakoeken dengen adat-istiadat.
Solicit	Minta dengen sanget.
Solicitor	Advocaat; procureur.
Solicitous	Ati-ati; beringin sanget.
Solicitude	Kekwatiran hati.
Solid	Barang jang berisi atawa keras; berisi atawa keras; oelet.
Solidity	Kakerasan; kaoeletan.
Solitary	Sepi; sendirian.
Solitude	Kasepian; keadaän jang sepi.
Solution	Barang antjoeran; ketrangan.
Solve	Kasi ketrangan.
Solvency	Hak boeat bajar oetang.
Sombre	Gelap-petang; kesel
Some	Sedikit; bebrapa.
Somebody	Sedikit orang; soeatoe orang.
Something	Sedikjt barang; soeatoe barang.
Sometimes	Kadang-kadang; sringkali.
Somnambulism	Ngigo; djalan pada waktoe tidoer.
Son	Anak lelaki.
Song	Njanjian; lagoe.
Songster	Toekang njanji.
Sonnet	Sairan dari 14 baris.
Soon	Lekas; tiada lama.
Soot	Sawang api.
Sooth	Betoel; setia.
Soothe	Bikin diam; hiboerin.
Sop	Roti sedoe.
Sophist	Orang jang pande adoe omong.
Sophisticate	Bikin djelek atawa boesoek.

Soporific	Obat tidoer.
Soprano	Bagian paling tinggi dari soeara prempoean.
Sorcery	Perboeatan dengen kemat atawa djimat; goena-goena.
Sordid	Sekaker; kotor.
Sore	Tempat loeka; sakit.
Sorrow	Kadoekaän; kakeselan.
Sorry	Doeka; kesel, menjesel; sajang.
Sort	Matjem; pili dengen matjemnja.
Sot	Pemabokan jang soeda kawakan.
Sough	Soeara mengaoeng dari angin atawa ombak.
Sound	Soeara; moeara ketjil; klemboengan ikan; enak; tiada koerang soeatoe apa.
Soup	Soep; makanan berkoewa.
Sour	Asem.
Source	Mata aer; asal-oesoelnja.
Souse	Lompat ka dalem aer.
South	Salatan; kidoel.
Southerly	Di sebla Salatan; dari sebla Salatan.
Souvenir	Tanda peringetan.
Souvereign	Radja; oewang Inggris dari 20 *shillings* atawa satoe pond sterling; mempoenjai kekwasaän besar.
Sow	Babi oetan prempoean.
Sow	Sebar.
Spa	Mata aer dari aer Olanda.
Space	Kamar; tempat kosong; djaoenja; bikin dengen lét-lét.
Spacious	Mempoenjai roewangan besar.
Spade	Patjoel.
Span	Djengkal.
Spare	Simpen; himat; tiada pake; sempet; ampoenken; kasi.
Spark	Kembang api; lelatoe.
Sparkle	Menkredep.
Spatter	Kipratin atawa kepretin.

Spawn	Telor ikan ; troeboek ; bertelor sebagi ikan.
Speak	Bitjara ; omong.
Spear	Toembak.
Special	Loear-biasa ; tjoema satoe-satoenja.
Specie	Sembarang matjem oewang.
Species	Matjem ; roepa.
Specific	Obat ; loear-biasa ; memang adatnja.
Specification	Soerat contract.
Specify	Namaken dengen perkataän.
Specimen	Tjonto ; monster.
Speck	Tilik ; toetoel ; noda.
Spectacle	Pengliatan ; pemandangan.
Spectacles	Katja mata.
Spectator	Pengliat ; penonton.
Spectre	Setan ; iblis.
Speculate	Pikir diam-diam ; simpen boeat kaoentoengan.
Speculation	Seta ; simpenan boeat kaoentoengan ; speculatie.
Speech	Omongan ; bahasa.
Speechless	Bisoe ; gagoe.
Speed	Lekasnja ; ladjoenja.
Spell	Goena-goena ; spel perkataän.
Spend	Blandja ; ilangin ; liwatin.
Spendthrift	Orang jang boros.
Sphere	Bola doenia ; tempat.
Spherical	Boender.
Spice	Boemboe ; boemboein.
Spider	Kawa-kawa atawa lawa-lawa.
Spike	Pakoe besar.
Spill	Toempaken.
Spin	Bikin benang.
Spindle	As ; djaroem.
Spine	Toelang blakang.
Spinster	Gadis ; prempoean jang belon menika.
Spiral	Melilit.
Spire	Tjiongtjit ; woewoengan paling atas dari gredja atawa roema.

Spirit	Roh atawa aloes menoesia ; iblis atawa setan ; kegagahan ; arak-api.
Spiritual	Boekan terbikin oleh menoesia ; berhoeboeng dengen barang soetji.
Sirituous	Berisi arak-api atawa alcohol.
Spit	Pakoe pandjang ; oedjoeng ; tana ; berloeda.
Spite	Dendeman-hati ; sakit-hati ; tiada perdoeli ; ganggoe.
Spiteful	Dengki hati.
Spittle	Loeda.
Splasch	Kitjretin aer.
Splendid	Bagoes ; termashoer.
Splendour	Kebagoesan ; nama jang termashoer.
Splice	Samboeng tambang ; menika.
Split	Tjopotin ; keset.
Spoil	Rampasan ; rampas ; bikin roesak.
Spoke	Palang roda ; soeda bitjara.
Spokesman	Orang jang wakilin laen orang boeat bitjara.
Sponge	Spons ; gosok dengen spons.
Spontaneous	Dari kemaoehan sendiri.
Spoon	Sendok.
Spoonful	Sasendok penoe.
Spoor	Tanda kaki bekas djalannja binatang liar.
Sport	Permaenan sport ; memaen.
Sportsman	Orang jang soeka dengen permaenan sport.
Spot	Toetoel ; noda ; tempat ; tandain.
Spout	Tjongtjot ; toewang dengen paksa.
Sprain	Sala-lakoe.
Sprawl	Reba melondjor.
Spray	Semprotan aer.
Spread	Siarken ; pentang.
Sprig	Moentjoek ketjil ; tjabang ketjil.
Sprightly	Tiada bisa diam ; gesit.
Spring	Mata-aer ; lompatan ; veer ; moesin semi ; lompat.
Spring	Mempoenjai veer ; bisa lompat sendiri.

Sprinkle	Kipratin aer.
Sprout	Moentjoek ; semi.
Spruce	Bersi ; netjis.
Spume	Boesa.
Spur	Spoor ; besi di blakang sepatoe boeat bikin koeda lari ; goembiraken ; gara-garain.
Spurious	Palsoe ; tiroean atawa tetiron.
Spy	Mata-mata ; intip ; liat.
Squabble	Riboet moeloet.
Squad	Koempoelan ketjil.
Squadon	Barisan kapal prang; barisan soldadoe koeda.
Squalid	Keliwat mesoem.
Squall	Angin riboet jang dateng dengen koenjoeng-koenjoeng ; soeara treakan ; bertereak.
Square	Pesegi.
Squeak	Soeara njaring.
Squeamish	Terlaloe tjerewet ; maoe sakit.
Squeeze	Tekenan ; tindian ; teken ; tindi.
Squib	Kembang-api ; ijan-hwee.
Squirrel	Badjing.
Squirt	Saringan ketjil ; boewang dari pipa.
Stab	Loeka ; tikem.
Stability	Katetepan ; kealotan.
Stable	Istal koeda ; tetep ; tiada begeming.
Stack	Toemploekan roempoet kering ; toemploekin.
Stadium	Lapangan adoe koeda.
Staff	Toengket ; garisan dalem noot musiek ; koempoelin orang jang melakoeken pakerdjahan.
Stage	Panggoeng.
Stagger	Djalan sempojongan.
Stagnant	Tiada bisa bergerak.
Stagnation	Kadiaman ; koerang gerakan.
Staid	Tetep.
Stain	Titik ; noda ; bikin noda.
Stair	Tangga ; loteng.

Stake	Kajoe jang tadjem ; oewang tarohan ; bertaro.
Stale	Basi ; tiada segar.
Stalk	Batang ; djalan dengen angkoe.
Stall	Goeboek ; panggoeng.
Stallion	Koeda bibit.
Stammer	Omong titi-tata.
Stamp	Indjekan ; pekakas dan tjapnja ; postzegel ; tjap ; indjek ; taro tjap.
Stand	Tempat brenti ; station ; berdiri ; tahan.
Standard	Bendera ; klass.
Staple	Soempe besi ; hasil boemi jang paling oetama ; oetama.
Star	Bintang.
Starch	Tadjin atawa kandji ; tadjinin atawa taro kandji ; bikin kakoe.
Stare	Awasan ; awasin.
Stark	Kakoe sama sekali.
Start	Brangkatnja ; lontjatan ; brangkat ; lontjat.
Startle	Kaget ; terkedjoet.
Starve	Kelaparan atawa mati-kelaparan.
State	Keadaän ; negri ; kekwasaän civiel ; kata.
Stated	Soeda dibikin slese ; soeda didiriken.
Stately	Bagoes ; agoeng.
Statement	Pritoengan ; staat.
Statesman	Staatsman ; politicus atawa orang jang pande dalem hal politik.
Station	Djabatan ; station atawa post kreta api ; bernti ; dikasi pegang djabatan atawa ditempatin.
Stationary	Tetep ; tiada begeming.
Stationer	Toekang tjitak.
Stationery	Perabot toelis.
Statistics	Tjatetan dan atoeran tentang hal-hal jang bener soeda terdjadi.
Statue	Patoeng.
Stature	Tingginja.
Statute	Wet atawa oendang-oendang negri jang didjalank

Stay	Tinggalnja ; tinggal.
Stead	Peganti ; giliran.
Steadfast	Tetep ; oelet.
Steady	Tetep ; gaga.
Steak	Potongan daging aken dimasak; biefstuk.
Steal	Tjoeri; tjolong.
Stealth	Djalanan resia ; pentjoerian.
Steam	Stoom ; asep poeti.
Steed	Koeda prang.
Steel	Wadja ; bikin keras.
Steelyard	Timbangan.
Steep	Djoerang ; tjelep.
Steeple	Woewoengan jang paling atas dari gredja atawa roema ; tiong-tjit.
Steer	Anak banteng ; kemoedi-in.
Steerage	Bagian sebla depan dari kapal.
Stellate	Beroman sebagi binatang.
Stem	Batang ; tahan.
Stench	Baoe jang tiada enak.
Senography	Toelisan tjara pendek.
Stentorian	Njaring ; bising.
Step	Tindakan ; tangan ; bertindakan ; djalan.
Sterile	Tiada gemoek ; tiada mengaloearken hasil.
Sterling	Harga jang ditentoeken.; toelen.
Stern	Bagian sebla blakang dari kapal ; bengis.
Stew	Reboes dengen api pelahan.
Steward	Toean-tana ; pengoeroes.
Stick	Toengket ; tempel atawa lengketin.
Sticky	Lengket.
Stiff	Kakoe.
Stigma	Tanda maloe.
Still	Pekakas boeat bikin minoeman ; diam ; masi.
Stilt	Djangkoengan.
Stimulant	Jang geraken pengrasaän ; jang mengoewat- ken badan.
Stimulate	Geraken pengrasaän ; gara-garain.

19

Sting	Antoek.
Stingy	Pelit.
Stink	Baoe jang tiada enak.
Stipend	Gadji.
Stipulate	Tawar harga.
Stir	Keriboetan ; bergerak.
Stitch.	Toetoesan ; toetoesin.
Stiver	Oewang Olanda jang beharga 5 cent.
Stock	Pongkot poehoen ; bangsa ; simpenan ; barang dagangan; helwan; lengkepin; simpen.
Stocking	Kous kaki jang pandjang.
Stomach	Hampedal. .
Stone	Batoe; timbangan dari 14 pond ; terbikin dari batoe.
Stool	Bangkoe.
Stoop	Djongkok.
Stop	Pembrenti ; brenti.
Stoppage	Brentinja ; halangan.
Store	Djoembla jang banjak ; goedang ; simpen.
Storehouse	Goedang.
Storey	Tingkatan roema.
Storm	Angin riboet.
Story	Tjerita ; hikajat ; djoebin roema.
Stout	Bier jang keras ; gemoek.
Stoutness	Kagemoekan ; keberanihan.
Stove	Tempat api jang terkoeroeng ; anglo.
Stow	Simpen ; boengkoes.
Straight	Lempeng.
Straightway	Lantes ; dengen sigra.
Strain	Sala-lakoe ; tenaga ; njanjian ; londjorin ; tindi ; saring.
Strainer	Saringan ; ijskan.
Strait	Selat ; kesoesaän ; sempit ; kalang-kaboet.
Straiten	Bikin sempit ; bikin soesa.
Strand	Darat ; tali tambang ; kandas.
Strange	Heran ; asing.

Stranger	Orang asing ; orang jang tiada dikenal.
Strangle	Tjekek.
Strap	Gesper ; tali koelit.
Stratagem	Akal ; tipoe-daja.
Strategy	Kepinteran dalem ilmoe prang.
Stratum	Tatakan.
Straw	Roempoet kering ; terbikin dari roempoet kering.
Stray	Djalan-djalan ; kesasar ; berboeat kesalaän
Stream	Djalanan aer ; kali atawa soengei ketjil.
Streamer	Barang jang anjoet.
Street	Straat ; djalanan besar.
Strength	Tenaga ; kekoewatan.
Strenuous	Bertenaga ; koewat.
Stress	Tenaga ; tindian.
Stretch	Londjorin.
Stretcher	Grobak jang disoeroeng dengen tangan.
Strew	Sebar.
Strict	Bengis.
Stride	Tindakan jang lebar ; bertindak
Strife	Berkoetet-koetetan ; pertengkaran.
Strike	Poekoel ; toeroenin ; masoekin ; mogok.
Striking	Menggeraken hati orang.
String	Tali.
Stringent	Bengis ; aseran.
Strip	Keping ketjil ; bikin telandjang ; roesakin. .
Stripe	Streep ; tjamboekin.
Stroke	Tepokan ; poekoelan.
Stroll	Djalan-djalan.
Strong	Koewat.
Stronghold	Benteng.
Strop	Koelit boeat gosok piso tjoekoer.
Structure	Arkoe ; pembikinan.
Struggle	Kesoesaän ; pertjobaän ; berkoetet-koetetan.
Strut	Tindakan jang angkoe ; djalan dengen angkoe.

Stubborn	Bandel atawa bengal ; berkepala batoe.
Stud	Kantjing knob ; kajoe ; koempoelan koeda-koeda ; pakein kantjing knob.
Student	Moerid ; orang jang beladjar.
Studied	Soeda dipikir baek-baek ; soeda bladjar.
Studio	Bengkel toekang gambar.
Studious	Giat beladjar.
Study	Peladjaran ; jakinan ; beladjar ; jakinen.
Stuff	Barang ; djedjel.
Stumble	Djato.
Stump	Oedjoeng jang katinggalan ; doezelaar pranti teeken gambar.
Stun	Bikin pengeng dengen poekoelan.
Stunt	Tjega toemboenja.
Stupefy	Bikin bodo.
Stupendous	Mengagetin ; bikin orang terkedjoet.
Stupid	Bodo ; goblok.
Sturdy	Bisa bekerdja keras ; meneradoeng·
Stutter	Omong titi-tata
Stye	Kandang babi ; belintit di mata.
Style	Model ; matjem ; namaken ; panggil.
Stylish	Perlente ; rébo.
Subdivide	Bagi lagi.
Subdue	Kalaken ; petjoendangin ; djinekin.
Subject	Anak-rahajat ; kalimat ; pakerdjahan ; di bawa pengaroe ; termasoek dalem bilangan.
Subject	Kalaken ; pertjoendangin.
Subjection	Keadaän di bawa pengaroe laen orang.
Subjoin	Samboeng di oedjoeng.
Subjugate	Taloeken ; koempoelken.
Sublime	Tinggi ; agoeng.
Submarine	Kapal silem ; di bawa laoet.
Submission	Pengalaän ; penjeraän.
Submissive	Renda ; soeka mengala.
Submit	Mengala ; seraken.
Subordinate	Lebi renda.

Subscribe	Berlangganan ; teeken ; soembang.
Subscription	Oewang berlangganan atawa soembangan ; teekenan.
Subsequent	Berikoet.
Subside	Tenggelem ; tinggal tetep.
Subsidiary	Orang jang membri pertoeloengan atawa oewang oeroenan ; membantoe.
Subsidy	Bantoean oewang.
Subsist	Mempoenjai penghidoepan.
Subsistence	Daja boeat hidoep.
Subsoil	Tana di bawa moeka boemi.
Substance	Barang ; kekajahan.
Substantial	Tiada roepanja ; berisi.
Substantiate	Menetepken dengen ketrangan.
Substitute	Peganti ; gantiken.
Subtile	Tipis ; tadjem.
Subtle	Berakal ; berilmoe.
Subtract	Potong ; koeroengin.
Subtraction	Itoengan potong (-).
Suburbs	Tempat jang berdamping dengen kota.
Subway	Djalanan di bawa tana.
Succeed	Gantiken ; djadi madjoe.
Success	Kemadjoean ; kebroentoengan.
Successful	Madjoe ; broentoeng.
Succession	Stellan ; prangkat.
Successor	Peganti ; orang jang menggantiken pakerdjahannja orang laen.
Succour	Penoeloengan ; toeloeng.
Succulent	Bergeta ; banjak patinja.
Succumb	Mengala ; menjera.
Such	Begitoe ; samatjem itoe.
Suck	Isep.
Sucker	Moentjoek dari akar.
Suckle	Soesoein ; tetein.
Sudden	Koenjoeng-koenjoeng ; dengen tida terdoega lebi doeloe ; lantes.
Sue	Sita ; minta dengen sanget.

Suffer	Rasa sakit.
Suffice	Menjoekoepin.
Sufficient	Tjoekoep.
Suffocate	Tjekek.
Suffrage	Hak mengasi soeara dalem sidang Parliament ; soeara.
Suffragette	Orang prempoean jang minta hak boeat mengasi soeara dalem Parliament.
Suggest	Voorstel ; kasi pikiran.
Suicide	Pemboenoehan diri sendiri ; orang jang memboenoe diri sendiri.
Suit	Stellan ; prangkat ; haloean dalem wet ; lamaran ; sebanding ; sedeng.
Suite	Prangkatan kamar-kamar ; kawanan pengikoet.
Suitor	Orang jang meminang atawa melamar ; orang mendakwa
Sulky	Beroman asem.
Sullen	Mendendem mara ; aseran.
Sully	Bikin noda ; bikin kotor.
Sultry	Panas dan rapet.
Sun	Djoembla ; itoengan ; djoemblain.
Summary	Tjerita pendek ; tarikannja ; pendek.
Summer	Moesin paras.
Summit	Poentjak goenoeng atawa boekit.
Summon	Panggil mengadep.
Summons	Pembrian taoe tentang hal jang bakal kedjadian.
Sun	Matahari.
Sunder	Pisaken.
Sundry	Tjampoer-tjampoer ; matjem-matjem.
Sup	Sedotan ; makan malem.
Superb	Bagoes ; gaga.
Supercilious	Sombong ; angkoe.
Superficial	Tjetek ; mengambang.
Superfine	Kliwat bagoes.

Superfluous	Keliwat banjak ; tiada perloe.
Superintend	Mandoorin ; tilik.
Superintendent	Mandoor ; eigenaar ; kwasa.
Superior	Orang jang pernanja lebi toea toewa atas lebi toea atawa atas.
Superlative	Dalem tingkatan jang paling tinggi.
Supernatural	Meliwatin kebisahannja natuur.
Supersede	Gantiken ; wakilken.
Superstition	Katachajoelan.
Superstitious	Tachajoel.
Supervisor	Mandoor ; kwasa.
Supper	Makanan malem.
Supplant	Gantiken dengen djalan jang koerang baek.
Supple.	Gampang bengkok.
Supplement	Lampiran tambahan.
Supplicant	Orang jang masoeken permoehoenan.
Supplicate	Minta dengen sanget ; bermoehoen.
Supply	Kalengkepan ; pengasihan ; lengkepin ; kasi.
Support	Toendjangan ; toendjang.
Supporter	Penoendjang.
Suppose	Kira doega.
Suppress	Pademken.
Supremacy	Pengaroe atawa kekwasaän jang paling besar ; hak dipertoean.
Supreme	Paling tinggi ; paling oetama.
Surcharge	Bikin laen pembajaran ; ganti harga.
Sure	Tentoe pantes.
Surely	Dengen tentoe ; dengen pasti.
Surety	Tanggoengan ; borgtocht.
Surf	Boesa.
Surface	Moeka ; bagian sebla loear.
Surge	Beloembang ; ombak besar ; bangoen dan mengglinding.
Surgeon	Doktor potong.
Surgery	Ilmoe mengobatin.
Surly	Asem berengoet.
Surmount	Kalaken ; petjoendangin.

Surname	Nama toeroenan ; she.
Surpass	Liwatin.
Surplus	Keadaän terlaloe banjak.
Surprise	Pengrasaän kaget ; kaget ; terkedjoet ; terprandjat.
Surrender	Serain ; menjera.
Surround	Koeroeng.
Survey	Tilik ; oekoer ; preksa.
Surveyor	Orang jang menilik dan preksa.
Survive	Hidoep kombali.
Suspect	Sangka ; doega.
Suspend	Gantoeng ; toenda.
Suspence	Keadaän jang tiada tentoe.
Suspicion	Sangkahan ; doegahan.
Sustain	Tahan ; toendjang.
Sustenance	Makanan ; barang toendjangan.
Suzerain	Orang jang paling berkwasa.
Swagger	Menjombongin ; djalan dengen angkoe.
Swain	Soeami ; ketjintahan.
Swallow	Boeroeng sala goenting ; tenggorokan ; telen ; tarik ka dalem.
Swamp	Tana jang legit.
Swan	Gangsa.
Sward	Tana roempoet.
Swarm	Kawanan besar ; berkawan.
Swarthy	Berparas gelap.
Swath	Garisan ; roempoet jang dipotong dengen arit.
Swathe	Band ; iketan ; iket.
Sway	Pamerentahan ; memerenta ; berajoen ; berkwasa.
Swear	Soempa ; pake perkataän kotor.
Sweat	Kringet ; berkringet.
Sweep	Sapoe.
Sweet	Manis ; merdoe.
Sweet-heart	Toendangan ; katjintahan.

Sweet-meat	Manisan.
Sweell	Bengkak ; tambahan ; djadi bengkak ; menamba.
Swelling	Bisoel.
Swift	Lekas ; tjepet.
Swiftly	Dengen lekas ; dengen tjepet.
Swill	Tjoetji dengen aer ; minoem dengen rakoes.
Swim	Bernang ; mengambang.
Swindle	Tipoe-daja ; tipoe.
Swindler	Penipoe atawa toekang tipoe.
Swine	Babi.
Swing	Ajoenan ; berajoen.
Switch	Tjabang ketjil ; poekoel.
Swoon	Keadaän loepa orang; kelenger atawa pangsan.
Swoop	Samber.
Sword	Pedang.
Sycophant	Orang jang bisa bermoeka-moeka ; pendjilat-kaki.
Syllable	Bagian perkataän jang dibatja dengen satoe soeara.
Symbol	Tanda.
Sympathize	Menoeroet doeka tjita.
Sympathy	Pengrasaän doeka tjita; sympathie
Sympton	Tanda.
Syndicate	Persariketan ; persakoetoean ; syndicaat.
Synonym	Perkataän jang mempoenjai maksoed jang bersamaän dengen laen perkataän.
Synopsis	Pemandangan jang terkoempoel.
Syntax	Koempoelan dari perkataän boeat menjataken pikiran.
Synthesis	Penarohan sama-sama.
Syringe	Saringan.
Syrup	Sirop ; aer goela.
System	Atoeran ; peta pendapetan.
Systematic	Dilakoeken menoeroet atoeran atawa peta pendapetan.

Tab — 298 — Tamely

T.

Tab	Tali sepatoe.
Tabard	Badjoe pendek.
Tabby	Bewarna ; bolang-bolang.
Tabernacle	Tanda jang gampang-di pinda-pindaken ; berdiam boeat samentara waktoe.
Table	Medja ; tjatetan dari barang-barang jang perloe ; tabel atawa takwim.
Tableau	Tableau ; pertoendjoekan sebagi gambar mati.
Tablet	Medja ketjil ; moeka jang rata ; samatjem koewe.
Tack	Pakoe ketjil ; tjantoem ; djalanan kapal.
Tackle	Kerekan dan tambang.
Tag	Oedjoeng rinda
Tail	Boentoet ; oedjoeng.
Tailor	Toekang badjoe ; tjaij-hong.
Taint	Noda ; kotor.
Take	Tangkepan ; ambil.
Tale	Tjerita ; lelakon.
Talent	Kapandean ; oewang sadjoembla 243 pond sterling dan 15 shillings ; beratnja.
Talented	Pinter ; mempoenjai kepandean.
Talisman	Djimat boewat lawan kadjahatan.
Talk	Omongan ; pembitjaraän ; omong ; bitjara.
Tall	Tinggi.
Tallow	Minjak kerbo atawa kambing ; olesin dengen minjak.
Tally	Perdjandjian ; kajoe wasiat ; bikin perdjandjian.
Talon	Koekoe.
Tame	Djinek ; bikin djinek.
Tamely	Dengen djinek.

Tamper	Berlakoe tjoerang ; tjampoer tangan.
Tan	Koelit kajoe *oak* ; bikin djadi koelit meteng ; djadi koening toea.
Tandem	Kreta jang memake doeda.
Tangle	Libetan tambang ; roempoet laoet ; libet.
Tank	Tahang ; bak.
Tankard	Tjangkir minoem.
Tanner	Toekang tjelep koelit.
Tantalize	Mendongkol ; permaenan.
Tantamount	Sama rata.
Tap	Tepok ; kraan ; tepok kaloearin.
Tape	Pita.
Taper	Lilin ketjil ; trang samar-samar ; lantjip ; bikin lantjip.
Tapestry	Gantoengan jang tersoelam boeat riasin tembok.
Tar	Teer.
Tardy	Lambat ; geremet.
Tare	Saroepa roempoet ; onkost pak barang ; barang.
Target	Boelan-boelan.
Tariff	Tarief ; tjatetan.
Tarnish	Goerem.
Tarry	Tinggal ; berlambat ; seleder.
Tart	Koewa taartje ; asem ; tadjem.
Tartan	Kaen jang soeda diploei.
Task	Pakerdjahan.
Tassel	Roentje-roentje ; koentjir.
Taste	Rasa ; rasain.
Tatter	Kaen rerombengan ; robek.
Tattle	Omongan iseng-iseng.
Tattoo	Soeara poekoelan drenden ; taptoe ; toesoek.
Taunt	Hinaken ; bikin maloe.
Tavern	Roema makan
Taw	Koelit jang soeda dibikin poeti.
Tawdry	Perlente ; rébo.

Tawny	Koening toea.
Tax	Padjek ; terka.
Taxicab	Kreta zonder koeda ; automobilen.
Tea	Thee.
Tecah	Adjar.
Team	Kawanan ; barisan ; bagian.
Tear	Aer mata ;˙robek.
Tease	Sisiran ; ganggoein.
Teat	Pentil tete.
Technical	Berhoeboeng dengen ilmoe pertoekangan.
Tedious	Bekerdja berat ; tjape.
Teem	Kaloearken banjak sekali.
Teeth	Gigi-gigi.
Telegram	Telegram ; soerat kawat.
Telegraph	Telegraaf ; machine ketok 'kawat.
Telephone	Telefoon.
Telescope	Keker djaoe.
Tell	Bilangin.
Temper	Prangi ; tabiat ; adat ; menoendjoekin ; bikin lembek.
Temperament	Tabiat ; adat.
Temperance	Pembikinan se.leng.
Temperate	Bikin sedeng ; sedeng ; tiada panas tiada dingin.
Temperature	Hawa boemi.
Tempest	Angin riboet.
Temple	Klenteng ; gredja ; pelengan kepala.
Temporal	Berhoeboengan dengen penghidoepan atawa djiwa.
Temporary	Boeat samentara waktoe ; boeat sabentaran.
Tempt	Boedjoek atawa pikat ka dalem perboeatan djahat.
Temptation	Boedjoekan atawa pikatan ka dalem perboeatan djahat.
Tenable	Boleh ditoendjang.
Tenancy	Pindjeman pake ; roema. sewahan ; tana sewahan.

Tenant	Toean roema; orang jang menjewa roema atawa tana.
Tenantable	Boleh disewaken; boleh dipindjemin.
Tend	Djaga; djoedjoein; hadepken.
Tendency	Djoedjoehan; hadepan.
Tender	Namanja saroepa praoe ketjil; penawaran; lembek; tjinta; tawarken; kasi.
Tendon	Zinuw; oerat daging.
Tenement	Roema; tempat-kediaman.
Tenet	Oedjar-oedjar agama; atoeran jang aseli.
Tennis	Permaenan bola tennis atawa kaatsbal.
Ternor	Djalanan; prilakoe; bagian lebi tinggi dari soeara orang lelaki,
Tense	Tempo; bagian dari *verb* boeat menoendjoeken temponja soeatoe perboeatan.
Tension	Tenaga jang dipake berkoetet-koetetan; gentakan.
Tent	Tenda.
Tenure	Keadaän atawa atoeran dari memegang tana particulier.
Term	Tempo jang diwatesin; perkataän; per-djandjian; namain.
Termagant	Prempoean jang rewel atawa bawel.
Terminate	Watesin; bikin abis.
Termination	Watesnja; abisnja; boentoetnja.
Terminus	, Oedjoengnja djalanan kreta api.
Terrace	Toemploekan tana.
Terrible	Menakoetin.
Terrific	Menerbitken rasa takoet.
Terrify	Bikin takoet.
Territorial	Soldadoe schutterij; termasoek dalem bilangan soeatoe district.
Territory	Tana djadjahan.
Terror	Pengrasaän takoet; ketakoetan.
Test	Pertjobaän; tjoba.
Testament	Kamaoehan; satoe dari antara doea bagian dari kitab soetji.

Testator	Orang jang membikin soerat peninggalan.
Testify	Saksiken.
Testimonial	Soerat kesaksian; certificaat.
Testimony	Ketrangan ; kesaksian.
Testy	Gampang dibikin mara ; brangasan.
Tether	Tambang; rante; iket dengen tambang atawa rante.
Teutonic	Berhoeboeng dengen bangsa Duitsch di djeman doeloe.
Text	Pakerdjahan ; kalimat.
Textile	Tertenoen.
Texture	Tenoenan.
Than	Dari pada.
Thank	Pengrasaän trima kasi ; bri trima kasi.
Thankful	Merasa trima kasi.
That	Itoe ; jang ; bahoewa.
Thatch	Atep ; atepin.
Thaw	Loemeran dari aer batoe; saldjoe dan sebaginja ; loemer.
The	Itoe.
Theatre	Roema-komedi.
Theatrical	Berhoeboeng dengen komedi; mengasi pertoendjoekan.
Thee	Kau (Perkataän Inggris koeno dipake di boentoet omongan).
Theft	Katjoerian; kerampokan.
Theme	Kalima pakerdjahan.
Then	Di itoe waktoe ; kamoedian ; dari itoe sebab.
Thence	Dari itoe tempat ; dari sana.
Thenceforth	Dari itoe waktoe.
Theology	Ilmoe peladjaran dari barang-barang soetji.
Theory	Theorie ; doega-doegahan.
There	Disana ; disitoe.
Therefore	Dari itoe sebab ; sebab itoe.
Thermometer	Oekoeran panas.
These	Ini (dipake boeat menoedjoeken barang-barang lebi dari satoe).

They	Ia-orang ; marika.
Thick	Bagian jang tebel ; tebel.
Thicket	Oetan jang rapet.
Thickness	Tebelnja.
Thief	Maling ; pentjoeri.
Thieve	Malingin ; tjoeri ; tjolong.
Thigh	Paha.
Thimble	Bidal.
Thin	Tipis ; koeroes.
Thine	Kau poenja (Perkataän Inggris koeno).
Thing	Barang.
Think	Pikir.
Thirst	Pengrasaän aoes ; keaoesan.
Thirsty	Aoes ; kring.
This	Ini (dipake boeat menoendjoeken barang tjoema satoe).
Thistle	Saroepa poehoen bidoeri.
Thither	Ka itoe tempat ; ka sana
Thong	Gesper ketjil.
Thorax	Dada.
Thorn	Doeri.
Thorough	Tjoekoep ; sampoerna.
Thoroughfare	Djalanan jang menemboes.
Thou	Kau (perkataän Inggris koeno, dipake di kepala omongan).
Though	Maski ; kendati.
Thought	Pikiran ; soeda pikir.
Thoughtful	Berpikiran ; mempoenjai pikiran.
Thrash	Toemboek padi ; poekoel.
Thread	Benang,
Threat	Antjem ; bikin takoet.
Threatening	Mengantjem ; menakoetin.
Threshold	Djalanan masoek.
Thrift	Kahimatan ; kapelitan.
Thrifty	Bisa himat ; bisa pelit-pelit.
Thrill	Toesoekan ; toesoek.

Thrive	Djadi madjoe, broentoeng.
Throat	Tenggorokan.
Throb	Kedoet-kedoetan; kekedoetan.
Throne	Tachta keradjaän.
Throng	Koempoelan orang; berkoempoel.
Throttle	Pipa hawa; tjekek.
Through	Teroes; dari lantaran.
Throughout	Koeliling; di ampat pendjoeroe.
Throw	Lempar; timpoek; boewang.
Thrush	Saroepa boeroeng jang bisa menjanji; bisoel di moeloet.
Thrust	Toesoek.
Thumb	Djempol.
Thump	Poekoelan jang keras; poekoel dengan keras.
Thunder	Goentoer; gledek; geloedoek.
Thunderstruck	Terperandjat; kaget.
Thus	Begitoe; dengen tjara begitoe.
Thwart	Tangkis; kalaken.
Thy	Kau poenja.
Tick	Koetoe andjing; bulzak atawa djok; ber= soeara tik-tok sebagi lotjeng.
Ticket	Kaartjis; tandain dengen kaartjis.
Tickle	Kitik.
Ticklish	Bagoes; penting.
Tide	Aer pasang.
Tidings	Kabar.
Tidy	Netjis.
Tie	Iketan; hoeboengan; perdjandjian; dasi; koende; iket; hoeboengken.
Tier	Barisan; derekan.
Tiffin	Makanan tengahari.
Tiger	Matjan.
Tight	Kentjeng; rapet-
Tile	Genteng; gentengin.
Till	Tjelengan; peti-oewang; sampe; hingga; loekoe.

Tillage	Pakerdjahan meloekoe ; pakerdjahan menani.
Tiller.	Gagang kemoedi ; toekang loekoe ; orang tani.
Tilt	Dojongin.
Timber	Kajoe ; balok.
Timbrel	Tamboer ketjil ; rembana.
Time	Tempo ; **waktoe** ; penghidoepan atawa djiwa ; tetepin.
Timely	Ada waktoenja ; ada moesimnja.
Timid	Penakoet ; pengetjoet.
Timidity	Penakoetan ; hati jang pengetjoet.
Tin	Tima ; kaleng ; peti dari kaleng ; blik.
Tinder	Oempan api.
Tinge	Warna ; warnain ; tjelep.
Tingle	Berboenji ; bergoemeter.
Tinker	Toekang kaleng.
Tinkle	Berboenji ; berklontongan.
Tint	Warna ; warnain.
Tiny	Ketjil ; moengil.
Tip	Oedjoeng ; nasehat ; bikin beroedjoeng atawa tadjem ; poekoel pelahan-pelahan.
Tipple	Minoem terlaloe banjak.
Tipsy	Mabok.
Tire	Karet boeat roda ; band karet ; bikin tjape.
Tired	Tjape ; lela.
Tiresome	Menjapein ; melelain.
Tissue	Kaen perada ; pembikinan.
Tithe	Bagian ka sapoeloe.
Title	Kalimat ; gelaran.
Titter	Tertawa menjengir.
To	Pada ; ka ; boeat atawa aken.
Toad	Kodok.
Toast	Roti panggang ; poedji-poedjian ; minoem boeat kahormatannja ; panggang.
Toe	Djeridji kaki.
Together	Sama-sama.

Toil	Pakerdjahan berat ; bekerdja berat.
Toilsome	Berat dikerdjaken.
Token	Tanda.
Tolerable	Jang boleh ditahan ; sedeng ; tiada bagoes tiada djelek.
Tolerate	Rasain ; imbangin ; andelin ; biarin.
Toleration	Pengrasaän ; imbangin ; andelin; biarnja.
Toll	Padjek ; gojang klenengan.
Tomb	Koeboeran ; bong.
Ton	Satoe ton, jaitoe **2240** pond atawa **40** kubiek kaki ; keadaän djeman.
Tone	Soeara lagoe ; kekoewatan.
Tongs	Sepit.
Tongue	Lida ; bahasa negri sendiri.
Tonic	Mengoewatin ; obat bikin koewat badan.
Tonnage	Beratnja kapal.
Tonsil	Anak-lida.
Tonsure	Tjoekoeran ramboet.
Too	Djoega ; terlaloe.
Tool	Pekakas ; perabot.
Tooth	Gigi ; rasa.
Top	Bagian paling atas ; gangsing.
Topaz	Batoe permata jang berwarna koening.
Topic	Kalimat omongan.
Tompost	Paling tinggi.
Topple	Djato kadepan.
Torch	Obor api.
Torment	Sakit jang heibat.
Torpedo	Kapal torpedo.
Torpid	Poentoel ; geremet.
Torpor	Ilangnja kakoeatan.
Torrent	Anjoetan jang deres.
Torrid	Panas ; angoes.
Torture	Sakit jang heibat ; persakiti.
Toss	Lempar ; amoek.
Total	Djoembla sama sekali ; sama sekali.

Totter	Djalan sempojongan.
Touch	Pengrasaän ; perhoeboengan ; rasa ; kena.
Touching	Menggeraken pengrasaän atawa hati orang.
Touchwood	Kajoe jang soeda boesoek.
Touchy	Brangasan ; bo-sioh.
Tough	Oelet ; alot.
Tour	Perdjalanan ; pelantjongan ; pasiar.
Tourist	Pelantjongan ; toekang pasiar.
Tournament	Permaenan sport.
Tourniquet	Band dari doktor boeat pangpetin dara.
Tout	Tjari langganan ; orang jang tjari langganan.
Tow	Lawe jang kasar ; tambang-nila ; tarik.
Toward	Ka pada ; ka hadepan ; sedia.
Towel	Handoek.
Tower	Mertjoe ; roema jang tinggi ; menara.
Town	Kota.
Toy	Barang permaenan ; pandang ketjil.
Trace	Tanda ; djalanan ; ikoetin.
Track	Djalanan.
Tract	Onder-district ; tempat ; rentjana pendek.
Tractable	Denger kata ; djinek.
Traction	Penarikan ; pikatan.
Trade	Perniagaän ; dagangan ; berniaga ; berdagang.
Tradesman	Soedagar ; toekang djoewal bli.
Tradition	Pembitjaraän jang ditinggalken ; omong-omongan orang doeloe.
Traffic	Perniagaän ; dagangan.
Tragedy	Lelakon jang ngenes ; hal jang menakoetin.
Tragical	Mengenesin ; menjedi-in.
Trail	Djalanan ; baoe ; ikoetin djalanannja ; baoein.
Train	Pengikoet ; bagian sebla blakang dari pakean ; stel ; djalanan ; kreta api ; adjar ; apalken.
Trait	Katjoerangan hati.

Traitor	Penghianat negri ; dorna atawa kansin.
Tram	Kreta tram.
Tranquil	Diam ; dami.
Tranquilize	Bikin diam ; bikin dami.
Transact	Lakoeken ; kerdjaken ; oeroes.
Transaction	Haloean ; pakerdjahan ; oeroesan.
Transcribe	Kopier ; tiroc.
Transcript	Kertas kopier ; concept ; tiroean.
Transfer	Pengasihan over ; kasi over.
Transfigure	Roba romannja.
Transfix	Toesoek temboesin.
Transform	Salin roepa ; pian-hoa.
Trangress	Berdosa.
Transgressor	Orang jang berdosa.
Transient	Meliwatin ; melintasin.
Transit	Liwatnja ; melintasnja.
Transition	Perobahan.
Transitive	Menoendjoeken perboewatan ada liwat ka-hadepan, seperti dari satoe *vreb*.
Transitory	Meliwatin pergi.
Translate	Salin ; vertal.
Translation	Salinan ; vertaling.
Transmission	Pindahan dari satoe ka laen tempat.
Transmit	Pindain atawa kirim dari satoe ka laen tempat.
Transmute	Salin ; toekar.
Transparent	Bening; teges.
Transpire	Djadi terkenal.
Transplant	Tanem di laem tempat.
Transport	Angkoetan ; kapal pengangkoet barang ; angkoet.
Transportation	Angkoetannja.
Transpose	Roba haloean.
Transposition	Perobahan haloean.
Transverse	Melintang ; menjebrang.
Trap	Djebakan ; djebak.
Trappings	Barang periasan.

Trash	Barang jang tiada beharga ; tek-tek-bengek.
Travail	Kalahirannja anak ; bekerdja berat.
Travel	Melantjong ; pasiar.
Traveller,	
Traveler	Orang pelantjongan ; toekang pasiar.
Traverse	Kamoengkiran , barang jang melintang ; melintang ; djalan meliwatin.
Tray	Nenampan ; lojang ; djoeroe-rawat.
Treacherous	Tiada setia ; berchianat.
Treachery	Hati jang tiada setian atawa chianat.
Tread	Indjek.
Treadle	Indjekan kaki dari machine mendjait.
Treason	Perboeatan chianat bagi radja atawa negri sendiri.
Treasure	Harta-banda ; simpen ; hargaken.
Treasury	Kas negri.
Treat	Rawatan ; pesta ; rawatin ; pegang ; berdami.
Treatise	Boekoe ; rentjana.
Treatment	Rawatan ; kelakoean.
Treaty	Kontract ; perdjandjian jang sah.
Treble	Bagian jang paling tinggi dalem musiek ; tiga kali lipet ganda ; kali atawa poekoel (×) dengen tiga.
Tree	Poehoen.
Tremble	Bergoemeter.
Tremendous	Besar ; menakoetin.
Tremulous	Bergoemeter.
Trench	Solokan ketjil ; gali solokan.
Trenchant	Tadjem ; membikin peri.
Trencher	Piring kajoe.
Trend	Hadepken ; inginin.
Trepidation	Bergoemeter.
Trespass	Kesalaän njang diboewat pada laen orang ; dosa ; masoekan dalem orang poenja tana dengen zonder hak ; berboeat kesalaän atawa dosa.

Tress	Ramboet jang riap-riap.
Trestle	Toendjangan jang boleh dipinda-pindaken.
Tret	Penambahan ; pegantian boeat barang jang roesak
Trial	Pertjobaän ; pamereksaän.
Triangle	Tiga pesegi.
Tribe	Kaoem ; bangsa.
Tribulation	Hoekoeman jang kedji.
Tribunal	Pengadilan.
Tributary	Tjabang kali atawa soengei ; berhoeboeng.
Tribute	Padjek ; barang persembahan ; oepeti atawa tjin-kong.
Trice	Tempo sabentaran.
Trick	Akal ; akalin.
Trickle	Menetes ; anjoet pelahan-pelahan.
Tricoloured	Bewarna tiga.
Triennial	Tiap-tiap tiga taon.
Trifle	Barang jang tiada beharga ; boewang per-tjoema.
Trifling	Dengen males ; ketjil ; tiada beharga.
Trigonometry	Ilmoe peladjaran aken mengoekoer *angles ; driehoeksmeting.*
Trill	Bergoemeternja soeara ; bikin soeara ber-goemeter.
Trim	Keadaän ; netjis ; bikin netjis ; benain.
Trinity	Pengangkatan soedara antara tiga orang.
Trinket	Barang periasan ; mas-inten.
Trio	Musiek boeat tiga orang; tiga orang djadi satoe.
Trip	Terpeleset ; kesalaän ; perdjalanan ; djato ter-peleset ; djalan.
Triple	Tiga kali ganda.
Triplets	Kelahiran dari tiga anak di satoe waktoe.
Trisyllable	Perkataän dari tiga soeara bitjaraän.
Trite	Loemrah ; biasa.
Triumph	Kagirangan besar ; kamenangan ; bergirang menang.

Triumphant	Bergirang.
Triune	Tiga dalem satoe.
Trivial	Ketjil ; tiada berharga.
Trombone	Trompet trombone.
Troop	Barisan koeda ; balatentara.
Trooper	Soldadoe toenggan koeda.
Trophy	Tanda kamenangan ; prize atawa barang bingkisan.
Tropical	Termasoek ·dalem bilangan negri-negri panas.
Trot	Djalan sebagi koeda ; tjongklang.
Troth	Kapertjaiaän.
Trouble	Kesoesaän ; bikin soesa.
Troublesome	Menjoesaken.
Trough	Kobakan.
Trowsers, •Trousers	Tjelana.
Truant	Anak jang soeka-mangkir dari sekola; toekang mahtjauw ; mangkir dari sekola atawa mahtjauw.
Truce	Perdamian boeat samentara waktoe.
Truck	Grobak jang disoeroeng dengen tangan ; toekar.
Truckle	Roda ketjil ; terpoeter.
Truculent	Biadab ; liar.
Trudge	Djalan dengen tetep.
True	Betoel ; bener ; berhati djoedjoer atawa lempeng.
Truism	Kabeneran jang tiada bisa disangkal.
Truly	Betoel-betoel ; dengen sabenernja ; dengen berhati-djoedjoer atawa lempeng.
Trumpery	Barang tetek-bengek ; tiada bergoena.
Trumpet	Trompet ; kasi kabar di loearan.
Trundle	Mengglinding.
Trunk	Pongkot poehoen ; telale gadja ; peti atawa koffer
Trust	Kapertjajaän ; ketang jang dikasi ; kasi oetang ; pertjaia.

Truslee	Ahliwaris; orang jang oeroes harta-banda boeat orang laen.
Trusty	Berhati djoedjoer atawa lempeng, setia.
Truth	Kabeneran.
Truthful	Pegang kabeneran; djoedjoer.
Try	Tjoba; preksa.
Tub	Tahang.
Tubercle	Bisoel.
Tuberculosis	Sakit paroe.
Tubular	Beroman sebagi pipa.
Tuck	Kepangan, oelatan; kepang; oelat.
Tuft	Rentjengan; tangkean
Tug	Tarikan jang keras; kapal api ketjil boeat tarik praoe; tarik dengen keras.
Tuition	Pengadjaran
Tulip	Saroepa roempoet jang mempoenjai kembang bagoes.
Tumble	Djatoan; djato; terplanting.
Tumbler	Glas besar.
Tumour	Bisoel; bengkak.
Tumult	Kalang-kaboetan; kekaloetan
Tumultos	Kalang-kaboet; kaloet
Tun	Tong atawa tahang besar; leger.
Tune	Lagoe-lagoein.
Tuneful	Enak; merdoe.
Tunnell	Lobang dalem tana.
Turbid	Berloempoer; boetek.
Turbot	Saroepa ikan besar.
Turbulent	Soeka bikin perkara onar.
Tureen	Djemboeng.
Turf	Tana jang beroempoet.
Turkey	Ajam kalkoen; rahajat dari Toerki.
Turmoil	Ganggoean; ganggoe.
Turn	Balikan; djalanan moendar-mandir; balik; poeter.
Turnip	Lobak besar.

Turnkey	Pendjaga pendjara; cipier boei.
Turnpike	Djalanan jang meneboes.
Turpentine	Minjak terpentijn
Turret	Benteng ketjil.
Tusk	Tjaling gadja; geeti.
Tutor	Goeroe; adjar.
Twaddle	Omongan jang pelo.
Twain	Kembar doea.
Twang	Soeara pang.
Tweak	Tjoebit dan gentak.
Tweezers	Djepitan ketjil.
Twice	Doea kali; lipet ganda.
Twig	Tjabang ketjil.
Twilight	Menggerip; sore.
Twin	Anak kembar, kembar.
Twine	Benang nanas; lipet.
Twinkle	Kelap-kelip.
Twirl	Poeteran jang lekas; poeter dengen lekas
Twist	Benang jang terkepang; kepang; lipet.
Twitch	Kakedoetan; tarikan jang keras; tarik dengen keras.
Twitter	Bertjrowat-tjrowet; bersoeara sebagi boeroeng.
Type	Tanda; soerat tjitak.
Typhoid	Demem typhus.
Typhus	Demem typhus.
Typical	Haroes diboeat toeladan.
Typify	Trangin dengen teekenan.
Typography	Ilmoe menjitak.
Tyrannical	Sebagi djago; kedjem.
Tyrannise	Berlakoe sebagi djago; berboeat menooroet soeka sendiri.
Tyranny	Kedjagoan.
Tyrant	Djago.
Tyro	Orang jang baroe moelai beladjar.
Tzar, Csar	Keizer Rusland.

U.

Udder	Mangkok tadaän soesoe sampi.
Ugliness	Kadjelekan,
Ugly	Djelek ; tiada kroewan matjem.
Ulterior	Di loewar doegahan ; meliwatin wätes.
Ultimate	Pengabisan ; paling boentoet.
Umbrella	Pajoeng.
Umpire	Hakim ; referee.
Un	Perkataän tambahan jang bermaksoed *tida* atawa *boekan*. Ampir semoea perkataän dalem bahasa Inggris jang dimoelai dengen letter U ada mempoenjai kepala Un, dan bermaksoed sebaliknja dari perkataän jang mengikoet di blakangnja. Perkataän jang mempoenjai kepala Un dan tida bisa terdapet di sini ada berdasar atas ini atoeran.
Unaccountable	Tida bisa di itoeng atawa dikasi ketrangan.
Unadvisedly	Tida bisa dikasi omongan baek ; lantjang.
Unadulterated	Toelen.
Unalloyed	Toelen ; boekan tjampoeran.
Unanimity	Persariketan.
Unanimous	Bersariken ; bersatoe hati.
Unassumiug	Taoe adat ; hormat.
Unavailing	Pertjoema ; tida bergoena.
Unawares	Dengen tidat terdoega ; dengen kaget.
Unbar	Boeka.
Unbelief	Hati jang tida pertjaia dengen barang soetji.
Unbend	Bikin lempeng ; longgarin.
Unbending	Tida lemes ; kakoe.
Unblushing	Tida taoe maloe ; bo-pan.
Unbosom	Pentang ; boeka.
Unbroken	Boelet ; baek ; tida petja.
Unburden	Senangin pikiran.

Uncertain — Tida ; tentoe sangsi.

Uncivil — Koerang adjar ; tida taoe adat.

Uncivilized — Biadab ; tida sopan.

Uncle — Soedara lelaki dari ajah atawa iboe ; oom.

Uncleanness — Kamesoeman ; kakotoran.

Uncommon — Djarang ; boekan biasa.

Uncompromising — Tida menoeroet ; tida taloek ; tida lemes.

Unconcern — Tida tersangkoet ; tida dipikirin

Unconditional — Berkwasa besar ; tjoan-tji.

Unconnected — Tida berhoeboeng ; terlepas.

Unconscionable — Tida bisa dikasi pikiran ; tida bisa masoek omongan.

Unconscious — Tida taoe ; tida mendoesin.

Uncork — Tjaboet peropnja.

Uncorrupt — Poeti bersi ; tida makan soewapan.

Uncouth — Djelek ; tida kroewan matjem.

Uncover — Boekan toetoepin.

Unction — Taro minjak ; bergerak pikiran.

Unctuous — Meminjak.

Undaunted — Tida penakoet.

Under — Di bawa.

Undergo — Tahan.

Underground — Di bawa moeka boemi.

Underhan — Dengen resia ; berakal.

Underlie — Reba di bawa.

Underline — Geret ; garisin.

Undermine — Gali di bawa ; bikin loeka.

Undermost — Paling renda.

Underneath — Di bawa.

Underrate — Di bawa harga.

Understand — Mengarti.

Understanding — Pengartian.

Undertake — Lakoeken ; kerdjaken.

Undertaker — Orang jang oeroes pengoeboerannja soeatoe orang jang meninggal.

Undertaking	Haloean.
Underwrite	Tanggoeng ; pastiken.
Undesigned	Tida sengadja.
Undignified	Di bawa prentanja laen orang.
Undo ✦	Boeka ; adoek.
Undoing	Keroesakan ; teradoekan.
Undress	Boeka pakean.
Undulate	Naek toeroen seperti ombak.
Undulation	Gerakan ombak.
Unearth	Gali ; boeka.
Unearthly	Boekan masoek bilangan doenia ; memang soeda dasarnja ; thian-djian.
Uneasiness	Tida bisa diam ; tida bisa lega pikiran.
Uneasy	Tida gampang, tida lega pikiran.
Unequal	Tida sama ; boekan bandingannja.
Unerring	Tentoe ; pasti.
Uneven	Tida rata ; bendjat-bendjoet.
Unexpected	Tida terdoega ; koenjoeng-koenjoeng ; tiba-tiba.
Unfair	Tida adil ; tjoerang.
Unfaithful	Tida setia.
Unfasten	Boeka ; longgarin.
Unfeeling	Bengis ; kedjem.
Unfeigned	Boekan belaga ; bener.
Unfilial	Tida berbakti ; poet-hauw.
Unfold	Boeka ; pentang.
Unforeseen	Tida didoega lebi doeloe ; koenjoeng-koenjoeng.
Unfortunate	Tida broentoeng ; sial.
Unfurl	Boeka ; pentang ; longgarin.
Ungainly	Djelek ; boeroek.
Ungodliness	Pelanggaran atoeran soetji.
Ungodly	Djahat ; melanggar atoeran soetji.
Unguent	Zalf ; kojoh.
Unhand	Terlepas dari tangan.
Unhappiness	Kasengsaraän.

Unhinge	Boeka ; tjaboet.
Unicorn	Koeda dengen satoe tandoek ditenga ke-palanja.
Uniform	Pakean soldadoe ; sama rata.
Uniformity	Sama ratanja.
Union	Persariketan ; perhoengan ; karageman.
Unique	Tida ada bandingannja; tjoema satoe-satoenja.
Unit	satoe ; satoe orang atawa barang.
Unite	Bersariket ; bersatoe hati ; beragem.
Unity	Tjoema satoe-satoenja ; persariketan ; per-hoeboengan.
Universal	Sama sekali ; berikoet semoea.
Universe	Atoeran mendjelemaken barang ; doenia ; boemi.
University	Sekola besar ; tay-hak ; midrasa.
Unkempt	Mesoem ; djorok.
Unleess	Kaloe tida ; sebaliknja.
Unlikely	Bole djadi.
Unlimited	Tida berwates.
Unman	Ilang pengharepan ; djadi hati ketjil.
Unmanly	Tida djadi orang ; berhati ketjil.
Unmask	Boeka pakean menjaroe.
Unmoor	Terlepas dari djangkar.
Unnatural	Boekan menoeroet natuur atawa alam.
Unnerve	Bikin lema.
Unofficial	Tida officiel ; tida sah.
Unpretending	Tida belaga ; betoel-betoel.
Unprincipled	Tida mempoenjai pri-boedi.
Unquestionable	Di loewar sangkahan ; tida bisa ditjari taoe.
Unremitting	Tida brentinja.
Unreserved	Teroes trang ; tida berdjaga.
Unruffled	Diam ; soenji ; tiada berombak.
Unruly	Tida boleh dioeroesin ; bentahan.
Unsearchable	Tersemoeni ; tida bisa ditjari.
Unsettle	Belon slese ; kaloet.

Unshaken	Tida bergojang ; tegoe.
Unsparing	Tida sajang barang ; tida bisa kesian orang.
Unspeakable	Tida bisa dioetjapken dengen perkataän ; tida bisa diseboet dengen perkataän.
Unspotted	Tida bernoda ; poeti-bersi.
Unstable	Tida tetep ; tida tentoe.
Until	Sampe ; hingga.
Untimely	Boekan moesimnja.
Untiring	Tida djadi tjape.
Unto	Ka pada ; ka dalem.
Untruth	Djoesta ; kepalsoean.
Unusual	Tida biasa ; djarang.
Unvarnished	Tida dipoles ; polos.
Unwary	Tida teliti ; tjompong.
Unwell	Tida baek atawa sehat ; sakit.
Unwholesome	Tida baek boeat pri-kewarasan.
Unwieldy	Besar ; blongkotan.
Unwittingly	Dengen bodo ; dengen goblok.
Unwonted	Tiada biasa.
Up	Di atas ; bangoen dari tidoer.
Upbraid	Terka sala.
Uphill	Soesa dikerdjaken ; soesa dilakoeken.
Uphold	Tahan ; toendjang.
Upholsterer	Penoendjangan ; orang jang menoendjang.
Uplift	Angkat ka atas.
Upon	Di atas.
Upper	Lebi atas.
Uppermost	Paling atas.
Upright	Berhati lempeng ; teroes-trang.
Uprightness	Hati jang lempeng atawa teroes-trang.
Uproar	Ganggoean jang heibat.
Upset	Terbalikin ; keleboein.
Upshot	Oedjoeng ; hasil.
Upstart	Orang jang koenjoeng-koenjoeng djadi ber-kwasa besar.
Upward	Ka atas.

Urban	Termasoek dalem bilangan kota besar.
Urchin	Anak ; landak.
Urge	Boedjoek ; paksa.
Urgent	Perloe ; penting.
Urn	Paso atawa mangkok pranti taro aer panas. toko.
Us	Kitaorang ; kita.
Usage	Rawatan ; kebiasaän.
Use	Kagoenaän ; pakenja ; goenaken ; pake.
Useful	Bergoena terpake.
Useless	Tida bergoena ; pertjoema.
Usher	Djoeroe rawat tetamoe ; pengawal pintoe.
Usual	Biasa ; seringkali.
Usurper	Linta-darat ; toekang kasi pindjem oewang ; penghianat negri.
Usurp	Terdjang ; tangkep dan pake dengen paksa ; perkosa ; rampok.
Usury	Rente atawa boenga jang berat.
Utensil	Sendok.
Utility	Kagoenaän ; pakenja.
Utilize	Pake ; goenaken.
Utmost	Paling banjak.
Utter	Meliwatin wates ; terlaloe banjak ; kata ; seboet.
Utterance	Seboetan ; soeara batja soerat.
Uttermost	Takeran jang paling moendjoeng ; wates jang paling tinggi.
Uxorious	Terlaloe soeka dan sajang istri.

V.

Vacancy	Pakerdjahan terboeka ; tempat kosong.
Vacant	Kosong ; tida dipikirin.
Vacate	Lepas ; brenti.
Vacation	Vacantie ; kalepasan vry ; brentian boeat samentara waktoe.
Vaccinate	Soentik.
Vacillate	Gojang.
Vacuum	Tempat jang kosong betoel maski dengen hawa oedara.
Vagabond	Boeaja darat ; badjingan.
Vagary	Pikiran jang lapat-lapat.
Vagina	Kemaloean orang prempoean.
Vagrant	Orang jang tida mempoenjai tempat tinggal ; mengglandangan.
Vague	Tida tentoe ; belon pasti.
Vain	Tokkong ; sombong ; angkoe.
Vale	Lemba ketjil.
Valet	Boedjang ; djongos.
Valiant	Brani ; tida penakoet.
Valid	Baek ; satoedjoe.
Valley	Lemba ; djalanan antara doea goenoeng ; tana jang terapit oleh goenoeng.
Valour	Kabranihan.
Valuable	Beharga ; mahal.
Valuation	Harga jang ditetepin.
Value	Harga ; kabagoesan ; hargain ; taksir.
Valve	Kraan ; pekakas jang memboeka djalanan atawa ngaliran.
Vamp	Koelit sepatoe jang pernanja lebi atas ; betoelin.
Van	Moekanja barisan ; grobak.
Vane	Ajam djago dari tembaga boeat menoemdjoekin hawa moesim.

Vanguard	Soldadoe di moeka barisan.
Vanilla	Poehoen bersama boewanja.
Vanish	Ilang dari pemandangan.
Vanity	Kasombongan jang boekan-boekan ; kadoer-djanaän.
Vanquish	Tangkis ; poenaken.
Vapid	Podol atawa poentoel ; rata.
Vapour	Hawa stoom ; hawa jang kaloear dari napas ; menjombongin.
Variable	Gampang ditoekar-toekar atawa diroba-roba
Variance	Perselesihan ; pertengkaran.
Variation	Toekarang atawa robahan
Variegate	Diwarnain.
Variety	Matjem-matjem ; segala roepa.
Various	Matjem-matjem ; roepa-roepa.
Varlet	Boedjang atawa djongos ; bangsat.
Varnish	Vernish ; tjat jang bikin mengkilap.
Vary	Beda ; toekar atawa roba.
Vase	Pot kembang.
Vassal	Boedak laskar.
Vast	Besar ; banjak.
Vat	Tong atawa tahang ; leger.
Vaticination	Ramalan.
Vaudeville	Banjolan dalem permaenan komedi.
Vault	Pintoe artja jang teroes meneroes ; tempat simpen minoeman ; lompat.
Vaulted	Tertoetoep dengen pintoe artja.
Vaunt	Menjombongin ; kasombongan.
Veal	Daging anak sampi ; daging sampi moeda.
Veer	Roba haloean.
Vegetable	Sajoer-sajoeran ; mempoenjai tabiat seperti sajoer-sajoeran.
Vegetate	Toemboe seperti sajoer-sajoeran.
Vegetation	Toemboenja sajoer-sajoeran.

Vehicle	Kreta dari segala matjem ; kandaran.
Veil	Toetoepan moeka ; klamboe ; toetoepin ; klamboein.
Vein	Oerat biroe jang mengangkoet dara kotor.
Velocipede	Sepeda , roda angin.
Velocity	Tjepetnja ; spoed.
Velvet	Beloedroe.
Venal	Boleh dapet dibli.
Vend	Djoewal.
Veneer	Keping-keping kajoe ; tatakin.
Venerable	Soetji ; beroemoer toea.
Veneration	Kasoetjian ; kealiman.
Vengeance	Pembalesan djahat.
Venial	Boleh diampoenken atawa dimaäfken.
Venison	Daging mendjangan.
Venom	Ratjoen binatang.
Vent	Djalanan kaloear ; kasi kaloear
Ventilate	Kasi masoek hawa.
Ventricle	Lobang dalem hati menoesia.
Ventriloquy	Ilmoe mengomong sebagi dari djaoe.
Venture	Brani korbanken.
Venturous	Brani ; gaga.
Verandah	Pekarangan.
Verb	Perkataän jang menjataken perboeatan atawa menjeritaken tentang satoe barang.
Verbal	Dioetjapken dengen moeloet.
Verbatim	Perkataän bales perkataän.
Verdant	Idjo ; seger.
Verdict	Poetoesannja satoe hakim.
Verdure	Warna idjo ; kaidjoan.
Verge	Rotan ; toengket ; pinggiran ; deketin ; melengketin.
Verger	Orang jang pegang rotan atawa toengket.
Verify	Terboekti.
Verily	Betoel-betoel ; dengen sasoenggoenja.
Verity	Kabeneran ; kapastian.

Vermicelli	Sohoen.
Vermillion	Mera toea.
Vermin	Koetoe jang bisa mengantoek ; orang djahat.
Vernacular	Tana-aer poenja berhoeboeng dengen tana-aer.
Verse	Garisan ; roentoenan.
Versed	Pande.
Version	Salinan ; ketrangan.
Versus	Contra ; bertentangan.
Vertex	Oedjoeng ; poentjak.
Vertical	Berdiri lempeng.
Vary	Amat ; sanget.
Vessel	Kapal ; mangkok.
Vest	Rompi; pake; djadiken milik.
Vested	Ditetepin sebagi milik.
Vestment	Pakean.
Veteran	Soldadoe jang soeda pensioen.
Veterinary	Berhoeboeng dengen ilmoe mengobatin ber-bagi-bagi penjakit binatang.
Veto	Larangan ; larang ; tahan.
Vex	Bikin mara ; ganggoe ; oesil.
Vexation	Ganggoean ; oesilan.
Viaduct	Djembatan di atas djalanan.
Vial	Botol ketjil.
Viands	Barang makanan.
Vibrate	Mengeter ; bergojang.
Vibration	Mengeteran ; gojangnja.
Vicar	Wakil kepala padri ; agent ; oetoesan.
Vicarage	Tempat tinggalnja wakil kepala padri, agent atawa oetoesan.
Vicarious	Diwakilken ; didjadiken wakil.
Vice	Kedjahatan; pekakas tindian jang pake schroef.
Vicegerent	Oetoesan ; wakil radja.
Viceroy	Radja moeda ; tjong-tok.
Vicinity	Tempat jang berdamping.
Vicious	Djahat ; berhati serong.

Victim	Korban.
Victimize	Tipoe ; akalin.
Victor	Orang jang menang; orang jang beroentoeng.
Victorious	Beroleh kamenangan ; broentoeng.
Victory	Kamenangan ; kabroentoengan.
Victual	Dilengkepin dengen makanan.
Victuals	Barang makanan.
Vie	Berkoetet-koetetan.
View	Pengliatan ; pemandangan ; pikiran; liat oekoeran.
Vigilant	Teliti.
Vignette	Barang oekiran jang ketjil.
Vigorous	Koewat ; gaga-perkasa.
Vigour	Kakoewatan ; kegagahan.
Viking	Badjak laoet dari tana Norse.
Vile	Djahat ; renda ; hina.
Vilify	Toedoe boeta-toeli ; terka sembarangan.
Villa	Roema dalem kebon.
Village	Kampoeng ; desa.
Villain	Orang djahat ; boeaja ; badjingan.
Villainous	Djahat ; kedjem.
Vindicate	Boektiken boeat djadi betoel ; belaken.
Vindication	Pembelaän.
Vindictive	Soeka membales sakit hati.
Vine	Poehoen anggoer.
Vinegar	Tjoeka.
Vintage	Pengngengetan atawa pemetikan boea anggoer
Vintner	Toekang djoewal anggoer.
Violate	Petjaken ; langgar.
Violence	Kakoewatan ; rasa amarah.
Violent	Berkoewat ; berkeras.
Violet	Saroepa kembang ; bewarna oengoe.
Violin	Viool ; biola.
Viper	Oeler santja.
Virago	Prempoean gaga perkasa.

Virgin	Anak prawan ; gadis ; roemadjapoetri.
Virtile	Sebagi orang ; gaga.
Virtual	Kalantesan ; kadjadian.
Virtue	Pri-boedi kebedjikan ; to tek.
Virtuous	Mempoenjai pri-boedi kebedjikan ; oe-to-tek.
Virus	Ratjoen.
Viscera	Oesoes atawa oetjoes.
Viscidity	Kalengketan.
Viscount	Gelaran di bawa graaf.
Visible	Keliatan ; bisa diliat.
Vision	Kabisahan aken meliat ; impian.
Visit	Koendjoengin ; melantjongin ; tilik ; koen-djoengan.
Visor	Kedok.
Vital	Perloe bagi penghidoepan.
Vitality	Kaperloean bagi penghidoepan.
Vitiate	Loekain ; bikin djadi djelek.
Vituperate	Salain ; toedoe sala.
Vivacious	Bagoes ; bertjahia.
Vivid	Senang bagi penghidoepan ; terang.
Vivify	Bikin hidoep ; kasi djiwa.
Vixen	Rase prempoean ; prempoean jang bawel.
Vocabulary	Kitab logat jang ketjil
Vocal	Dioetjapken dengen moeloet.
Vocation	Oetjapan ; panggilan ; dagangan.
Vogue	Roman ; perhoeboengan.
Voice	Soeara.
Void	Tempat jang kosong ; kosong ; blon di-tempatin ; kosongin.
Volatile	Gampang djadi hawa ; gampang terbang.
Volcanic	Berhoeboeng dengen goenoeng api.
Volcano	Goenoeng api ; hwee-swa.
Vole	Tikoes aer.
Volition	Pengrasaän ingin.
Volley	Tembakan senapan.
Voluble	Tetes dalem omongan.

Volume	Boekoe ; djilid ; bagian.
Voluntary	Dengen pilihan.
Volunteer	Orang jang bekerdja dengen kamaoehan sendiri ; barisan schuttery ; langgar ; tawarin
Vomit	Moenta ; toempa.
Voracious	Rakoes ; kelaparan.
Voracity	Kerakoesan ; kelaparan.
Votary	Orang jang geraken napsoe ; orang jang soeda diangkat djadi pengoeroes ; orang jang angkat soempa.
Vote	Pilihan ; pili.
Vouch	Tanggoeng ; djadi saksi.
Voucher	Orang jang menanggoeng ; soerat kesaksihan.
Vow	Soempa ; dipake boeat bekerdja.
Vowel	Letter jang bisa mengeloearken soeara-batja.
Voyage	Pelajaran.
Vulcanite	Karet jang soeda dibikin keras.
Vulgar	Biasa ; renda ; kasar ; orang kasar.
Vulgarity	Kakasaran dalem omongan atawa pri-lakoe.
Vulnerable	Jang boleh dibikin loeka.
Vulture	Boeroeng alap-alap jang besar.

W.

Wabble	Pinda-pinda.
Wad	Saiket atawa sagaboeng ; soempelan moeloet senapan.
Wad, Wadd	Tima item
Wadded	Djadiken iketan atawa gaboengan ; soempel.
Wadding	Barang jang digoenaken boeat soempel moeloet senapan ; kapas.
Waddle	Djalan sebagi bebek.
Wade	Menggrobok ; djalan di aer.
Wafer	Opak ; koewe tipis.
Wafer	Lak ; taroken lak atas envelop soerat.

Waft	Gojang ; kiberken ; mengambang di moeka aer.
Wag	Gojang ajoen-ajoen.
Wag	Orang jang soeka berbanjol.
Wage	Maloemken ; bales ; bertarohan oewang.
Wager	Pertarohan oewang.
Wages	Gadji.
Waggery	Kasenangan ; permaenan sport.
Waggish	Senang : berbanjol.
Waggishly	Dengen senang atawa berbanjol.
Waggle	Gojang ; ajoen-ajoen.
Waggon, Wagon	Grobak kreta api.
Wagoner	Djoeroe-moedi grobak kreta api ; toekang rem.
Wagonette	Kreta jang boleh didoedoekin dari ampat sampe sapoeloe orang.
Waif	Barang jang terdapet ; orang jang tida mempoenjai roema-tangga.
Wail	Bersoesa hati ; berdoeka.
Wailing	Tangisan jang menjataken kasoesahan hati.
Wain	Wagon ; grobak kreta api.
Wainscot	Alingan ; palangan ; alingin ; palangin.
Waist	Pinggang.
Waistband	Band tjelana ; iketan pinggang.
Waistsoat	Rompi ; badjoe koetang orang lelaki
Wait	Toenggoe ; lajanin.
Waiter	Orang jang menoenggoe ; djoeroe-lajan.
Waiting-maid	Baboe prempoean ; boedjang prempoean.
Waive	Soengkan ; tida maoe.
Wake	Mendoesin ; bangoen.
Wake	Pendjagaän ; bekasnja djalanan kapal di aer.
Wakeful	Tida bisa poeles ; selaloe melek.
Waken	Mendoesin ; bangoen.
Wale	Ploeian di atas pakean ; papan di samping kapal.
Walk	Djalan ; djalan-djalan ; djalanan.

Wall	Tembok ; tembokin.
Wallet	Kantong atawa dompet.
Wall-flower	Poehoen jang mengaloearken kembang koening jang tjantik.
Wallow	Mengglandangan ; djalan sana sini dengen tida katentoehan.
Walnut	Boea kenari ; poehoen berikoet boeanja.
Waltz	Lagoe waltz.
Wampum	Sipoet atawa kiong jang digoenaken sebagi oewang dan barang periasan oleh bangsa Indiaan koelit mera di Amerika.
Wan	Poetjoet ; poeti.
Wand	Toengket ; toja.
Wander	Djalan ; kesasar.
Wanderer	Orang jang djalan ; toekang djalan.
Wandering	Berdjalan sana-sini mengglandangan.
Wane	Koerangin ; koerangnja.
Wanton	Soeka plesir ; orang jang soeka plesir.
Wantonly	Dengen keadaän jang soeka plesir.
Wantonnes	Tabiat jang soeka plesir ; kaperlentean.
War	Paprangan.
Warble	Menjanji dengen soeara bergoemeteran.
Warbler	Boeroeng jang bisa menjanji.
War-cry	Kabar jang menjataken prang.
Ward	Djaga ; lindoengin ; orang di bawa perlindoengan.
Warden	Cipir boei ; president dari satoe midrasa ; kepala gredja.
Warder	Pendjaga ; orang jang melindoengin.
Wardrobe	Lemari boeat gantoeng pakean ; pakean.
Ward-room	Kamar di kapal pranti sekalian officier bersantap.
Wardship	Kapal pendjaga ; kapal jang membri perlindoengan.
Ware	Barang dagangan.
Ware	Teliti ; hati-hati.

Warehouse	Goedang; tempat pranti simpen barang-barang.
Warfare	Paprangan; oeroesan prang.
Warily	Dengen teliti; dengen hati-hati.
Warlike	Mempoenjai prilakoe sebagi orang papra-ngan; berhoeboeng dengen oeroesan prang.
Warm	Anget; panas ingin; bikin anget; soeka korbanken djiwa.
Warmly	Dengen anget; dengen bersoekoernja hati.
Warmth	Rasa anget; kainginan; kagiatan.
Warn	Kasi nasehat.
Warning	Nasehat.
Warp	Sala benang; benang jang sala.
Warrant	Tanggoengan; tanggoengan.
Warrantable	Boleh di tanggoeng.
Warranty	Pertanggoengan; perboeatan menanggoeng.
Warren	Tempat pranti mempiara klentji, ajam, atawa ikan.
Warrior	Orang paprangan; soldadoe.
Wart	Tai laler di atas koelit menoesia.
Wary	Teliti; hati-hati.
Was	Soeda ada.
Wash	Tjoetji; tjoetjian.
Wash-board	Papan menjoetjian.
Washerwoman	Toekang tjoetji prempoean; dobi prem-poean.
Washy	Beraer; lema.
Wasp	Tawon tjeking.
Waspish	Gampang mara; bo-sioh; sebagi tawon tjeking.
Waspishly	Dengen gampang mara; dengen bo-sioh.
Wassail	Barang minoeman jang terbikin dari anggoer. goela, pala, dan boea appel jang dikringin; sairan pemabokan.
Waste	Boeang pertjoema-tjoema; barang jang di-boeang pertjoema-tjoema; tana jang belon digoenaken.

Wasteful	Rojaal ; borós.
Waste-gate	Pintoe boeat boeang aer kotoran.
Watch	Djaga ; pendjagaän ; horloge.
Watcher	Pendjaga ; orang jang mendjaga.
Watchful	Berhati-hati boeat mendjaga.
Watch-house	Roema pranti orang-djaga.
Watchman	Orang-djaga.
Watchtower	Benteng boeat soldadoe pendjaga.
Watchword	Perkataän resia dari soldadoe pendjaga.
Water	Aer ; aerin atawa sirem dengen aer.
Water-course	Djalanan aer.
Water-fall	Djatohan aer.
Waterish	Sebagi aer ; beraer.
Waterman	Toekang pikoel aer.
Watermelon	Boea semangka.
Water-pot	Pot atawa boejoeng pranti moeat aer.
Water-power	Kakoeatan aer.
Water-proof	Bisa mendjaga masoeknja aer ; tida temboes aer.
Water-spout	Aer jang naek lantaran ditioep angin poejoe.
Water-tight	Begitoe kentjeng atawa rapet hingga aer tida bisa menemboes.
Watery	Berhoeboeng dengen aer ; tipis ; rasa tawar.
Wattle	Tjabang kajoe ; pager ; kalangin ; pagerin.
Wave	Gojang ; ajoen-ajoen.
Wave	Ombak di laoet.
Waver	Bergojang ; tjoeriga.
Wax	Lilin ; lak.
Waxen	Terbikin dari lilin. ·
Wax-work	Hoeroef jang terbikin dari lilin.
Waxy	Sebagi lilin.
Way	Djalanan ; atoeran.
Way-bill	Lijst nama-nama penoempang dan barang-barang jang terbawa dalem kreta.
Wayfarer	Orang pelantjongan.
Wayfaring	Melantjong.

Waylay	Semoeni ; potong orang poenja djalanan.
Wayward	Madjoe ; bentahan ; berkepala besar.
Waywardness	Kemadjoean ; madjoenja.
We	Kitaorang.
Weak	Lema ; kenji.
Weaken	Bikin kenji atawa lema.
Weakly	Dengen kenji atawa lema.
Weakness	Kakenjian atawa kalemahan.
Weal	Kasenangan ; kabroentoengan.
Wealth	Kekajahan.
Wean	Tahan napsoe.
Weapon	Gegaman ; sendjata.
Wear	Pake ; menahan.
Weariness	Katjapehan.
Wearisome	Menjapein.
Weary	Tjape ; bikin tjape.
Weasand	Pipa angin dalem toeboe menoesia.
Weasel	Binatang marmoet ; tikoes Olanda.
Weather	Moesim ; hawa.
Weather-cock	Ajam djago tembaga jang ditaro di atas gredja atawa roema pranti menoendjoekin hawa ; orang jang paling gampang menoeroet kamaoeanja laen orang.
Weather-gage	Pertandaän jang menoendjoekin djalannja hawa.
Weatherglass	Oekoeran hawa.
Weatherwise	Bisa membilang hawa jang blon dateng.
Weave	Tenoen kaen.
Weaver	Toekang tenoen.
Web	Barang jang tertenoen ; kaki sebagi bebek ; sarang lawa-lawa.
Webbed	Mempoenjai kaki sebagi bebek.
Webbing	Kaen jang terbikin dari lawe.
Webbed-footed	Mempoenjai kaki sebagi bebek.
Wed	Kawin ; berhoeboeng rapet.
Wedding	Kawinan ; nikahan.

Wedge	Linggis ; pahat ; bersifat sebagi pahat.
Wedlock	Perkawinan ; nikahan.
Wednesdy	Hari rebo.
Weed	Roempoet aer ; roempoet jang tiada bergoena.
Week	Minggoe ; toedjoe hari,
Week-day	Hari selaennja hari minggoe.
Weekly	Saban minggoe ; tiap-tiap minggoe.
Ween	Pikir.
Weep	Menangis ; meratap.
Weeping	Tangisan ; soeara ratapan.
Weevil	Koetoe jang meroesakin padi.
Weigh	Beratnja ; timbang.
Weight	Beratnja ; timbangan.
Weighty	Berat ; perloe.
Weird	Goena-goena atawa kongtauw
Welcome	Selamat dateng.
Weld	Leboer djadiken satoe.
Welfare	Kabaean ; kaslamatan ; kabroentoengan.
Welkin	Langt ; awan.
Well	Soemoer ; baek.
Wellbeing	Kabaean ; kabroentoengan.
Wellbred	Terpladjar baek ; sopan.
Well-nigh	Deket ; ampir.
Wellspring	Mata-aer ; mantjoeran aer.
Welt	Pinggiran ; wates
Welter	Mengglinding atawa terpoeter sana-sini ; kalang kaboet
Wen	Bendjoet di koelit.
Wench	Prempoean moeda.
Went	Soeda pergi.
Were	Soeda ada.
West	Barat ; koelon.
Westerly	Mengadepin atawa dari sebla Barat.
Westeren	Di sebla Barat.
Westward	Ka sebla Barat.
Wet	Basa ; bikin basa.

Wether	Kambing kebiri
Whale	Ikan paoes.
Whalebone	Toelang jang terdapet dari moeloet ikan paoes
Wharf	Boom atawa pelaboean boeat naekin barang-barang dari kapal ka darat.
Wharfage	Oewang sewa boom atawa pelaboehan.
Wharfinger	Pendjaga boom atawa pelaboean.
What	Apa.
Whatever	Ada djoega
Whatsoever	Apa djoega; baek apa djoega.
Wheat ·	Poehoen gandoem; padi Olanda.
Wheaten	Terbikin dari gandoem.
Wheedle	Boedjoek.
Wheel	Roda.
Wheel-barrow	Grobak angkoet barang dengen satoe roda; pedati.
Wheel-wright	Toekang bikin roda.
Wheeze	Sengal-Sengal; mengap-mengap.
Whelk	Sipoet; kiong; djerawat jang ngangkoet nana.
Whelm	Rendem dalem aer; moeatin terlaloe sarat.
Whelp	Anak andjing.
When	Kapan.
Whence	Dari tempat mana; dari mana.
Whenever	Kapan djoega; kapan sadja.
Whensoever	Kapan djoega; kapan sadja.
Where	Di mana.
Whereabout	Deket tempat apa; deket mana; dari jang mana; tempat-tinggal.
Whereas	Padahal; asalnja.
Whereat	Pada jang mana.
Whereby	Dengen atawa oleh jang mana.
Wherefore	Dari lantaran mana; dari lantaran apa.
Wherein	Dalem jang mana; dalem apa.
Whereof	Dari jang mana; dari apa.
Whereto	Pada jang mana; begimana achirnja.

Whereupon	Atas atawa lantaran mana.
Wherever	Dimana djoega ; dimana sadja.
Wherewith	Dengen atawa sama jang mana ; dengen atawa sama apa.
Wherry	Sekotji ; praoe jang bisa berdjalan lekas.
Whet	Gosok ; bikin tadjem.
Whetstone	• Batoe gosok.
Whey	Aer jang terdapet dalem soesoe.
Which	Jang mana.
Whichever	Jang mana djoega ; jang mana sadja.
Whiff	Semprotan hawa atawa asep.
Whiffle	Gojang-gojang ; brantakin.
Whig	Party politiek ; pakoempoelan resia jang ambil bagian dalem oeroesan negri.
Whiggery, Whiggism	Haloeanja satoe party politiek.
While	Selagi ; begitoe lama ; padahal.
Whilst	Selagi ; sabegitoe lama ; padahal.
Whim	Pikiran jang melajang.
Whimsical	Penoe dengen pikiran melajang.
Whimsically	Dengen penoe pikiran melajang ; dengen melajang atawa lapat-lapat.
Whine	Menggrendeng ; menjomel.
Whinny ·	Berboenji sebagi koeda.
Whip	Tjamboek ; petjoet.
Whir	Berboenji ; bersoeara.
Whirl	Terpoeter ; poeteran.
Whirlwind	Angin jang terpoeter.
Whisk	Keboet ; sapoe ; bergerak dengen lekas ; sesapoe roempoet.
Whisker	Tjambang ; djenggot.
Whisky	Whisky ; minoeman keras.
Whisper	Berbisik.
Whist	Permaenan kartoe ; diam.
Whistle	Bersoeit ; soeitan.
Whit	Tanda ; titik.

White	Poeti.
Whiten	Bikin poeti·
Whiteness	Keadaän poeti bersi.
Whitewash	Sapoe kapoer.
Whitewasher	Toekang sapoe kapoer.
Whither	Ka mana ; ka tingkatan mana.
Whithersoever	Ka mana djoega.
Whiting	Samatjem ikan laoet ; kapoer tana.
Whitish	Semoe-semoe poeti.
Whitleather	Koelit jang dipakein tawas.
Whitlow	Tjantengan di tangan.
Whittle	Koepas atawa potong dengen piso ; piso ketjil.
Whiz	Soeara mengaoeng dan njaring.
Who	Siapa.
Whoever	Siapa djoega ; siapa sadja.
Whole	Boelet ; sama sekali.
Wholesale	Djoeal borongan; pendjoealan dengen borongan.
Wholesome	Baek bagi prikewarasan badan.
Wholly	Sama sekali ; antero.
Whom	Siapa.
Whomsoever	Siapa djoega ; siapa sadja.
Whoop	Soeara treakan jang keras.
Whore	Djobong besar ; prempoean hina jang soeda karatan.
Whoredom	Perboeatan tiada baek dari satoe djobong.
Whose	Siapa poenja.
Whosoever	Siapa djoega ; siapa sadja.
Why	Kenapa.
Wich	Soemboe lampoe.
Wicked	Djahat ; berdosa.
Wickedly	Dengen djahat ; dengen berdosa.
Wickedness	Kedjahatan ; kadosahan.
Wicker	Terbikin dari tjabang-tjabang ketjil.
Wicket	Pintoe ketjil.

Wide	Lebar.
Widely	Dengen lebar.
Widen	Bikin lebar.
Wideness	Lebarnja
Widespread	Terpentang lebar.
Widow	Prempoean djanda.
Widowe	Lelaki djanda.
Widkwhood	Keadaän orang jang djanda,
Width	Lebarnja.
Wield	Pake ; goenaken.
Wife	Bini ; istri.
Wifehood	Keadaän atawa prilakoenja satoe istri.
Wig	Ramboet palsoe.
Wight	Orang ; menoesia ; brani ; berpengaroeh.
Wigwam	Pondok orang Indiaan koelit mera.
Wild	Liar ; galak ; oetan.
Wilderness	Tegalan ; oetan.
Wildly	Dengen galak.
Wildness	Kegalakan.
Wile	Tipoe-daja ; akak ; tipoe ; akalin.
Wilful	Bengal ; berkepala batoe.
Wilfully	Dengen bengal ; dengen sengadja.
Wilfulness	Kabengalan ; kakoekoetan.
Wiliness	Akal ; tipoe-daja.
Will	Kamaoean ; nanti.
Willing	Menoeroet kamaoean ; soeka bekerdja.
Willingly	Dengen menoeroet kamaoean ; dengen hati jang soeka bekerdja.
Willingness	Hati jang soeka bekerdja ; hati jang menoeroet kamaoean.
Willow	Poehoen Lioe.
Wily	Berakal.
Wimble	Bore ; poesoet.
Win	Menang.
Wince	Mengkirik ; kisoet
Winch	Pekakas poeteran.

Wind	Angin.
Wind	Poeter.
Wind-bound	Tertjegat angin
Windfall	Boea-boeahan jang djato lantaran katioep angin ; hasil jang tiada terdoega.
Wind gun	Senapan angin.
Winding-sheet	Kaen toetoepan orang mati ; kaen pranti toetoep mait.
Windlass	Kerekan pranti angkat barang-barang.
Windmill	Penggilingan jang didjalanken dengen ka- koeatan angin.
Window	Djendela.
Window-glass	Katja djendela.
Window-sash	Lyst atawa arkoe boeat menoesia boeat
Windpipe	Pipa hawa dalem toeboe masoekin katja bernapas.
Windward	Menoeroet angin.
Winday	Angin ; berangin.
Wine	Anggoer (minoeman).
Wine-bibber	Toekang minoem anggoer ; pemabokan.
Wing	Sajap.
Wink	Kedip-kedip dengen mata ; maen mata.
Winner	Orang jang menang.
Winning	Menarik hati ; menjoekain hati.
Winnow	Toemboek padi ; preksa.
Winter	Moesin dingin.
Wipe	Gosok ; seka.
Wire	Kawat ; iket dengen kawat ; ketok kawat.
Wiry	Terbikin dari kawat ; oelet.
Wisdom	Kapinteran ; kapandean.
Wise	Pinter ; pande.
Wisely	Dengen pinter ; dengen pande.
Wish	Kapengen ; memoedjiken.
Wisp	Sagaboeng roempoet kering.
Wistful	Teliti ; hati-hati ; ingin.
Wistfully	Dengen teliti ; dengen hati-hati ; dengen kainginan besar.

Wit	Akal ; tipoe-daja ; kapinteran.
Witch	Doekoen ; orang prempoean jang soeka pake goena-goena.
Witchcraft	Ilmoe doekoen ; Ilmoe goena-goena.
Witchery	Ilmoe doekoen ; katoeroenan.
With	Sama ; dengen.
Withdraw	Tarik poelang.
Withdrawal	Tarikan poelang.
Withe	Tjabang poehoen Lioe (willow)
Wither	Lajoe.
Withers	Toelang poendak dari koeda.
Withhold	Tahan.
Within	Di dalem.
Without	Di loear ; zonder.
Withstand	Protest ; bantah.
Witness	Saksi ; kasaksian ; saksiken.
Witty	Berakal.
Wives	Bini-bini ; istri-istri.
Wizard	Doekoen lelaki ; orang jang pande dalem ilmoe hikmat.
Wizen	Dibikin kering.
Woe, Wo	Ketjilakaän ; kesoesaän.
Woful	Bertjilaka ; bersoesa.
Wofully	Dengen sengsara.
Wolf	Andjing oetan.
Wolfish	Sebagi andjing oetan.
Woman	Orang prempoean.
Womanhood	Keadaän atawa prilakoenja orang prempoean.
Womanish	Prempoean.
Womb	Kantong anak ; lobang jang dalem.
Women	Orang-orang prempoean.
Wonder	Kaheranan ; heran.
Wonderful	Heran ; loear biasa.
Wonderment	Kaherenan ; kakagetan.
Wondrous	Heran ; loear-biasa.

Wondrously	Dalem keadaän jang heran.
Wont	Biasa ; adat-kebiasaän.
Wonted	Soeda biasanja.
Woo	Minta kawin ; bikin pertjintaän.
Wood	Oetan ; kajoe.
Wooded	Tertoetoep dengen poehoen-poehoenan.
Wooden	Terbikin dari kajoe.
Wood-engra-Wving	Ilmoe mengoekir kajoe.
Wood-land	Tana jang kaloearken hasil kajoe.
Woody	Penoe kajoe ; penoe poehoen-poehoen.
Wooer	Orang jang minta kawin ; orang jang bikin pertjintaän.
Woof	Benang boeat menenoen.
Wool	Wol ; boeloe kambing.
Woollen	Terbikin dari wol.
Woolly	Penoe dengen wol.
Wool-pack	Kantong wol.
Wool-sack	Tempat doedoek jang terbikin dari wol; kadoedoekan ferdana mantri dalem sidang 1e Kamer.
Word	Perkataän.
Wordy	Penoe dengen perkataän.
Wore	Soeda pake.
Work	Kerdja ; pakerdjahan.
Works	Fabriek.
Worker	Toekang kerdja.
Work-house	Roema miskin.
Work-man	Orang pakerdjahan.
Workmanlike	Pande bekerdja.
Workmanship	Pakerdjahannja ; kapandeannja
Workshop	Bengkel ; toko pakerdjahan.
World	Doenia ; boemi.
Worldly	Berhoeboeng dengen ini doenia.
Worm	Tjatjing.
Wormy	Banjak tjatjing ; tjatjingan.

Worn	Soeda pake.
Worried	Bersoesa ; bersengsara.
Worry	Keset dengen gigi ; robek ; kasoesaän ; sengsaraän.
Worse	Lebi djelek; lebi djahat.
Worship	Poedja ; soedjoet.
Worshipful	Boleh dihormat atawa disoedjoet.
Worshipfully	Dengen kahormatan atawa soedjoetan.
Worshipper, Worshiper	Orang jang bersoedjoet
Worst	Paling djelek ; paling djahat.
Worsted	Benang wol.
Worth	Beharga.
Worthless	Tida beharga.
Worthy	Haroes ; bagoes ; orang jang haroes dihormat.
Would	Soeda nanti.
Wound	Loeka ; bikin loeka.
Wound	Soeda poeter.
Wove	Soeda tenoen.
Wrangle	Perbantahan sengit ; berbantah dengen sengit.
Wrangler	Orang jang berbantah dengen sengit.
Wrap	Boengkoes.
Wrapper	Boengkoesan ; pakean loear,
Wrapping	Boengkoesan ; toetoepan.
Wrath	Goesar hati ; rasa amarah.
Wrathful	Goesar ; mara.
Wreak	Bales sakit hati.
Wreath	Barang jang dibebet ; boeket kembang ; krans.
Wreathe	Bebet ; lilit ; pelintir.
Wreck	Kapal petja ; katjilakaän kapal.
Wren	Saroepa boeroeng ketjil.
Wrench	Tarik dengen pelintir ; pelintiran ; kakatoea pranti menjaboet pakoe.
Wrest	Sentak dengen paksa ; rampas.
Wrestle	Bergoelet (dalem berklai) ; bergoeletan,

Wrestler	Orang jang pande bergoelet dan djatoken moesoenja.
Wrestling	Bergoeletan dan saling djatoken orang.
Wretch	Orang jang menanggoeng sengsara ; orang jang tida beharga.
Wretched	Sengsara ; tida beharga.
Wretchedly	Dengen sengsara ; dengen tida beharga.
Wriggle	Bertindak madjoe moendoer.
Wright	Toekang atawa baas ; orang pakerdjahan.
Wring	Pelintir ; rampas ; betot.
Wrinkle	Letjek ; mengkeroet.
Wrist	Meh atawa nadi tangan.
Writ	Toelisan.
Write	Toelis.
Writer	Penoelis ; orang jang menoelis.
Writhe	Rampas ; pelintir ; betot.
Writing	Toelisan ; jang di toelis ; karangan.
Written	Ditoelis ; terkarang.
Wrong	Sala ; kasalahan.
Wrongful	Menanggoeng sala ; tida adil.
Wrongfully	Dengen menanggoeng sala atawa tida adil.
Wrongly	Dengen sala ; dengen tida adil.
Wrote	Soeda toelis.
Wroth	Mara besar.
Wrought	Dikerdjain ; dilakoeken.
Wry	Miring ; mengok.
Wynd	Gang sempit.
Wyvern	Oeler terbang ; naga.

X.

Xanthin, Xanthine	Sepoehan koening.
Xebec	Kapal ketjil bertiang tiga jang digoenaken di Laoetan Tenga.

Xylographic	Berhoeboeng dengan pakerdjahan mengoekir kajoe.
Xylography	Ilmoe mengoekir dalem kajoe.
Xylophageous	Makan kajoe ; hidoep dengen kajoe.
Xystus	Lapangan baris.

Y.

Yacht	Praoe plesiran ; belajar dalem praoe plesiran.
Yachtsman	Djoeroe-moedi praoe plesiran.
Yankee	Laen gelaran boeat orang Amerikaan.
Yard	Oekoeran pandjangnja 3 kaki ; pekarangan ; tiang kapal.
Yardstick	Kajoe oekoeran jang pandjangnja 3 kaki.
Yarn	Boeloe kambing, benang nanas, atawa kapas jang soeda didjadikan benang.
Yataghan	Piso belati jang pandjang.
Yawl	Praoe ketjil jang didjalanken dengen anam penggajoe ; praoe ikan.
Yawn	Mengoewap ; ngangain moeloet.
Ye	Kauorang.
Yea	Ia ; soeda tentoe.
Yean	Melahirken.
Yeanling	Anak kambing.
Year	Taon ; doea-blas boelan.
Yearling	Machloek jang beroemoer satoe taon.
Yearly	Saban taon ; tiap-tiap taon.
Yearn	Ingin ; kapengen ; rindoein.
Yearning	Kainginan ; kapengenan ; pengrasaän rindoe.
Yeast	Dek pranti bikin koewe.
Yell	Bertereak dengen soeara keras ; soeara bertreak.
Yellow	Koening ; warna koening.
Yellowish	Semoe-semoe koening.

Yelp	Mengoeing atawa bergonggong sebagi andjing.
Yelping	Gonggongan jang santer sekali.
Yeoman	Orang jang melakoeken pakerdjahan tani ; orang tani.
Yeomanry	Koempoelan orang-orang tani.
Yes	Ja ; betoel.
Yesterday	Kemaren.
Yesternight	Kemaren malem.
Yet	Djoega ; tetapi toch ; doeloe.
Yew	Namanja saroepa poehoen jang selamanja idjo.
Yield	Kaloearken hasil ; mengala ; hasil kaloearan.
Yoke	Pekakas boeat hoeboengken kerbo-kerbo aken melakoeken pakerdjahannja ; dibawa prenta atawa pengaroehnja ; sapasang.
Yoke	Hoeboengken ; djadiken satoe.
Yoke-fellow	Sobat ; temen.
Yokel	Toekang loekoe sawa ; orang tani.
Yolk	Mera telor.
Yon	Di sebrang.
Yonder	Di sebrang jang masi kliatan.
Yore	Dari tempo doeloe.
You	Angkau ; kamoe.
Young	Moeda.
Younger	Lebi moeda.
Youngest	Paling moeda.
Youngish	Sada-sada moeda.
Youngster	Anak moeda.
Your	Angkau poenja ; kamoe poenja.
Yourself	Angkau sendiri ; kamoe sendiri.
Youth	Tempo masi moeda ; anak moeda.
Youthful	Moeda ; seger ; gaga.
Youthfulness	Keadaän jang masi moeda, seger, atawa gaga.
Yule	Nama jang doeloe boeat hari Natal (Kerstmis).

Z.

Zany	Orang jang bermoeka trang.
Zeal	Kainginan atawa kapengenan jang sanget.
Zealot	Orang jang mempoenjai kainginan atawa kapengenan jang sanget.
Zealous	Berhati ingin atawa bernapsoe kapengen.
Zera	Koeda loreng; koeda belang.
Zebu	Kerbo jang terdapet di Oost Hindia (bilangan Amerika).
Zemindar	Gelaran jang dikasi pada toean-tana di Hindia Inggris.
Zend	Bahasa Persi jang paling koeno.
Zenith	Oedjoeng langit
Zephyr	Angin jang menioep pelahan.
Zero	Nul; kosong.
Zest	Koelit djeroek; rasa.
Zigzag	Legat-legot; belak-belok.
Zinc	Zink; logam jang bermirip kaleng.
Zincography	Ilmoe boeat bikin gambar atas zink; ilmoe bikin cliche.
Zodiac	Djalanan mata-hari.
Zodical	Berhoeboeng dengen djalanan mata-hari.
Zone	Bagian moeka boemi.
Zoogony	Ilmoe peladjaran mentjari taoe prihal kelahirannja machloek di doenia.
Zoographer	Orang jang mentjeritaken prihal penghidoepannja machloek di doenia.
Zoological	Berhoeboeng dengen peladjaran prihal machloek (binatang).
Zoologist	Orang jang pande dalem ilmoe peladjaran prihal machloek.
Zoology	Ilmoe peladjaran prihal machloek.
Zoonomy	Peladjaran jang menjeritaken prihal penghidoepannja machloek.

Zoophyte	Machloek jang beroepa sebagi tetaneman; spons
Zouave	Soldadoe kaki bangsa Prasman jang berpakean satjara Arab
Zulu	Bangsa Kaffir jang mendoedoekin negri Afrika Salatan.
Zygomatic	Berhoeboeng dengen toelang pipi.
Zymology	Ilmoe peladjaran boeat jakinken asal-oesoelnja minoeman jang bikin orang djadi mabok.
Zymotic	Berhoeboeng sama pemabokan.

CPSIA information can be obtained
at www.ICGtesting.com
Printed in the USA
BVHW082133050521
606533BV00002B/162